# Lecture Notes in Computer Science 1094

Edited by G. Goos, J. Hartmanis and J. van Leeuwen

Advisory Board: W. Brauer    D. Gries    J. Stoer

# Springer

*Berlin*
*Heidelberg*
*New York*
*Barcelona*
*Budapest*
*Hong Kong*
*London*
*Milan*
*Paris*
*Santa Clara*
*Singapore*
*Tokyo*

Ron Morrison   Jessie Kennedy   (Eds.)

# Advances in Databases

14th British National Conference on Databases
BNCOD 14
Edinburgh, United Kingdom, July 3-5, 1996
Proceedings

 Springer

Series Editors

Gerhard Goos, Karlsruhe University, Germany

Juris Hartmanis, Cornell University, NY, USA

Jan van Leeuwen, Utrecht University, The Netherlands


Volume Editors

Ron Morrison
University of St Andrews
School of Mathematical and Computational Sciences
North Haugh, St Andrews, Fife KY16 9SS, Scotland, UK

Jessie Kennedy
Napier University, Department of Computer Studies
Canal Court, 42 Craiglockhart Ave, Edinburgh EH14 1LT, Scotland, UK

Cataloging-in-Publication data applied for


Die Deutsche Bibliothek - CIP-Einheitsaufnahme

**Advances in databases** : proceedings / 14th British National
Conference on Databases, BNCOD 14, Edinburgh, United
Kingdom, July 3 - 5, 1996. Ron Morrison ; Jessie Kennedy (ed.).
- Berlin ; Heidelberg ; New York ; Barcelona ; Budapest ;
Hong Kong ; London ; Milan ; Paris ; Santa Clara ; Singapore ;
Tokyo : Springer, 1996
  (Lecture notes in computer science ; Vol. 1094)
  ISBN 3-540-61442-7
NE: Morrison, Ron [Hrsg.]; British National Conference on Databases
  <14, 1996, Edinburgh>; GT


CR Subject Classification (1991): H.2-5

ISSN 0302-9743
ISBN 3-540-61442-7 Springer-Verlag Berlin Heidelberg New York

© Springer-Verlag Berlin Heidelberg 1996
Printed in Germany

Typesetting: Camera-ready by author
SPIN 10513186    06/3142 – 5 4 3 2 1 0    Printed on acid-free paper

# Foreword

The British National Conference on Databases has been held annually since 1981 with this year's event, BNCOD14, being held at Napier University, Edinburgh, in July 1996. The aim of the conference series is to act as a forum for database workers and as a focus for database research by attracting high quality papers from many countries and providing an excellent opportunity for academics and industrialists to meet, discuss ideas, debate current developments and anticipate the future.

The conference has maintained its record of international appeal by attracting 47 paper submissions from 21 countries: Argentina, Australia, Belgium, Canada, China, France, Germany, Ireland, Italy, Japan, Netherlands, New Zealand, Norway, Russia, Slovenia, South Africa, Spain, Sweden, UK, USA, and Venezuela. Each paper received at least three reviews and 13 were selected for presentation at the conference. The selected papers join two invited lectures, an invited industrial session with three speakers, one panel session and six five-minute formally presented poster sessions to complete the programme.

The first invited speaker is Professor Stan Zdonik from Brown University, USA. His talk entitled "Dissemination-based information systems: your data may be where you least expect it" examines a new architecture for distributed information systems that is based on the idea that asymmetry in communication channels will require a new approach to data delivery. He discusses the use of broadcast as a method of delivering data, analyses how servers should organise broadcasts, and says how clients should utilise their local cache to tune to a particular broadcast.

The second invited speaker is Dr Matthew Chalmers from Ubilab, the Union Bank of Switzerland. His talk entitled "Pearls, swines and sows' ears: interface research inside a multinational bank" analyses the mismatch in expectation between what bank employees, such as traders and analysts, and computing researchers see as state-of-the-art. The talk discusses the risk of new technology unbalancing established business practices, and goes on to highlight some of the contrasts and similarities between the bank's database use and Ubilab's research in systems and interfaces.

An innovation this year is a session based on three invited talks from industry. Nigel Stanley, from ICS Solutions Ltd., presents "Microsoft database technologies: an inside view" which gives a technical overview of Microsoft database technologies and their application within commercial settings. Steve Ross-Talbot, from Nomura International, presents "Predicate-maintained queries: an active OODBMS for financial applications" which describes part of a system claimed to be one of the largest object-oriented developments being undertaken in the City of London's financial community. Andy Bailey, from Oracle, presents "Universal data management for all types of data and all types of applications" which starts by highlighting some of the key industry trends and basic computing models and moves onto information management within these models, highlighting the requirements and techniques for managing different types of data, such as relational, multimedia, spatial and text.

The selected papers are partitioned for presentation into four themes: Object-Oriented Databases, Integrity, Query Optimisation/Performance, and Database Language Issues. It is the contents of these papers that constitute this volume.

## Acknowledgements

The staging of BNCOD14 was made possible by the cooperation of many different organisations and people. In recognition of this fact we would like to extend our thanks to everyone who contributed to the success of the conference:

- To the authors, both those whose papers were accepted and those who were unsuccessful this time. A conference is nothing without papers and we are grateful to those people who submitted work to the programme committee.
- To the programme committee who ensured that all papers received at least three reviews, and whose hard work in selecting the 13 accepted papers is reflected in the quality of the conference.
- To the invited speakers who took the trouble to travel a considerable distance to give the British database community the benefit of their experience and knowledge.
- To the industrial speakers who brought to the conference their practical experience of the application of database technology.
- To Alfred Hofmann and everyone at Springer-Verlag involved with the publication of the proceedings.
- To the British Computer Society who recognised the conference as a contribution to their Continuing Professional Development (CPD) scheme.
- To the conference sponsors: Lothian and Edinburgh Enterprise Ltd who provided seed funding; International Thomson Publishing who sponsored the céilidh; VIGLEN who provided financial assistance; Office and Training Consumables who supplied part of the conference kits. We also wish to acknowledge sponsorship received after the proceedings went to press!
- To the steering committee for their help and guidance in the organisation of conference.
- Finally to the organising committee who made it all happen. In particular we would like to mention Dr Peter J. Barclay for his work in putting together the proceedings, Kenny Mitchell for constructing the WWW pages, and Amanda Coulter for her help with the administration of the conference.

May 1996                                      Ron Morrison and Jessie Kennedy

# Conference Committees

## Organising Committee

| | | |
|---|---|---|
| J.B. Kennedy | (Chair) | Napier University |
| P.J. Barclay | (Publishing) | Napier University |
| J. Owens | (Publicity) | Napier University |
| A.E. Varey | (Local Arrangements) | Napier University |
| K. Chisholm | (Social) | Napier University |
| A. Coulter | (Administrator) | Napier University |

## Programme Committee

| | |
|---|---|
| R. Morrison (Chair) | University of St. Andrews |
| P.J. Barclay | Napier University |
| T.J. Bourne | SIAM Ltd. |
| W.P. Cockshott | University of Strathclyde |
| R. Connor | University of St Andrews |
| R. Cooper | University of Glasgow |
| C. Goble | University of Manchester |
| P.M.D. Gray | University of Aberdeen |
| W.A. Gray | University of Wales, Cardiff |
| M. Jackson | University of Wolverhampton |
| K.G. Jeffrey | DRAL |
| M. Kay | ICL |
| J.B. Kennedy | Napier University |
| J. Kerridge | Napier University |
| R.J. Lucas | Keylink computers |
| J. Mariani | University of Lancaster |
| J.K.M. Moody | University of Cambridge |
| S. Lavington | University of Essex |
| N.W. Paton | University of Manchester |
| A. Poulovassilis | King's College, London |
| W. Samson | University of Abertay, Dundee |
| M. Shave | University of Liverpool |
| P. Thanisch | University of Edinburgh |
| S. Todd | IBM (UK) |
| B. Theodoulidis | UMIST |
| M.H. Williams | Heriot-Watt University |
| M.F. Worboys | Keele University |

# Steering Committee

| | |
|---|---|
| W.A. Gray (Chair) | University of Wales, Cardiff |
| T.J. Bourne | SIAM Ltd. |
| C. Goble | University of Manchester |
| P.M.D. Gray | University of Aberdeen |
| J.B. Kennedy | Napier University |

# Table of Contents

# Abstracts of Industrial Papers

# Schema Integration Meta-knowledge Classification and Reuse

R. M. Duwairi*        N. J. Fiddian        W. A. Gray

Department of Computer Science
University of Wales College of Cardiff, U. K.
Fax: +44 - 01222 - 874598
E-mail: R.Duwairi@cs.cf.ac.uk, N.J.Fiddian@cs.cf.ac.uk and
W.A.Gray@cs.cf.ac.uk

* Jordan University of Science and Technology, Irbid, Jordan.

**Abstract.** Recent progress in communication and database technologies has drastically changed user data processing capabilities. The present situation is characterised by a growing number of applications that require the ability to access and manipulate data from various pre-existing database sources. A possible solution to deal with multiple databases is to logically integrate the component databases by the provision of one or more tailored global schemas. The end-user therefore is presented with a homogeneous and consistent view of the (possibly heterogeneous) multidatabase. Schema integration is an involved process that requires the supervised detection of similarities and dissimilarities between the component schemas, reconciling the dissimilarities once detected and providing a homogeneous view to the end-user. We are currently investigating the schema integration problem in object-oriented multidatabase systems. This paper describes one aspect of our work, namely, the classification and reuse of the knowledge accruing from the schema integration process. Such knowledge is classified into the knowledge that accrues from detecting and reconciling semantic heterogeneity between local schemas and the knowledge that accrues from generating the global schemas. We argue that reuse in schema integration is a vital issue and proves most valuable in saving the integrator's effort, simplifying the generation of new global schemas and supporting global schema evolution.

## 1. Introduction

The need to access a collection of independently designed databases is inevitable in most organisations due to the increasing use of diverse database management systems and the rapid rate of change in technology. In particular, the ever increasing power of computers and the development of high speed networks have laid a sound basis for the rapid and reliable transfer of bulk information either locally (LANs) or remotely (WANs) [CAS95]. This means that computer users are more aware of other databases, the information they hold and the potential resource if they can be linked together. These pre-existing databases will probably be heterogeneous since they were designed independently. This heterogeneity may exist at three basic levels [DOG95]. Firstly, at the platform level - database systems reside on different hardware, use different operating systems and communicate with other systems using different communication protocols. Secondly, at the database management system (DBMS) level - data is managed by a variety of database management systems based on different data models and languages. Thirdly, at the semantic level - semantic (logical) heterogeneity may arise [BAT86] because different designers have different viewpoints in modelling the same objects in the application domain or because of equivalence among constructs of the given data model, where several combinations of these constructs can be applied equivalently. It may also arise because of incompatible design specifications which lead to different naming, types and integrity constraints. In this paper we are concerned with logical heterogeneity alone.

Physically integrating heterogeneous databases by creating a composite database as a means for interoperability between these databases is an expensive and thus unfeasible solution [BRE90]. Several frameworks for integrating heterogeneous databases without physical integration exist in the literature. The two extremes are the global conceptual schema approach [COL91, DOG95, MOT87, QUT92] and the multidatabase language approach [KRI91, KUH93, LIT86, LIT93, SCH94]. The former builds a global schema that contains all the information in the multidatabase and the integration linkage information. The latter provides a multidatabase language that is capable of accessing several databases with the ability to reconcile some of the heterogeneity encountered in such an environment; in this approach the user must explicitly specify links in every set of statements performing a retrieval. An important aspect the above approaches fail to address is the reuse of the information generated during the integration process [ROS94]. We call this form of information "integration meta-knowledge". Integration meta-knowledge is costly to collect and maintain, so one wishes to reuse it whenever possible.

In this paper we describe a novel approach for integrating a set of logically heterogeneous object-oriented (OO) databases. It is based on using a schema integration language called the Multidatabase View Definition Language (MVDL) to generate *multiple* global schemas. Since our approach employs an integration language to construct several persistent schemas, it may be classified as an intermediate approach between the above two approaches for database integration. The integration language (i.e. MVDL) gives the user control over the global schema generation process by choosing its contents and structure; the generated global schemas and the integration linkage information are persistent and therefore may be queried repeatedly compared with session based integration (e.g. [LIT86]); finally, the global schemas' history is stored to facilitate the generation of new global schemas. Our focus here will be on integration meta-knowledge classification and reuse in our system, i.e. the potential to reuse a global schema when appropriate or to create new, alternative global schemas if required. An important feature is that our system will use previously derived meta-knowledge to assist users in the integration process.

## 2. Background

Here we briefly describe our approach for integrating a set of OO databases. The component databases are integrated by building several tailored global schemas as a semantic layer over them (see figure 1). Having several global schemas rather than one (possibly very large) global schema has the advantages of providing customised and tailored global schemas that suit different user needs, accommodating databases with large schemas and accommodating a large number of component databases.

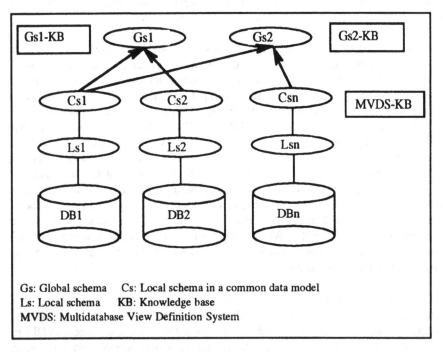

**Figure 1: Integrating a Set of Databases by Generating Multiple Global Schemas**

In the next section we describe our schema integration language (MVDL) that is used to generate the global schema(s), while in section 2.2 we describe global attribute selection strategies. In section 2.3 we list our schema integration algorithms and in the last section (i.e. section 2.4) we describe the Multidatabase View Definition system (MVDS), a prototype software system we have developed to implement our schema integration algorithms.

## 2.1 MVDL Operators

MVDL is a schema integration language that is capable of reconciling conflicting local classes and constructing homogeneous and customised global classes. It is based on a small set of fundamental operators that integrate local classes according to their semantic relationships. Each operator, when materialised by passing local classes to it, has three interfaces (dimensions). Firstly, a user-interface where the user sees the integrated local classes as a consistent and conflict-free global class; this interface is dynamically specified through interaction with the user (see section 2.2). Secondly, a system-interface which consists of a set of rules that links each global class to its origins (i.e. the local classes from which it was constructed) and reconciles heterogeneous representations through the definition of transformations. The third interface is the reuse-interface, this defines the rules for reusing the generated global classes.

Table 1 shows the usage of each operator. The second column states how the arguments (local classes) of the operator are integrated. For example, in the case of the Combine operator they are merged into one class, while in the case of the Intersect operator they are integrated by generating a common subclass. The third column shows the contribution of each operator to the global schema. For instance, the Union operator will generalise two local classes into a common superclass and add the whole generalisation hierarchy (i.e. the three classes) to the global schema, while the Union1 operator will generalise two local classes into a common superclass and add the generated superclass only to the global schema. The fourth and last column defines the extension (instances) of the generated global classes. For example, in the case of the Combine operator the generated global class instances are equal to the union of the instances of its corresponding local classes. Note that the generated global classes are not populated with actual instances, rather, their instances are derived from the local class instances. The rules that specify how to define the instances of each global class are specified in the system interface of each operator.

| Operator | Usage | Contribution | Instances at the global level |
|---|---|---|---|
| C=Combine (C1, C2) | merges two classes into one class. | | $ext(C) = ext(C1) \bigcup ext(C2)$ |
| C=Union (C1, C2) | generates a superclass for two classes. | | $ext(C) = ext(C1) \bigcup ext(C2)$ <br> $ext(C1') = ext(C1)$ <br> $ext(C2') = ext(C2)$ |
| C=Union1 (C1, C2) | generates a superclass for two classes. | | $ext(C) = ext(C1) \bigcup ext(C2)$ |
| C=Intersect (C1, C2) | generates a subclass for two classes. | | $ext(C1') = ext(C1)$ <br> $ext(C2') = ext(C2)$ <br> $ext(C) = ext(C1) \bigcap ext(C2)$ |
| C=Intersect1 (C1, C2) | generates a subclass for two classes. | | $ext(C) = ext(C1) \bigcap ext(C2)$ |
| Connect (C1, C2) | generates is-a link from C1 to C2. | | $ext(C1') = ext(C1)$ <br> $ext(C2') = ext(C2)$ |
| C=Include (C1) | imports a class. | | $ext(C) = ext(C1)$ |
| C=Include1 (C1) | imports the subset of instances of a class that satisfy a selection predicate. | | $ext(C) = $ subset of $ext(C1)$ |

WHERE: C1 is a local class and C1' its global version.
C2 is a local class and C2' its global version.
ext. is the extension of a class.

**Table 1: MVDL Operators and Their Effect on the Global Schema**

## 2.2 Global Attribute Selection Strategies

In the previous section we said that each operator of MVDL has three interfaces. When an operator is applied to a set of local classes an intermediate construct (IC) is created. The three interfaces of this IC have to be specified. System and reuse interface specification is carried out automatically by MVDS, while the specification of the user-interface of each IC can be achieved by following one of two possible options, namely: the default and the user-specified options. The IC user-interface specification process is actually the process of choosing the global attributes for the generated class(es). For default IC user-interface specification we provide the "default global attribute selection" option. Here the set of global attributes for each generated global class is determined automatically. For example, the default attributes for a global class generated by applying the Combine operator to a set of local classes is the union of the local class attributes. Note that some of the local class attributes will be equivalent rather than identical, which necessitates the use of transformations (mappings) to map between the global representation and the local ones. For user-specified IC user-interface specification we provide the "user-specified global attribute selection" option. In this case the user is able to choose the attributes for the generated global classes. In the previous example the user may be interested in a subset of the possible attributes or he/she may prefer to add derived attributes to the generated global class to customise it further. We have defined a set of semantic preserving rules to validate the user's decisions. The reason behind providing this latter method of selecting the global attributes is to give the user more control over the global schema definition process. Table 2 shows the global attribute selection rules for each operator under the default global attribute selection (column 2) and the user-specified global attribute selection (column 3) options.

## 2.3 Schema Integration Algorithms

The local schema integration process, in our approach, passes through three phases. The first phase is a translation phase where the local schemas are translated from their DDL specification to our intermediate model, which is an OO model. Once all the participating local schemas are translated into the common model, the global schema construction starts, this is phase two. The global schema is generated by applying MVDL operators to the translated local classes. The generated global schema is expressed initially in the intermediate model. During phase three the global schema is translated from the intermediate model to a user-specified DDL. Global schemas in MVDS may be generated from scratch by integrating local schemas (this is addressed in figure 2) or by modifying an existing global schema (this is addressed in figure 3). The latter option demonstrates the reuse aspect of the global schema generation process.

| Operator | Default Attributes | User-Specified Attributes |
|---|---|---|
| Combine | • The generated class attributes are equal to: $A \cup B \cup C$ | • The generated class attributes are equal to: $\text{subset}(A \cup B \cup C) \cup D$ |
| Union | • The generated superclass attributes are equal to: C<br>• The generated first subclass attributes are equal to: $A \cup C$<br>• The generated second subclass attributes are equal to: $B \cup C$ | • The generated superclass attributes are equal to: $\text{subset}(C) \cup D$<br>• The generated first subclass attributes are equal to: $\text{subset}(A \cup C) \cup D \cup D1$<br>• The generated second subclass attributes are equal to: $\text{subset}(B \cup C) \cup D \cup D2$ |
| Union1 | • The generated superclass attributes are equal to: C | • The generated superclass attributes are equal to : $\text{subset}(C) \cup D$ |
| Intersect | • The generated first superclass attributes are equal to: $A \cup C$<br>• The generated second superclass attributes are equal: $B \cup C$<br>• The generated subclass attributes are equal to: $A \cup B \cup C$ | • The generated first superclass attributes are equal to: $\text{subset}(A \cup C) \cup D1$<br>• The generated second superclass attributes are equal to: $\text{subset}(B \cup C) \cup D2$<br>• The generated subclass attributes are equal to: $\text{subset}(A \cup B \cup C) \cup D \cup D1 \cup D2$ |
| Intersect1 | • The generated subclass attributes are equal to: $A \cup B \cup C$ | • The generated subclass attributes are equal to: $\text{subset}(A \cup B \cup C) \cup D$ |
| Connect | • The generated superclass attributes are equal to: C<br>• The generated subclass attributes are equal to: $C \cup A$ | • The generated superclass attributes are equal to: $\text{subset}(C) \cup D$<br>• The generated subclass attributes are equal to: $\text{subset}(C \cup A) \cup D \cup D1$ |
| Include or Include1 | • The generated local class attributes are equal to: $C \cup A$ | • The generated local class attributes are equal to: $\text{subset}(C \cup A) \cup D$ |

WHERE A: is the set of attributes that belong to the first class only,
B: is the set of attributes that belong to the second class only,
C: is the set of attributes that belong to both classes,
D, D1, D2 are user-defined sets of derived attributes.

**Table 2: Global Attribute Selection Rules in MVDS**

a. Building a global schema from scratch:

REPEAT:
    1. Apply the appropriate MVDL operator to the relevant local classes.
    2. Detect the semantic relationship between the chosen classes to
       determine related information and reconcile heterogeneous
       representations.
    3. Choose the attributes for the generated global class(es).
UNTIL the global schema definition is complete
4. If required, import global classes from other global schemas.
5. Close the global schema by importing all local classes that it refers to.
6. Infer is-a relationships (if possible) between the generated global classes.
7. Represent the global schema in a user-specified DDL.
8. Generate the mappings to populate the generated global schema.

**Figure 2: Algorithm for Generating a Global Schema from Scratch**

b. Building a global schema by modifying another global schema:

1. Choose the global schema to modify.
2. Apply some of the allowed modifications to that global schema
   (cf. figure 8).
3. Close the new version of the global schema
   (i.e. after modifying the old one).
4. Infer is-a relationships (if possible) between the generated global schema
   classes.
5. Represent the generated schema in a user-specified DDL.
6. Generate the mappings to populate the generated global schema.

**Figure 3: Algorithm for Generating a Global Schema by Modifying Another Global Schema**

## 2.4 MVDS Architecture and Operation

MVDS's external architecture is shown in figure 4. It consists of three interfaces, namely: a local DDL to MVDS intermediate representation interface, a global schema construction interface and a MVDS intermediate representation to user-specified DDL interface. Using the first interface, the local OO schemas, expressed in a particular DDL, are transformed into an intermediate representation. It is based on a DAG (Directed Acyclic Graph) where an OO schema is seen as a single graph with one root and no cycles [KIM90]. This interface allows MVDS to integrate different sets of local schemas expressed in different DDLs. The second and major interface is responsible for constructing a global schema by following either the algorithm presented in figure 2 or the algorithm presented in figure 3. Finally, the third interface is responsible for transforming the generated global schema from MVDS intermediate form to a user-specified DDL. MVDS is implemented using Quintus Prolog [QUI91] while its graphical user interface is implemented using Quintus Prolog with OSF/Motif [HEL94].

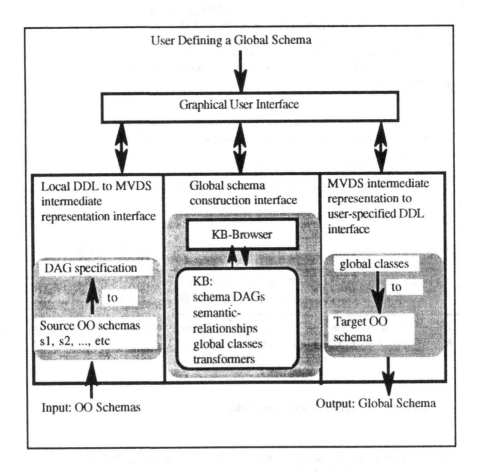

**Figure 4: External Architecture of MVDS**

# 3. Meta-Knowledge Classification and Reuse

In our approach, schema meta-knowledge is classified into two categories. Firstly, knowledge accrues from detecting and reconciling semantic heterogeneity between local classes. Secondly, knowledge accrues from generating global schemas. In the next two sections we show how these two categories of meta-knowledge are derived and reused in MVDS.

## 3.1 Semantic Heterogeneity Detection, Reconciliation and Reuse in MVDS

Irrespective of the approach taken to integration, the designers are faced with the problem of comparing the information content of the various databases concerned [SPA91]. It is important to know to what extent the databases share related information and it is equally important to instruct the integration system about such commonalities so that it can manage global schema(s) over the underlying databases.

Since we are integrating a set of OO schemas written in a particular Data Definition Language (DDL), i.e. we are dealing with structured information rather than unstructured information such as text and voice, class structure (i.e. layout) plays an important role in detecting semantic relationships between local classes. Semantic heterogeneity detection and reconciliation in MVDS is a semi-automatic process that depends on lexical matching between local class properties and on user advisory interaction. In general, two classes may be related by [QUT93, SAV91] equivalence, homonymity, containment, intersection and common real-world-semantics (RWS) relationships. Heterogeneous representations are reconciled by defining the proper conversion formulae (e.g. to convert degrees Centigrade to degrees Fahrenheit), mapping tables (e.g. to convert grades represented as letters to grades represented as integers) and structural transformers (e.g. to reconcile conflicts arising because the same real world concept has been represented as an attribute in one schema and as a class in another schema).

Integration meta-knowledge accruing from the above process consists of semantic relationship types, local attribute correspondences and conversion tables, formulae and structural transformers. For example, assume we want to compare *Schema1-Employee(name:string, address:string, salary:float)* and *Schema2-Employee(name: string, address:string, salary:float, dept:string)*. Assume further that salary in Schema1-Employee represents an annual salary while Schema2-Employee salary represents a monthly salary. Figure 5 shows the integration meta-knowledge resulting from the comparison process between these two classes.

This meta-knowledge may be *reused* in many different ways. For example, if we want to integrate the same classes in another global schema, we do not have to

equiv_to(schema1_employee, schema2_employee, ac([att(name, name),
        att(address, address), att(salary, salary), att(***, dept)],
        [dom(string(1), string(1)), dom(string(1), string(1)),
        dom(float(1), float(1), y_salary_to_m_salary),
        dom(***, string(1))])).

formula(name(y_salary_to_m_salary),
        expression('schema1_employee.salary/12'),
        expression_inverse('schema2_employee.salary*12'),
        first_class(schema1_employee),
        first_attribute(salary),
        second_class(schema2_employee),
        second_attribute(salary)).

equiv_att(schema1_employee, name, string(1), schema2_employee,
        name, string(1), _).
equiv_att(schema1_employee, address, string(1), schema2_employee,
        address, string(1), _).
equiv_att(schema1_employee, salary, float(1), schema2_employee,
        salary, float(1), y_salary_to_m_salary).

Where: y_salary_to_m_salary is a function that changes salary from
        salary/year to salary/month.

**Figure 5: Integration Meta-Knowledge Accruing from Comparing
Classes Schema1-Employee and Schema2-Employee**

compare them again because the knowledge accrued from the first comparison process
is already stored in the knowledge base (this form of reuse is called direct reuse). As
another example, consider a third class called *Schema3-Employee(name:string,
address:string, salary:float, dept:string)*, where salary is a monthly salary. Assume
further that this class has already been compared with class Schema2-Employee. Now
if the classes Schema1-Employee and Schema3-Employee are to be integrated we do
not need to detect the semantic relationship between them. The information can be
deduced from the meta-knowledge stored from the comparisons between classes
Schema1-Employee and Schema2-Employee and between classes Schema2-Employee
and Schema3-Employee. This is illustrated in figure 6 (this form of reuse is called
indirect reuse).

```
equiv_to(schema2_employee, schema3_employee, ac([att(name, name),
        att(address, address), att(salary, salary), att(dept, dept)],
        [dom(string(1), string(1)), dom(string(1), string(1)),
        dom(float(1), float(1)), dom(string(1), string(1))])).

equiv_att(schema2_employee, name, string(1), schema3_employee, name,
        string(1), _).
equiv_att(schema2_employee, address, string(1), schema3_employee, address,
        string(1), _).
equiv_att(schema2_employee, salary, float(1), schema3_employee, salary,
        float(1), _).
equiv_att(schema2_employee, dept, string(1), schema3_employee, dept,
        string(1), _).

==> THE FOLLOWING KNOWLEDGE IS INFERRED
    AUTOMATICALLY:

equiv_to(schema1_employee, schema3_employee, ac([att(name, name),
        att(address, address), att(salary, salary), att(***, dept)],
        [dom(string(1), string(1)), dom(string(1), string(1)),
        dom(float(1), float(1), y_salary_to_m_salary), dom(***, string(1))])).
```

**Figure 6: An Example of Integration Meta-Knowledge Reuse at the Semantic Relationship Level**

Such meta-knowledge may also be reused at a different level, namely: at the class attribute level. Under the OO model a class may inherit some of its properties from its superclass(es). So if a class under consideration inherits some of its attributes from a superclass which has already been analysed in a previous comparison, we can exploit the inheritance property to immediately deduce semantic information about the inherited attributes in the new class under consideration. Figure 7 shows some examples of this form of reuse in MVDS.

We have therefore demonstrated by example how integration meta-knowledge accruing from the semantic heterogeneity detection and reconciliation process can be reused in MVDS.

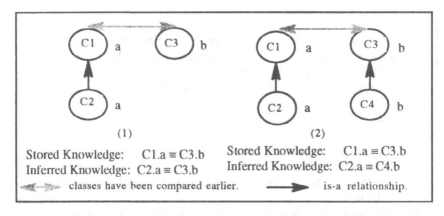

**Figure 7: Integration Meta-Knowledge Reuse at the Class Attribute Level**

## 3.2 Global Schema Generation Reuse in MVDS

User requirements and needs change over time [TRE93] and therefore an existing schema will have to be modified to reflect the new requirements or needs. This problem (i.e. evolving a database schema) is more interesting if we are dealing with a global schema that has been created by integrating a set of local schemas, because we have to consider the effect of such modifications on several databases rather than one database. In the rest of this section, we show how MVDS can be used to modify such a global schema.

Figure 8 shows the set of modifications that can be carried out on a global schema. Two issues need to be considered here. Firstly, the effect of schema modification must be propagated to its instances to enable them to conform with its new structure. Secondly the effect on existing application programs needs to be determined. In MVDS, global schema modification has no effect on existing local instances. Recall that the global schema does not have actual instances, rather its instances are derived from local schema instances. However the user is presented with the illusion that the schema and therefore its instances are modified. Also, the old version of the global schema is kept intact and therefore existing application programs are still operational.

In MVDS, a global schema consists of a set of virtual (global) classes created by applying an MVDL operator to a required set of local classes. Performing schema integration using an integration language (i.e. MVDL) supported by the declarative facilities of Prolog enabled us to store and consequently reuse the generated global classes' history. Each global class is represented internally as a Prolog frame (see figure 9) that carries the information necessary to populate it (i.e. to generate the mappings to its corresponding local classes), to reuse it in different global schema(s), if required, ... etc. This stored meta-knowledge facilitates the global schema modification task.

---

1. Import a global class as it is to the current global schema.
2. Import a global class hierarchy as it is to the current global schema.
3. Delete a global class.
4. Delete a global class hierarchy.
5. Change a global class name.
6. Create a new global class.
7. Add a derived attribute to a global class.
8. Delete an attribute(s) from a global class.
9. Change an attribute name in a global class.

Note that these modifications may overlap in practice.

---

**Figure 8: The Set of Allowed Global Modifications**

---

view-class(view-name(ViewName),
        class-name(ClassName),
        op-name(OperatorName),
        local-class-name(LocalClassName),
        own-attributes(OwnAttributes),
        own-domains(OwnDomains),
        all-attributes(AllAttributes),
        all-domains(AllDomains),
        own-rules(OwnRules),
        all-rules(AllRules),
        superclasses(Superclasses),
        subclasses(Subclasses),
        local-attribute-corres(LocalAttributeCorrespondence)).

---

**Figure 9: Global Class Internal Data Structure**

Global schema modification, in MVDS, is carried out by interacting with a software module developed for this purpose. Allowed modifications are implemented graphically and therefore user effort is minimal. Each modification has a predefined effect on the global schema that is carried out by using the global schema stored meta-knowledge (history). This characteristic of MVDS (i.e. generating a global schema by modifying an existing one) proves most valuable in saving the user time and effort because he does not have to integrate the required local information from scratch (i.e. it is possible to reuse and/or modify existing and integrated information).

## 4. Conclusions

This paper has described our method for integrating a set of logically heterogeneous OO databases. The method is based on using a Multidatabase View Definition Language (MVDL) to generate global schemas as a semantic layer over the participating databases. This language consists, currently, of eight operators, namely: Combine, Union, Union1, Intersect, Intersect1, Connect, Include and Include1. These operators enable a user to construct a global schema by generalising, specialising, merging and importing local database classes.

Putting integration rules at a definition language level rather than burying them in the integration "black box" process has enabled us to achieve the following objectives. Firstly, we have managed to divide the integration process into well defined steps. Secondly, it is possible to generate different global schemas tailored towards particular user groups. Thirdly, local classes can be integrated differently (i.e. customisability and evolution are supported). Fourthly, we have classified integration meta-knowledge into two distinct categories and defined rules for reusing such knowledge. The overall outcome is a flexible and productive integration facility.

Integration meta-knowledge is classified into knowledge accruing from the semantic heterogeneity detection and reconciliation process, and knowledge accruing from the global schema generation process. In this paper we have demonstrated how each category may be reused in schema integration. This latter aspect of our work proves most valuable in enhancing the integrator's productivity and in supporting global schema evolution.

## References

[BAT86]    Batini C., Lenzerini M. and Navathe S. B., "A Comparative Analysis of Methodologies for Database Schema Integration", ACM Computing Surveys, Vol. 18, No. 4, pp. 323-364, 1986.

[BRE90]    Breitbart Y., "Multidatabase Interoperability", SIGMOD RECORD, Vol. 19, No. 3, pp. 53-60, 1990.

[CAS95]    Case T. and Smith L., "Managing Local Area Networks", McGraw-Hill, 1995.

[COL91]     Collet C., Huhns M. N. and Shen W. M., "Resource Integration Using a Large Knowledge Base in Carnot", IEEE Computer, Vol. 24, No. 12, pp. 55-62, 1991.

[DOG95]     Dogac A. et al, "METU Interoperable Database System", SIGMOD RECORD, Vol. 24, No. 3, pp. 56-61, 1995.

[HEL94]     Heller D. and Ferguson M., "The Definitive Guides to the X Window Systems: Motif Programming Manual for OSF/Motif Release 1.2", Vol. 6A, O'Reilly & Associates Inc., 1994.

[KIM90]     Kim W., "Introduction to Object-Oriented Databases", MIT Press, 1990.

[KRI91]     Krishnamurthy R., Litwin W. and Kent W., "Interoperability of Heterogeneous Databases with Semantic Discrepancies", Proceedings of the First International Workshop on Interoperability in Multidatabase Systems, Kyoto, Japan, pp. 144-151, 1991.

[KUH93]     Kuhn E., "Multidatabase Language Requirements", Research Issues in Data Engineering: Interoperability in Multidatabase Systems (RIDE-IMS'93), Vienna, Austria, pp. 119-122, 1993.

[LIT86]     Litwin W. and Abdellatif A., "Multidatabase Interoperability", IEEE Computer, Vol. 10, No. 12, pp. 10-18, 1986.

[LIT93]     Litwin W., "O*SQL: A Language for Object Oriented Multidatabase Interoperability", in Interoperable Database Systems (DS-5), ed. by Hsiao D. K., Neuhold E. J. and Sacks-Davis R., Elsevier Science Publishers B. V., North Holland, pp. 119-137, 1993.

[MOT87]     Motro A., "Superviews: Virtual Integration of Multiple Databases", IEEE Transactions on Software Engineering, Vol. SE-13, No. 7, pp. 785-798, 1987.

[QUI91]     Quintus Prolog, Release 3, Quintus Corporation, 1991.

[QUT92]     Qutaishat M. A., Fiddian N. J. and Gray W. A., "A Schema Meta-Integration System for A Heterogeneous Object-Oriented Database Environment - Objectives and Overview", Proceedings of the NordDATA'92 Conference, Tampere, Finland, pp. 74-92, 1992.

[QUT93]     Qutaishat M. A., "A Schema Meta-Integration System for A Logically Heterogeneous Distributed Object-Oriented Database Environment", PhD Thesis, Department of Computing Mathematics, University of Wales College of Cardiff, 1993.

[ROS94]    Rosenthal A. and Seligman L., "Data Integration in the Large: The
           Challenge of Reuse", Proceedings of the 20th Conference on Very
           Large Databases (VLDB), Santiago, Chile, pp. 669-675, 1994.

[SAV91]    Savasere A. Sheth A. and Gala S., "Applying Classification to Schema
           Integration", Proceedings of the First International Workshop on
           Interoperability in Multidatabase Systems, Kyoto, Japan, pp. 258-261,
           1991.

[SCH94]    Scholl H. and Sheck H. J., "Object Algebra and Views for Multi-
           Objectbases", in Distributed Object Management, ed. by Ozsu T. M.,
           Dayal U. and Valduriez P., Morgan Kaufmann Publishers, 1994.

[SPA91]    Spaccapietra S. and Parent C., "Conflicts and Correspondence
           Assertions in Interoperable Databases", SIGMOD RECORD, Vol. 20,
           No. 4, pp. 49-54, 1991.

[TRE93]    Tresh M. and Scholl M. H., "Schema Transformation without Database
           Reorganisation", SIGMOD RECORD, Vol. 22, No. 1, pp. 21-27, 1993.

# View Mechanism for Schema Evolution in Object-Oriented DBMS

Zohra BELLAHSENE
LIRMM
UMR 9928 CNRS - Montpellier II
161 rue ADA 34392 Montpellier Cedex 5
France
e-mail : bella@lirmm.fr

**Abstract** :
This paper discusses the topic of using view mechanism to simulate schema modifications without database reorganisation in Object Oriented Database Systems. Our approach allows each user to specify the schema modifications to his own virtual schema rather than to the base schema shared by many users. One of the main advantages provided by this approach is the preservation of the independence of existing application programs from the schema evolution. The most important issue concerns the control and sharing of the information introduced by capacity-augmenting views. Furthermore, capacity augmenting schema modifications cannot be unambiguously propagated to the base schema when the related virtual class is derived from several classes. This paper proposes a solution based on the definition of a multi-level schema architecture, emphasising:
(i) The integration of this information into a federated schema.
(ii) Improvement of the sharing and re-use of information between views
Furthermore, we argue that view mechanism capabilities must be enhanced in order to be used as a uniform framework to manipulate both the schema and the database, thereby providing full data independence.

**Keywords** : object-oriented database systems, view mechanism, schema evolution, object views, virtual schema, capacity-augmenting views.

## 1. Introduction

Data independence developed in the relational model is defined to protect applications against change in storage structure and access techniques. Data independence can be achieved by supporting the view mechanism. Actually, no relational DBMS provides full data independence since views are only used as shorthand in queries because they cannot be freely updated.

Views in object-oriented databases have to provide the same functionalities as the relational context (restructuring, integration, query simplification and authorisation). Furthermore, view mechanism can extend the object paradigm by adapting object structure and object behaviour. For modelling, views are primarily used for defining different views or roles on a class, allowing different interpretations of the same class, without increasing the class hierarchy [1], [15], [5] [11]. How the virtual object identity is managed and how its correspondence with the base objects is maintained are key considerations for updating and querying an object-oriented database through a view.

The possibility of managing dynamically a database schema without losing data is crucial for advanced applications such as CAD/CAM, software engineering etc. The schema changes arise for many reasons : changed real world domain, reusability and extendibility of classes or cooperation with other systems, etc. To support these applications, certain object oriented DBMS provide schema modification operations [3]. The schema modifications should be propagated to the existing objects in order to ensure database coherence [10]. Besides, schema update operations have to ensure that a structurally-consistent schema is produced as a result of the update operation. Structural consistency is provided by using a set of "invariant" that define the consistency requirements of the class hierarchy [3]. However, propagation techniques are time consuming and alter system performance. Also, the system must ensure the compatibility of the modified schema with existing application programs referencing the original schema. For example, if the schema modification consists of deleting an existing attribute, all methods and programs referencing this attribute become incoherent with regard to the new schema. Furthermore, the value of this attribute is definitely lost.

To overcome the drawbacks listed above, views can be used straightforwardly to simulate some schema modifications without database reorganisation, since the definition of a view does not affect the schema of the underlying classes. We argue that views will provide logical data independence only if they are able to allow standard database manipulations : querying, updating the data and the schema. More precisely, concerning schema evolution, in our approach, a user specifies schema changes to his own virtual schema rather than to the shared schema. In this way, most of the schema modifications are allowed without database reorganisation. Furthermore, the views are no longer sub-schema and therefore they can have their own specific properties.

The idea of integrating the capabilities of schema evolution with view facilities was first introduced in [5]. In [16], a more elaborate mechanism is proposed : the simulation process is enhanced and included in an external schema. The issue of managing capacity- augmenting views is discussed in [13]. The proposal consists of propagating the added property to the base schema. This solution presents the following drawbacks: (i) The propagation of the added property to the base schema is not without ambiguity when the related virtual class is derived from more than one base classe. (ii) the added property remains invisible to other views and can therefore become a source of redundancy.

We propose a solution to overcome the drawbacks listed above, based on the definition of a multi-level schema architecture and emphasising:
(i) The integration of the added information into a federated schema.
(ii) Improvement of the sharing and re-use of information between views by
    introducing inter-view visibility.

The main contributions of this paper are: (1) discussion of the problem of data independence in object oriented database systems; more precisely, we indicate how database reorganisation might be avoided after schema modification, (2) a solution based on the definition of a multi-level schema architecture for federated views is proposed, (3) we propose a view language to define and update virtual schema enhancing view capabilities with schema evolution facilities for use as a uniform framework to manipulate both the schema and the database, thereby providing full data independence. The view definition and update languages presented in this paper are implemented on top of the O2 Database system as a small prototype named SETV(Schema Evolution Through Views) [8].

This paper is organised as follows. In section 2, we present the specific terms that we used to define and implement the views of our proposition. A multi-level schema architecture is presented in section 3. Section 4 describes our view specification language. How the virtual schema can be updated is discussed in section 5. Section 6, gives an overview of the implementation of our approach. Related work is presented in section 7. Finally, section 8 contains concluding remarks and future work.


## 2. Preliminaries

In this section, we introduce the specific concepts that we use to define and implement the views of our proposition. We suppose that object-oriented data model concepts such as object identity, class, inheritance are known to the reader [6], [7].

### 2.1 The core data model

We use the O2 data model [7] as a core data model for our view language. The O2 data model relies on two concepts : complex values and objects which consist of pairs of <identifier, value>. Objects having the same structure and the same behaviour (methods) are grouped into classes. Every class has an associated type describing the structure of its objects.
The O2 data model does not provide class extension at the logical level. Extension of a class is defined as a named set of objects which is a root of persistency. For example, the extension of the class Person may be defined as follows:
name People: set(Person);

### 2.2 Virtual schema

We use the term of *base class* to refer to classes that are defined during the initial schema and whose objects are explicitly stored. The object instances of a base class are denoted *base objects*.
In our proposition, a view is defined by a virtual schema which is in turn defined as a set of virtual classes. Every *virtual class* has an associated query allowing computation of its *virtual objects*. These objects are not explicitly stored, but rather computed on demand. A virtual class can be derived from one or several base classes. In what follows, virtual schema is taken as being synonymous with view.

In our approach, a virtual class may possess its own specific properties (i.e. non-derived attributes and methods). The data of specific properties are persistent and the corresponding virtual objects have persistent OIDs. Besides, views can be derived from other virtual schemas, i.e. the root schema of a view can be a virtual schema. A derivation relationship exists between a class C and a virtual class V when V is defined on top of C. However, V is not always a sub-class of C since it may have fewer properties.

The running example throughout this paper for defining and updating virtual schemas is presented in figure 1.

**Class Person**
type tuple (name: string,
          surname :string,
          birth-date: Date)
  method  age : integer
end;

**Class Laboratory**
  type tuple ( name : string,
          addr : Address)
end;

**Class Address**
type tuple ( number: integer,
      street : string,
      city : string,
      Zip_code: integer)
end;

**Class Researcher inherit Person**
  type tuple ( speciality:string,
        Rank:string,
        lab : Laboratory,
        publications: list (Publication))

end;

**Class    Publication**
  type tuple( title:string,
        editor:string,
        publi_date:Date)
  end;

**Fig. 1.** A Database schema example with O2 Data Definition Language

# 3. Federated Views

## 3.1 Motivations

The possibility of including additional (non-derived) properties in a virtual class allows the views to be augmented independently of the base classes. The second usage of additional properties is to support schema changes. However, capacity-augmenting schema modifications cannot be unambiguously propagated to the base schema when the related virtual class is derived from several classes. In our approach, the additional properties are not propagated to the base schema and are stored in a persistent class in the federated schema. The associated data are stored in a federated base. Our approach provides the following features :
- managing the storage of the additional properties,
- allowing nesting views,
- providing virtual schema modifications without database reorganisation

### 3.2 A multi-level schema architecture

The control of sharing and the management of the information introduced by capacity-augmenting views requires the definition of a multi-level schema architecture based on a federation of views. The federation notion means that each view is autonomous, although it can share some its own information with other views. In this way, the view mechanism becomes an enhanced form of schema versioning, since each view is a version of the base schema.
We define three levels of schema :
1. The *virtual schemata* or views level, which is the user interface,
2. The *federated schema*, built as the federation of existing views, includes the base classes and the virtual classes. This schema offers an overview of all the available structural components of an application. Thus it provides designers with a framework in which new virtual schemas can be created.
3. The *base schema* level which is a canonical representation of the real world. It includes the base classes from which views are originally derived. The following figure gives an overview of this architecture.

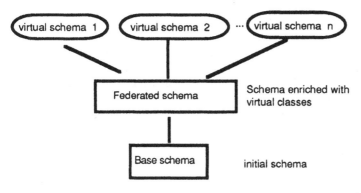

**Fig. 2.** A multi-level schema architecture

## Definitions

**Base schema**
Given a base schema $S_B = (C, <, M, N)$,
C is a set of base classes,
M is a set of method signatures,
< is a partial order on C which represents the inheritance link and N is a set of names (i.e. data base entry points)

**Virtual schema**
In a virtual schema, we have to specify the virtual classes, the existing classes from which they are derived and the signatures of the view methods, denoted $M_V$.
Then, a virtual schema SV is defined by the tuple (C $\cup$ $C_V$, derived_from, $M_V$)

Where

$C_V$ is a set of the virtual classes,

"derived_from" is a relationship relating each virtual class to a subset of $C \cup C_V$

$M_V$ is a set of method signatures defined in virtual classes $C_V$.

**Federated schema**

A federated schema $FS = (C \cup C_V, <, \text{derived\_from}, M \cup M_V)$

Where $C_V$ is a set of virtual classes,

and "derived_from" is a relationship relating each virtual class to a subset of $C \cup C_V$

In summary, our approach can be used to define virtual schemas in federated databases. The visibility notion may be used to specify the export and import parts of the local databases. However, issues concerning structural conflicts between the different databases must be solved. Moreover, the multi-schema architecture should be refined in order to fit with the federated databases requirements [17].

# 4. View specification language

In this section, we present the syntax of the main commands of our view definition language and informally describe their semantics. Our view definition language is an extension of the O2views [14] to support capacity-augmenting views. Therefore, a virtual schema may include its own properties (i.e. non-derived properties). The second difference with O2views lies in the fact that our view language also includes update operations on virtual schemas (see section 5).

### 4.1 Virtual schema definition

```
[CREATE] virtual schema <virtual schema-name> from < root schema
name>;
```

This command creates a virtual schema from a base or a virtual schema.

### 4.2 Virtual class definition

```
[CREATE] virtual class  <virtual class name>  [from <list of class
names>]
        [Inherit <virtual class name>,]
        [Extension : <extension name>]
        Query           : <query expression>;
        [Add Attribute : < ( additional attributes specification)>]
        [Add Method  : <( method specification)>],
        [Hide Attribute : <attributes names>]
end;
```

This command creates a virtual class under the current virtual schema. Extension clause gives the virtual class extension. If no extension name is given, the system provides a default name ("the_virtual class name").

The *add attribute* clause gives the specific attributes of the virtual class (i.e. attributes that do not belong to the base schema).

Methods can be defined already in existing classes or specially-defined for the virtual class purpose. In the latter case, only the signature of methods is required. The method body can be defined later. Defining customised methods is equivalent to allowing virtual attributes.

The *query* clause follows OSQL syntax. It returns a set of objets with type depending on the select clause. If it corresponds to a simple "selection"(i.e. relational selection or projection) then the query must return a set of instances of the base class referenced in the *from* clause. The type of the resulting objects is the same as the type of base class. Further, object identity is preserved[1]. If the query expression corresponds to a *join -projection* operation then it must return a set of unique tuples whose type is that defined by the (query) target attributes. In this case, a new identifier is assigned to each tuple to build a new object [2].

Finally, it is possible to hide some attributes from a class by using the *hide* clause.

**Example of virtual schema definition :** This example illustrates nesting views defined on the base schema presented in figure 1.

```
CREATE virtual schema Research_view;

Virtual class  Invited__researcher from Researcher
query : Select x
       From x in The_Researchers
       where x.status <> "permanent"
Add attribute  (original_lab: string)
end Invited__researcher;

Virtual class  Foreign_Invited__researcher  From Invited__researcher
query :        Select  x
               From x in The_invited_researcher
               Where x.original_country <> "France";
Add attribute  (original_country : string);
End  Foreign_Invited__researcher;
```

The virtual class "Invited_researcher" is derived from the base class Researcher described in figure1. The variable "The_researchers", defined as a named set, is a root of persistency. The attribute "original-lab" is specific to this virtual class and indicates the laboratory where the invited researcher comes from. Also, the virtual class Foreign_Invited__researcher possesses a specific attribute : "original-country".

## 4.3 Inter-view visibility

In object-oriented DBMS, the notion visibility allows the sharing of properties by classes of the same schema. We extended this form of visibility to allow the sharing of attributes and the reusability of methods defined in the different views. This concerns particularly the properties (attributes and methods) or classes added through views and which are not included in the base schema. Sharing classes is a relevant

---

[1] that is the virtual objects have the same identifiers as the selected base objects.

mechanism for avoiding redundant definitions of virtual classes but also for simplifying derivations. Visible properties are included in a virtual class which will be exported.

```
Export virtual class <virtual class name>
```

The semantics of the previous statement is to export a virtual class
The import command is :

```
Import virtual class <class name>;
```

# 5. Virtual schemas Modifications

Our proposal provides schema update primitives allowing a user to specify schema changes to his own (virtual) schema rather than to the base schema. Zicari [19] shows that the taxonomy of schema changes can be reduced to a minimal and complete set of basic schema primitives which can be combined to express more complex operators. This minimal set falls into categories : (i) changes to a class content and (ii) changes to the inheritance hierarchy [3].

We defined a virtual schema update language that includes the basic schema changes and more sophisticated modifications such as nest and unnest operations, affecting the aggregation hierarchy. We do not describe in detail all these classical schema changes due to space limitations [3], [5]. We concentrate our effort on those needing special processing with our approach, such as the adding and deleting operations. More complex operations needing object migration, which are not supported by the OODBMS may be supported by the view mechanism [5].

## 5.1 Restructuring a virtual class content

### • Adding an attribute to a virtual class

We describe in this section an algorithm for adding an attribute to a virtual class. Adding a property (an attribute or a method) must not produce side-effects on other existing virtual classes. This feature is called views independence [11]. For enforcing this constraint, the virtual class to be modified must be redefined if it is a derivation root[2] or if it is exported. In fact, our approach performs the modification on the virtual copy rather than on the original class. However, this manipulation is transparent to the user, who is provided with an alias of the original virtual class. The syntactic form of the add command is :

Add Attribute <additional attributes specification > to <virtual class name>

The semantics of the add attribute operator is to augment the type of a virtual class. The virtual class becomes persistent if it is the first specific(non-derived) attribute.

---

[2]Namely there exists at least one virtual class derived from it.

The propagation of the added attribute to the derived classes and sub classes is prohibited in order to preserve the independence of the other virtual schemas.

```
Add( A, V1)
If A exists then reject the operation
Else If   V1 <> derivation root class Then   Add Attribute A in
virtual class V1 ;
        Else  do  /* create a virtual class V'1 which will include A
*/
                create virtual class V'1 from V1
                query : select x from x in V1,
                add Attribute A in class V'1;
                end;
                V'1 used_as V1 /* providing an alias of the original
class*/
end;
```

**Example** : Add attribute hobby : string to Virtual class Invited_researcher;

Since Invited_researcher is a derivation root for Foreign_Invited_researcher , the insertion will not be actually performed on Invited_researcher, but on a virtual copy of it, as follows :

```
Virtual class Invited_Researcher_bis from
Invited_researcher
query :      Select  x
             From x in The_invited_researcher
             Add attribute hobby:string;
end;
Invited_Researcher_bis  used_as Invited_researcher;
```

• **Deleting an attribute of a virtual class**

As for adding a property, the deleting operation must preserve the views independence. For enforcing this constraint, and if the concerned virtual class is a derivation root, the deleting operation will be performed on a virtual copy of the original class. Before propagating an update, we need to know if the related property is currently used by an application program. We define a function named "f_used(p)" which returns a Boolean (true if p is currently used and false otherwise). The first usage of "f_used" is to avoid indefinitely keeping a property which is not actually used. The second usage is enforcing the consistency of application programs after schema modifications.

```
Delete Attribute <attribute name> in <Virtual class name>;
```

The semantics of the deleting operator is to remove the specified attribute from the type of the virtual class V1. The algorithm dealing with the delete-attribute operator is:

Delete (A,V1)

If ( A $\epsilon C_{exp}$ )) **and** non(fused(A)) )  /\* $C_{exp}$ is the set of exported classes \*/

Then `Hide A in the_exported class ;`

If V1 <> "derivation root"  Then do `Hide A in class V1`

Else /\* V1 is a derivation root \*/ do /\* create a copy V'1 \*/

```
        create virtual class V'1 from V1
        query : select x from x in V1,
        Hide A in class V'1
        end;
        V'1 used_as V1.
```

End;

**Example** : `Delete Attribute original_country in Virtual class Foreign_Invited_Researcher;`

This operation will be performed by a *Hide* command since Foreign_Invited_Researcher virtual class is not a derivation root class.

`Hide original_country in Virtual class Invited_Researcher`

### 5.2 Restructuring a virtual schema

#### • Class Creation and Inheritance link

A class may be declared as being the super-class of another one with the following statement :

`virtual class <super-class name> Superclass of <existing class name>;`

The inheritance link may be specified at the creation of the class or later as follows :

`virtual class <class name> Inherit <existing class name>;`

#### • Deleting a class

Deleting a virtual class in our approach must be examined by paying particular attention to derivation links. In particular, class deletions are guaranteed to be without side-effects on other existing virtual classes, in order to avoid data reorganisation and preserve the application programs from inconsistency. Thus, as for property deletion, the operation effects must be located within the single virtual schema from which a class must be removed. If the user intends to remove a virtual class having subclasses, the deletion is necessarily propagated to the sub-classes since, their semantics are captured through the definition query of their super-class.

### 5.3 Modifying the aggregation hierarchy

#### • Connecting classes

The first operator consists of connecting a virtual class to another virtual class by the following statement:

`connect <existing class name> to <existing class name>`

## • Class Decomposition

The operator *unnest* creates an intermediate class including a sub-set of its properties (including the "Properties list" ) and an aggregation relationship between the source class to the new class. This operator, called *aggregate* in [9], may be easily simulated by a view creation.

```
unnest <Properties list> of <source class name> into <new class
name>;
```

## • Nesting classes

The nest operator has the effect of deleting the aggregation relationship between the aggregate class and the source class and all the properties belonging to the aggregate class will be included in the source class. Furthermore, it is possible to perform more complex operations such as a "partial nesting" allowing only a sub-set of aggregate class properties to be included in the source class.

```
nest<aggregate class name> into <source class name>;
```

**Example** : This example illustrates the simulation of a nest operation which consists of including all properties of the Address class directly as properties of the class Laboratory.

```
nest Address into Laboratory;
```

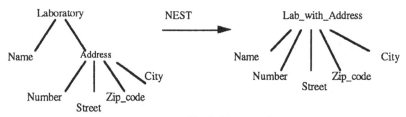

**Fig 3**. Nesting classes

This operation is performed by creating the following virtual class :

```
Virtual class  Lab_with_address from Laboratory
query:
Select (x.name,x.adr.number,x.adr.street,x.adr.Zip_code,
       x.adr.city)
From x in Laboratories; /* laboratories is the database
                                entry */
end;
```

# 6. Implementation Aspect

### 6.1 Virtual Object Identity

A view system must support object identity since it is a fundamental part of any object model. When a view includes only a "selection" (project or selection), virtual objects are then derived from a unique base class and the identity of base objects is preserved by the view query. Therefore, for each instance of a virtual class, there is a corresponding instance of its base class and these two related instances share the same object identity[3]. Some OODBMS support multiple class instantiation [15]. O2 System does not. In our implementation, the system keeps track of the relationship between a virtual object and its corresponding base object.

In contrast, virtual objects[4] derived by composite views are distributed over several underlying base objects. For these objects, a new identity would have to be created. In this case, a new identifier is assigned to each tuple to build a new object by the new operator.

Recall that in our approach, a virtual class may possess its own specific properties (i.e. non-derived attributes and methods). Therefore, a virtual object may encompass a real part and a virtual part. The real part is created by the "new" operator. An OID is then assigned to it by the system. Concerning the object value, the real part is affected by an "init" method and the virtual part is computed by the corresponding query.

### 6.3 An overview of our prototype

The work described in this paper is implemented as a prototype named SETV(Schema Evolution Through Views), on top of O2 DBMS[5]. The functionalities provided by SETV are:
- a view definition language (which does not currently implements the inheritance features between virtual classes)
- a virtual schema manipulation language

The first objective of the current prototype [8] was to validate our idea concerning the simulation of schema evolution. The following figure gives an overview of the SETV architecture which consists of a communicating set of modules:

---

[3]This feature is named multiple class instantiation, i.e. an object can be an instance of several classes.

[4]These objects are named imaginary objects in [ABBO 91].

[5]O2 is a registered trademark of O2Technology Corporation

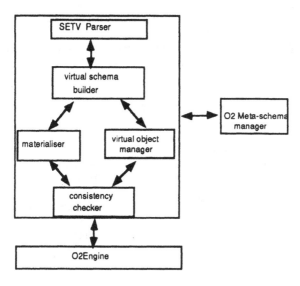

**Fig. 4.** The System Architecture of SETV

## SETV System classes

The components of SETV are implemented as system classes. A part of the SETV meta-schema hierarchy is presented in the following figure.

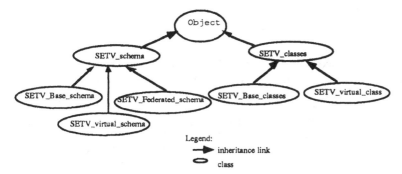

**Fig. 5.** The system classes of SETV

Due to space limitations, we give a short example including the system classes representing a virtual class with O2 data definition language :
class SETV_virtual_classes inherit SETV_classes public type
 tuple (
        range:string, /* represents the class visibility */
        from:set(SETV_base_classes), /* bases class names */
        extension:SETV_extensions, /* virtual class extension described below */
        attributes:set(SETV_attr), /* attributes belonging to the virtual class */

has_additional:integer, /*flag indicating if a virtual class has additional attributes */

has_init:integer /* flag indicating if an init method for additional attributes already exists*/

end;

class SETV_extensions public type / * class describing information on virtual class extension */

tuple(

name:string, /* extension name of the virtual class */

class:SETV_virtual_classes, /* related virtual class name */

is_materialized:integer, /* flag indicating if the virtual class is already materialised */

query:string /* the query allows to compute the base objects that populate the virtual class*/,

is_persistent : boolean, /* flag indicating if the extension is persistent */

)

end;

## 7. Related work

In this section we review the main approaches proposed to define views in an object-oriented database. This overview is organised according the contribution of each work.

**Pioneer Work :**

The concept of schema virtualisation was introduced by Tanaka et al. [18]. The view specification in this proposition does not include the view behavioural aspect. The integration of virtual classes in the class hierarchy has to be done by the user.

A more elaborate view language is proposed in [1] with the O2 object model. The contributions of this proposition are : the definition of a set of view primitives : ( virtual class , imaginary classes, virtual attributes,..), OID creation for composite (or imaginary) objects. A view may be thought of as a database that imports all its data from other databases. The concepts described in [1] are extended and implemented in the O2Views prototype on the top of the commercial OODBMS O2 [14].

O2Views provides a powerful view language, allowing composition of view primitives and cascade of virtual schemas. Its originality lies in the formalisation of the extended data model including an automatic resolution based on a new relationship named "maybe".

**Virtual classes Integration**

Rundensteiner's work [11] proposes a methodology for supporting multiple view schemata. The originality of this works lies in the integration of the virtual schema into one consistent global schema through a classification algorithm. The multi-view system is implemented on top of Gemstone. The integration approach gives rise to a more complex inheritance hierarchy containing classes that are semantically unmeaningful to the user. Algorithms for view integration can be found in [11]. In our approach, the federated schema is extended by a new relationship, called derivation relationship, allowing linkage of each virtual class to its derivation root class, as in [5].

## View updatability

The large majority of all previous papers do not address the problem of updating objects through views. Scholl et al.'s work [15] is one of the exceptions. These authors discuss the updates on views derived by the query language COOL. An object set-oriented algebra is proposed that can be used to customise the type structure and object membership of classes. This approach is based on a query language having the following properties : object preservation, type/class separation, multiple instantiation and multiple class membership. View updatability is guaranteed by object preservation.
This approach does not provide a solution for updating composite views that produce virtual objects built from several base objects and therefore not preserving object identity.

## Views for schema evolution

The idea of integrating the capabilities of schema evolution with view facilities was first introduced in [5]. In [16], the simulation process is enhanced and included in an external schema definition. An external schema is defined as a subset of base classes and a set of views that correspond to the schema modifications. More recently, the Multi-view system is enhanced with schema evolution support [13]. The originality of this work lies in the fact that the system provides versions of views. More precisely, given a schema change request on a view schema, the system computes a new view which simulates the schema change. The new view is assigned to the user, while the old one is maintained by the system, for as long as other application programs continue to operate on it. However, the issue concerning the augmentation of virtual class derived from several base classes is not addressed.

A comparative summary is given in figure 6 : it shows that view updatability is guaranteed by object preservation . Therefore view systems providing composite views (O2Views and SETV) provide restricted updatability.

| Approaches | virtual class integration | view = schema | schema evolution | composite view | updatability |
|---|---|---|---|---|---|
| Bertino | no | no | yes | yes | ? |
| CoCoon | yes | no | yes | no | yes |
| Multiview/TSE | yes | yes | yes | no | yes |
| O2Views | no | yes | no | yes | restricted |
| SETV | no | yes | yes | yes | restricted |

Fig. 6. Comparison of the different approaches

# 8. Conclusion

In the present paper, we show how database reorganisation might be avoided after schema modifications and we point out the problems arising when using view mechanisms for this purpose. We propose a view specification language that supports the extension of the database with new data introduced by capacity augmenting views. The most important issue concerns the management of these new data. The existing solution is not very satisfactory since the capacity augmenting operation cannot be simulated by views without data reorganisation if the added properties are inserted into the base schema [16], [13]. Furthermore, capacity augmenting schema modifications cannot be unambiguously propagated to the base schema when the related virtual class is derived from several classes. A solution based on the definition of a multi-level schema architecture is proposed here. Our approach provides the following features :
- The schema modifications are allowed without database reorganisation.
- Capacity-augmenting views
- Improvement of the sharing and reuse of information between views

The view definition and update languages presented in this paper are implemented on top of the O2 Database system [8]. We learnt from this that the object data model must be extended to facilitate the implementation of a view system, with the following capabilities :
- multi-instantiation and multi-classification,
- providing the extension of a class defined as the set of all objects belonging to this class,
- Assigning Identifiers to virtual composite objects.

Our future work will concern the study of view mechanisms to support the interoperability and schema evolution in federated databases. The view mechanism is essential to support customisation and to control access on local databases and on the federated level.

## Acknowledgements

I would like to thank Gilles Lucato for his implementation work of the SETV prototype on top of O2, Pascal Poncelet and Maguelonne Teisseire for their fruitful discussions on views.

## References

1. ABITEBOUL S., BONNER A. ,"Objects and Views", in Proc. ACM SIGMOD, Conference on Management of Data, pp 238-247, Denver, Colorado, May 1991.

2. ABITEBOUL S., HULL R, VIANU V, "Foundations of Databases", Addison Wesley, 1995.

3. BANERJEE J., KIM W., KIM K.J., KORTH H., "Semantics and Implementation of Schemas Evolution in Object-oriented databases", in Proc. ACM SIGMOD Conference on Management of Data, San Francisco, May 1987.

4. BELLAHSENE Z., "An Active Meta-model for Knowledge Evolution in an Object-oriented Database", in Proc. of CAISE'93, Paris 8-11 June, Lecture Notes on Computer Sciences, Springer-Verlag, 1993.

5. BERTINO E., " A View Mechanism for Object-oriented Database", 3rd International Conference on Extending Database Technology, March 23-24, Vienna(Austria),1992.

6. KIM W., "Introduction to Object-Oriented Databases", MIT Press, Cambridge, Massachusetts, London, England, 1990.

7. LECLUSE C., RICHARD P., VELEZ F., "O$_2$, An Object Oriented Data Model", in Proc. of the ACM SIGMOD Conference on Management of Data, Chicago, June 1988.

8. LUCATO G., "Evolution de schema au travers des vues", Rapport de DEA, University of Montpellier II, June 1995.

9. MOTRO A., "Superviews: Virtual Integration of Multiple Databases", IEEE Trans. on Software Engineering, Vol. SE-13, N°7, July 1987, PP. 785-798.

10. NGUYEN gian Toan, RIEU Dominique, "Schema Evolution in Object-oriented Database systems", Data&Knowledge Engineering, North Holland, vol.4 July, 1989.

11. RUNDENSTEINER E.A., "Multiview : A Methodology for Supporting Multiple Views in Object-Oriented Databases", in Proc. of the VLDB Conference, Vancouver, British Columbia, Canada 1992.

12. RA Y.G., RUNDENSTEINER E. A., "A transparent object-oriented Schema Changes Approach Using View Evolution", IEEE Int. Conference on Data Engineering, 1995, Taipei, Taiwan.

13. RA Y.G., KUNO H., RUNDENSTEINER E. A., "A Flexible Object-Oriented Database Model and Implementation for Capacity-Augmenting Views", Electrical Engineering and Computer Science and Engineering Division, university of Michigan, Ann Arbor, Technical report CSE-TR-215-94, May 1994.

14. SANTOS C., DELOBEL C., ABITEBOUL S., "Virtual Schemas and Bases", in Proc of the International Conference on Extending Database Technology, Cambridge, March 1994,.

15. SCHOLL H. M et al., "Updatable Views in Object-Oriented Databases", in Proc. of Deductive and object-oriented Databases, Germany, October 1991.

16. TRESCH M., SCHOLL M.H, "Schema Transformation without Database Reorganisation", in SIGMOD Record, 22(1), March 1993.

17. SHETH A.P, LARSON J.A., "Federated Databases Systems for Managing Distributed, Heterogeneous, and Autonomous Databases", ACM Computer Surveys, 22(3):183-236, September 1990.

18. TANAKA K., YOSHIKAWA M., KOSO I., "Schema Virtualization in Object-Oriented Databases", in Proc. of the IEEE Data Eng. Conference, Feb. 1988.

19. ZICARI R., "A framework for O2 Schema updates", in Proc. of 7th IEEE International Conference on Data Engineering, PP. 146-182, April 1991.

# An Active Rule Language for ROCK & ROLL

Andrew Dinn, Norman W. Paton†, M. Howard Williams and Alvaro A.A. Fernandes††

Department of Computing and Electrical Engineering,
Heriot-Watt University, Riccarton, Edinburgh, UK
email: <andrew,howard>@cee.hw.ac.uk
Department of Computer Science†,
University of Manchester, Oxford Road, Manchester, UK
email: norm@cs.man.ac.uk
Department of Mathematical Sciences††,
Goldsmiths College, New Cross, London SE14 6NW
email: a.fernandes@gold.ac.uk

**Abstract.** This paper presents an active rule language for the ROCK & ROLL deductive object-oriented database system. A characteristic feature of ROCK & ROLL is that it blends imperative and deductive programming styles so that both can be used together in support of passive database applications. The aim in developing an active extension is to allow declarative expression of aspects of active behaviour wherever possible, without imposing prohibitive restrictions on the power of the resulting system. The proposal which results is more powerful than most earlier declarative active rule systems, in both its language and execution model, without resorting to the wholly procedural approach supported by most proposals for active object-oriented databases. The paper indicates where retaining declarative features yields greatest benefits, but also where difficulties are encountered which lead to compromises.

## 1 Introduction

The ROCK & ROLL deductive-object-oriented database (DOOD) system [4, 3] supports an expressive object-oriented data model, a deductive language in which to write queries and rules, and an imperative database programming language. As such, it provides a comprehensive collection of passive facilities for defining database functionality. However, in the same way as the imperative and deductive mechanisms in ROCK & ROLL are complementary, an active extension can itself be seen as adding to the range of facilities available to a programmer. For example, there is no built-in mechanism for integrity checking in ROCK & ROLL, and while certain checks can be implemented using methods in the context of strict encapsulation, it is sometimes the case that the checking of integrity should not be done immediately an update is executed, but rather later, when any temporary inconsistencies should have been overcome. Essentially, active capabilities in a system such as ROCK & ROLL allow non-intrusive monitoring of activities in the database, with a view to enforcing integrity, maintaining derived information, keeping users informed of activities or refreshing displays (for an overview of active databases, see [25]).

Research into active databases leading to the development of complete systems has generally fallen into one of two camps:

- Active relational databases [24, 26], which are based on the query language of the underlying database system, and thus support declarative expression of conditions and straightforward facilities for performing updates. Such systems generally have simple event specification languages and execution models.
- Active object-oriented databases [12, 17, 11, 6], which are based on the programming language of the underlying database system, and thus support procedural mechanisms for the expression of conditions and for performing updates. Such systems generally have sophisticated event specification languages and execution models.

However, the trend that is emerging in standards, for example SQL-3 and ODMG [8], is towards systems which support both declarative query facilities and powerful programming capabilities. This raises the question as to how procedural and declarative mechanisms can be integrated effectively in active systems, without the introduction of arbitrary restrictions and inconsistent rule structures as are found in early commercial implementations of active facilities [19]. The experience reported in this paper for ROCK & ROLL indicates that while blending declarative and procedural mechanisms is not without its challenges, coherent and powerful rule systems can be developed.

This paper is structured as follows: section 2 outlines recent research on active database systems; section 3 summarises the passive capabilities of ROCK & ROLL; section 4 presents the language extensions of the active ROCK & ROLL system; section 5 describes the corresponding execution model; section 6 gives an example of an active application in ROCK & ROLL; section 7 outlines some distinctive features of the active extension to ROCK & ROLL; and section 8 presents some conclusions.

## 2 Related Work

### 2.1 Active Database Systems

Limited space prevents a comprehensive description of the characteristics of active database systems; for a classification and brief survey, see [21]. The distinguishing feature of an active database system is that it is able to respond automatically to situations that arise inside or outside the database itself. The active behaviour of a database is generally described using rules, which most commonly have three components, an *event*, a *condition* and an *action*. A rule with such components is known as an event-condition-action rule, or *ECA-rule*. Such a rule lies dormant until an occurrence of the event that it is monitoring, when the rule is said to be *triggered*. The condition of a triggered rule is subsequently evaluated, and if true, then the action of the rule is scheduled for execution.

The structural and behavioural characteristics of active database systems can be classified according to a number of dimensions, as outlined informally in [21]. For the purposes of this paper we classify the aspects to be described into two areas: *knowledge model* and *execution model*.

The knowledge model represents the syntactic view of active rules as seen by the rule programmer. This has three main facets:

**Event language:** a notation in which the situations that trigger a rule can be specified. Events are classified as *primitive*, in which case no components are distinguished (e.g. the *deletion* of an object), or *composite*, in which case a number of primitive occurrences are linked using the operations of an event algebra (e.g. the *salary* of a *person* has been updated and the person is given an increased *holiday* allowance within the same transaction).

**Condition language:** a notation used to enquire about the context in which the rule has been triggered, to ascertain if it is appropriate for the action to be carried out.

**Action language:** a notation used to specify the effect that the rule must have when it is executed.

The execution model describes how rules interact in the context of the whole database system. It has the following aspects:

**Coupling mode:** the temporal and causal relationship between triggering and execution. For example, it is possible that the action of a rule is executed as soon as possible after the evaluation of the condition of the rule (immediate), or at a later point, such as at end of transaction (deferred).

**Transition granularity:** the nature of the binding between event occurrences and rule activations. It is possible that an individual event occurrence will trigger a rule, or that a collection of occurrences of an event will together trigger a rule.

**Rule priorities:** the mechanism for indicating to the system the order in which rules are selected for processing when many are triggered at the same time.

## 2.2   Event Specification Languages

The event and the condition of an ECA rule between them describe the *situation* that is being monitored. The overall expressiveness of situation monitoring thus depends upon the capabilities of the event and condition description languages. In general, increasing the power of the event specification language means that more of the situation can be described using the event part of a rule, and that conditions are both evaluated less frequently and perform more straightforward tests. However, this is achieved at some cost – rich event description languages often require that considerable amounts of information be recorded about partially detected events, and thus impose space and time overheads on executing transactions.

An event specification language enables declarative queries to be posed about what is happening in the database. As such, event specifications can be seen as queries over the history of operations that have been applied to the database, although implementations do not generally implement event detection in this way for performance reasons. Rather, the only information that is recorded is on specific activities of interest to the application.

The best known languages for describing composite events are supported by ODE [18], SAMOS [16] and Sentinel [11]. These languages provide facilities, for example, for detecting:

- *Conjunctions* of events (the event $E_1$ and the event $E_2$ have taken place within some time interval).
- *Sequences* of events (the event $E_1$ followed the event $E_2$ within some time interval).
- *Repetition* of an event (the event $E$ occurred multiple times within some time interval).

The event detection language for ROCK & ROLL supports a range of facilities that are present in the languages mentioned above. However, it has several noteworthy characteristics: the syntax of the event detection language is comparable to that of the condition expression language, and the semantics of both languages are defined in terms of the semantics of logic programs; literals and unification within an event description are used to filter out irrelevant events early. Matching within event expressions is also supported in PFL [23], although in that system the considerable power of the event expression language could cause performance problems.

## 2.3 Architectures

There are two principal architectures for active database systems – *layered* and *integrated*. Of these, ROCK & ROLL has an integrated active rule system, in that event detection, scheduling, optimisation, etc are built into the kernel.

# 3 ROCK & ROLL

This section summarises the features of ROCK & ROLL that are relevant to the description of the active rule language that follows. The approach to the development of a DOOD adopted in ROCK & ROLL involves the derivation and subsequent integration of two languages, one a logic query language (ROLL), and the other an imperative programming language (ROCK), from a single object-oriented data model (OM). The architecture is presented in figure 1. This architecture remains largely untouched by the active extensions. The languages and the underlying model remain the same, although language facilities are now also used from within active rules which monitor the execution of programs and changes to databases described using the model. The following sections present the individual components of ROCK & ROLL and their integration.

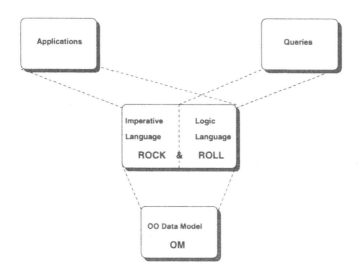

**Fig. 1.** Relationship between the principal components of ROCK & ROLL.

## 3.1 OM

The OM data model underpins the two languages ROCK and ROLL; it supports a range of modelling constructs familiar from semantic data models for describing sets, aggregates, inheritance, lists, etc. To illustrate some of the features of OM, the example power supply application from [10] will be used.

Information has to be stored on the elements that appear in the power supply network, and on the way in which these elements are connected together. The elements in the network are represented as shown in figure 2, using the types: **point**, which is an abstract type defining the property **location**, which is shared by the subtypes of **point**; **plant**, which is a source of power for the network; **user**, which is a sink drawing power from the network; and **node** which is the location of a connection in the network.

The connections between the elements in the network are represented as shown in figure 3, using the types: **link**, which identifies the **points** that are connected; **wire**, which describes the current carrying component of the connection; and **tube** which describes any container which is used to wrap the **wires**.

Note that this is rather a straightforward model which uses only a few of the features of OM; for examples of the use of ROCK & ROLL in a geographic application see [1].

## 3.2 ROCK

ROCK is an imperative object-oriented database programming language based upon OM (i.e. OM describes the structural characteristics of objects that can be

```
type point
   properties:
     public:
       location: string;
end-type

type plant:
   specialises: point;
   properties:
     public:
       power_output: float;
end-type

type user:
   specialises: point;
   properties:
     public:
       power_reqt: float;
end-type

type node:
   specialises: point;
   properties:
     public:
       power_loss: float;
end-type
```

**Fig. 2.** Elements in the power supply network

created and manipulated by ROCK). As such, ROCK can be used to implement complete applications over OM databases, as together ROCK and OM constitute an object-oriented database system. ROCK programs can either be free standing applications, or can be attached to OM types as methods. To illustrate some ROCK concepts, the following code fragment increases the **max_voltage** of every **wire** with a current **max_voltage** of less than **10.0** by **10%**:

```
foreach w in wire do begin
   if (get_max_voltage@w < 10.0) then
      put_max_voltage(get_max_voltage@w * 1.1)@w;
end
```

This fragment illustrates: iteration over the instances of a type using **foreach**; retrieval of the stored properties of an object using a system-generated method of the form **get_***attributename* invoked using the message sending operator **@**; and updating of the value of a stored property of an object using a system-generated method of the form **put_***attributename*.

ROCK can be considered to be a conventional imperative programming language operating in an object-oriented context. Standard facilities for object-

```
type link:
    properties:
      public:
        from: point,
        to: point;
end-type

type wire:
    specialises: link;
    properties:
      public:
        max_voltage: float,
        max_power: float;
        voltage:float,
        power_carried: float;
end-type

type tube:
    specialises: link;
    properties:
      public:
        protected: bool;
end-type
```

**Fig. 3.** Connections in the power supply network

oriented programming are supported, including encapsulation, overriding and dynamic binding. ROCK programs defined as methods on persistent types are stored in the database alongside the data to which they relate.

### 3.3 ROLL

ROLL is a logic query language based upon OM (i.e. OM describes the structural characteristics of objects that can be explored by ROLL queries and rules). ROLL is a conventional deductive database language, in that its semantics are defined by a mapping onto Datalog [9] in the context of an axiom set which describes the structural features of the OM data model [14]. ROLL is free from extensions to support updates or control, which are present in many other deductive database languages (e.g.[22]), as such facilities are provided by ROCK.

ROLL can be used to write queries or methods. As an example, the following ROLL query will retrieve the set of **user** objects that are indirectly connected to the **plant** with **location** equal to **Sizewell**.

```
[ALL User | get_to@Link == User:user,
            get_from@Link == Plant:plant,
            get_location@Plant == "Sizewell"]
```

The part of the query to the left of the | is the projection expression, which indicates that what is of interest is the set of bindings obtained for the variable `User` when the query to the right of the | is evaluated. The query looks for bindings for the variables `Link`, `Plant` and `User`, such that the `Link` joins the `Plant` to the `User` and the `location` of the `Plant` is `Sizewell`. The types of variables in ROLL queries are inferred by a type inference system, and thus need not be given explicitly except to resolve ambiguities. In the above example, the variable `User` is explicitly associated with the type `user` and the variable `Plant` is explicitly associated with the type `plant`. The subgoals to the right of the query can be listed in any order, and an optimiser plans an efficient execution strategy [13]. ROLL can also be used to define methods, expressed as deductive rules, as described in [1, 3, 13].

### 3.4 ROCK & ROLL

The languages ROCK and ROLL can be used together in the development of a single program. The following facilities are available for their combined use:

- ROLL queries can be embedded in ROCK programs. For example, the example query from the previous section can be embedded in ROCK thus:

```
var us := [ALL User | get_to@Link == User:user,
                      get_from@Link == Plant:plant,
                      get_location@Plant == "Sizewell"]
```

  The type of the ROCK variable `us` is inferred by the type inference system from the type of the logic variable `User`. ROLL queries can also access ROCK variables, which are named in ROLL with the prefix !.
- ROCK methods can be invoked from ROLL queries and rules, although with the restriction that the ROCK method must not have any side-effects. The check for potential side-effects is carried out at compile time.

The level of seamlessness offered by the integration of ROCK and ROLL is discussed in [4].

## 4 Knowledge Model

This section describes the languages available to the user for describing events, conditions and actions in ROCK & ROLL. Essentially, rules are constructed using the syntax:

$Rule ::=$ RULE $RuleId$ WHEN $EventSpec$ IF $CondSpec$ DO $Action$ END_RULE

The remainder of this section, along with section 5 will fill in the details of how rules are defined.

### 4.1 Event Language

ROCK & ROLL supports a variety of primitive event types and provides an event algebra for describing composite events.

$Event ::= PrimEvent \parallel CompEvent$

**Primitive Events:** Primitive events are able to monitor a wide range of structure operations and behaviour invocations, as well as more global activity, such as the start or the end of a session.

$$PrimEvent ::= MsgEvent \;||\; CreateEvent \;||\; DeleteEvent \;||$$
$$SessStartEvent \;||\; SessCommitEvent \;||\; SessAbortEvent$$

In ROCK & ROLL, structure operations are implemented using a message sending syntax to invoke system generated methods, and thus share the same syntax as user defined operations. Object creation and deletion occurs via special built-in operators which are also shared by the event syntax.

Message events must specify a method name, recipient and arguments, and are described using a syntax comparable to that used for method invocation:

$$MsgEvent \quad ::= Msg \text{ SENT} \;||\; Msg \;||\; Msg ==> Param$$
$$Msg \qquad\quad ::= \text{Id } OptParams \; @ \; Rcpt$$
$$OptParams ::= \epsilon \;||\; (\; Params.\;)$$
$$Params \qquad ::= Param \;||\; Param \;,\; Params$$

Message events must also specify whether the event occurs when the message is sent or after it has been processed. In the latter case it may also be desirable to know the return value from the method (where there is one). The keyword SENT can be appended to identify that the event occurs when the message is *sent* i.e. before executing the method. If the return value from a completed message is required in the event specification then the message send can be followed by the symbol ==> and a parameter for the returned value.

The parameters of a message event can be either variables which *bind* message arguments, constant values which *match* message arguments or anonymous variables (written as _), which unify with arguments that play no other role in the event detection process. Note that there is no way to specify an instance of a user defined type as a constant value so the recipient can only be supplied as a variable (or anonymous variable).

$$Param ::= Var \;||\; Val \;||\; \text{AnonVar}$$
$$Rcpt \quad ::= Var \;||\; \text{AnonVar}$$
$$Var \quad ::= \text{Id} \;||\; \text{Id : Id}$$

As an example of a message event, `put_max_voltage(0)@W:wire` detects when an attempt is made to assign 0 as the maximum voltage of wire `W`.

**Composite Events:** Composite events allow both conjunctions and disjunctions of events. Conjunctions may be either sequenced or unsequenced. In the present implementation, the interval over which the components of a composite event are accumulated is a single session.

$$CompEvent ::= OptPolicy \; Event \; \text{WITH } Event \;||$$
$$OptPolicy \; Event \; \text{THEN } Event \;||$$
$$Event \; \text{OR } Event \;||$$
$$\text{REPEATED Count TIMES } Event$$

The WITH keyword implies unordered conjunction whereas THEN implies sequenced conjunction.

As an example of a composite event:

`put_max_voltage(Max)@W:wire WITH put_min_voltage(Min)@W`

detects the setting of the maximum and the minimum value for the voltage of a wire within a single session. Note that unification of variable W between the two events ensures that the composite event is only triggered by two messages sent to the same wire. As a further example of a composite event, the following event specification detects when the maximum voltage of a wire is changed more than once within a session:

`REPEATED 2 TIMES put_max_voltage(Max)@W:wire`

In [11] it is shown that different *consumption modes* for composite events can be discerned, which indicates how component events are grouped together to form composite events (there is not space here to elaborate on the details). In ROCK & ROLL, three consumption modes are supported for conjunctive events, namely recent, chronicle and continuous. The keyword **LATEST** (the default) specifies recent consumption, **EARLIEST** specifies chronicle consumption and **ALL** specifies continuous consumption.

$$OptPolicy ::= \epsilon \parallel \text{LATEST} \parallel \text{EARLIEST} \parallel \text{ALL}$$

**Event Detection and ROLL:** As indicated in the introduction, one of the aims of this paper is to show what costs and benefits result from the integration of declarative language features with an active database system. Benefits which derive from the use of a declarative condition language include consistency of style with the event language, conciseness, and amenability to optimisation and analysis (see section 7). There are difficulties, however, with detection of events raised within a declarative language component. In ROCK & ROLL the problem arises when operations invoked from ROLL queries or methods are being monitored by events.

There are two basic problems. Firstly, the number of times a method is invoked and the parameters with which it is invoked depend on the evaluation strategy chosen by the optimiser. Secondly, certain operations appearing in the source of the program may be replaced by other operations when the program is compiled.

Consider the query in section 3.4 when a rule is monitoring the message event `get_location@P:plant ==> L`. The query might be executed naively by scanning class `user` traversing `links` to the relevant `plants` and testing the value of attribute `location`. Alternatively, class `plant` might be scanned first or, in the presence of an index on `location`, the relevant `plants` generated directly bypassing any access to attribute `location`.

The approach adopted in ROCK & ROLL is to raise an event for every set of bindings *generated* for a method invocation with unbound arguments or every set of bindings *validated* for a method invocation whose arguments are all bound. So, in the example, whatever plan the optimiser chooses, an event is raised for each plant/location pair generated during evaluation. If a plant is considered which has undefined location or location other than the required value `Sizewell` then no event is raised.

## 4.2 Condition Language

Rule conditions are essentially arbitrary ROLL expressions, although the pseudo-goal TRUE is also supported, effectively allowing optional conditions.

$$Condition ::= \text{TRUE} \parallel GoalCond$$

Alternative conditions can be expressed using a disjunction operator, so long as the condition as a whole is in Disjunctive Normal Form (DNF).

$$GoalCond ::= GoalList \parallel GoalList \text{ OR } GoalCond$$

Each disjunct is a list of ROLL goals, built-in, system-generated or user-defined, as appears in the right hand side of a normal query expression. Rule conditions can also access information about the event which has triggered the rule, as discussed in section 5.2. Conditions are thus expressed using the declarative language facilities of the ROCK & ROLL system, which makes them amenable to query optimisation, as discussed in section 7.3.

## 4.3 Action Language

Action specifications are operations to be performed either in addition to or in place of those mentioned in the event specification. Alternatives are only appropriate when a message event forms part of the rule event specification.

$$Action ::= Acts \parallel \text{INSTEAD } Acts \parallel Acts \text{ RETURN } Expr \parallel \text{INSTEAD } Acts \text{ RETURN } Expr$$

A list of actions (*Acts*) is a sequence of semi-colon separated ROCK & ROLL expressions or statements, which may also access information originating from the event or condition, as described in section 5.2.

$$Acts ::= \text{ROCKOp} \parallel \text{ROCKOp} ; Acts$$

Thus actions are expressed using the procedural language facilities of the passive ROCK & ROLL system, which allows direct execution of stored operations, updates, or user interaction commands.

## 4.4 Control Language

Language facilities are also provided to allow the user to control the way in which rules are executed. As these relate to the execution model, they are considered in section 5.

# 5 Execution Model

This section describes the execution model of the ROCK & ROLL active rule system, along with the syntactic constructs that relate to execution model features.

## 5.1 Coupling Modes

The coupling mode of a rule indicates when the event, condition and action of the rule are evaluated relative to each other. The coupling mode is described by a statement given separately from the rule definition:

*Coupling* ::= COUPLING *RuleId* CONDITION *Mode* ACTION *Mode* END_COUPLING
*Mode*    ::= IMMEDIATE || DEFERRED

The coupling mode is expressed separately for the condition and the action of the rule, and thus indicates when the condition is evaluated relative to the event and when the action is evaluated relative to the condition. For example, it would be possible to check a condition immediately after the event that the rule is monitoring, but to defer execution of the action to the end of the session.

As ROCK & ROLL has a very straightforward transaction model which is derived from that of the EXODUS system on which it is built [7] (a session is treated as a single transaction), deferred processing is initiated either in response to the top-level (i.e. not a program statement) command **ASSERT**, or, by default, at the end of a session.

Rules with **INSTEAD** actions always require immediate processing and rules which specify a set level transition granularity (see below) always require deferred mode processing. Furthermore, rules which perform actions on objects arising from a delete event must be processed immediately since it is not possible to perform such operations after the deletion has occurred. This is part of a wider difficulty which arises for all object-oriented models with explicit deletion, as information used as input to a rule may no longer be current when the rule is executed. This is handled in ROCK & ROLL by untriggering all rule activations that have deleted objects as parameters, but would be much more difficult to support in object-oriented databases with lower level data models.

An additional problem exists in supporting **IMMEDIATE** rule processing where rules are triggered by operations invoked from ROLL queries or rules. Not only is the order and number of events raised dependent upon the way in which the optimiser has planned the execution strategy, no updates can be performed during the execution of a piece of ROLL, which must operate over a static database. Thus when events are raised during the execution of a fragment of ROLL, rules defined for **IMMEDIATE** processing are deferred until ROLL code is no longer being processed, and are then scheduled for execution; a similar approach is adopted in PFL [23].

## 5.2 Transition Granularity

Deferred rules need to specify whether the condition is to be executed repeatedly, once each time the specified event occurs, or once only, even if the specified event occurs several times. As well as defining whether these occurrences should be processed individually or as a group, it is also necessary to specify how bindings for variables in the event are to be passed as parameters to the condition or action, and how bindings obtained from the condition are to be supplied to the action.

Projections from events and conditions use a comprehension syntax similar to that employed by ROLL queries. The right hand side contains a description of the relevant events or conditions. The left hand side contains a projection of the relevant bindings. To allow bindings from the event or condition to be referred to in the condition/action it is possible to bind the projected value(s) to a variable. Subsequent mention of the variable in the condition/action provides access to the relevant value(s).

$$EventSpec ::= \text{Var} <== [\ EProj \mid Event\ ] \mid\mid$$
$$[\ EGran \mid Event\ ]$$
$$CondSpec ::= \text{Var} <== [\ CProj \mid Condition\ ]\mid\mid$$
$$[\ \mid Condition\ ]$$

If the rule is fired *each* time the event is raised then the projection can retrieve a single value or a single aggregation of values from the event occurrence for subsequent use in condition or action processing. If the rule is only fired once in response to multiple raisings of the event then the projection can take one of two forms. It can pick a single value or a single aggregation of values from *any* of the event occurrences which raised the event, or it can retrieve bindings from *all* event occurrences supplying the collection of values to the condition and action as an association.

$$EProj ::= \text{EACH } Proj \mid\mid \text{ANY } Proj \mid\mid \text{ALL } Proj$$

An event projection which does not retrieve bindings specifies what to do when an event is raised more than once. The rule may be fired in response to *each* raising of the event or once only in response to *any* event occurrence.

$$EGran ::= \text{EACH} \mid\mid \text{ANY}$$

As an example of an event specification, the following raises an event for every wire that is assigned both a maximum and a minimum voltage during a session, and projects out the object identifier of the wire:

```
awire <== [EACH W |put_max_voltage(Max)@W:wire WITH put_min_voltage(Min)@W]
```

The following event specification raises a single event whenever one or more wires have had their maximum and minimum voltages set during a session, and projects out the set of wires modified in this way (this supports a form of nett-effect processing):

```
wires <== [ALL W |put_max_voltage(Max)@W:wire WITH put_min_voltage(Min)@W]
```

A condition specification includes a ROLL query expression specifying the condition to be evaluated. If the corresponding event specification produces a binding for the event variable $Var$ then the bound value may be employed as an input in the query expression by mentioning $Var$ prefixed with ! in the query body.

The projection part of the query uses the conventional query syntax producing either a boolean result, a single value or aggregation of values obtained from *any* solution to the expression on the right hand side of the query or a set of values or aggregations retrieved from *all* solutions to the expression. In all cases the action will only be executed if the query expression can be solved using the current state of the database.

$$CProj ::= \text{EACH } Proj \, || \text{ANY } Proj \, || \text{ ALL } Proj$$
$$CProj ::= \epsilon$$

If an **ANY** query is used then the action is run once should there be *any* solution to the query, with the bindings picked arbitrarily from one such solution. If an **ALL** query is used then the action is run once if the query has solutions, with bindings being collected from *all* solutions as an association. If an **EACH** query is used then the action is run once for each solution to the query with the relevant bindings projected out of the solution and made available to the action.

The syntax for specifying projected variables in event and condition specifications is the usual ROLL query projection syntax, in which aggregates are specified using angled brackets:

$$Proj ::= Id \, || \, \langle \, Id \, , \, Ids \, \rangle$$

Examples of condition specifications are given in section 6.

**Rule Priorities:** Where multiple rules or rule components (conditions/actions) are scheduled for execution at the same time, a priority mechanism can be used to indicate to the scheduler the order in which different items of processing should take place. In ROCK & ROLL a simple numerical scheme is used:

$$Priority ::= \text{PRIORITY } RuleId \, RealConst \text{ END\_PRIORITY}$$

## 6  Example Application

This section continues the power supply example from [10], showing how some constraints can be expressed using the ROCK & ROLL rule language.

**Example 1:** *All wires must be inside a tube.* The problem arises here when there exist some wires for which there is no corresponding tube. The condition to test for this situation exploits ROLL methods defined on **link** which associate a link with nodes that it links:

```
links(Point1,Point2)@Link :-
    get_from@Link == Point1,
    get_to@Link == Point2.

tube_linked(To)@From :-
    links(To, From)@T:tube.
```

The constraint can only be broken when the end points of a **wire** or a **tube** are changed, or when a tube is deleted. Each case has to be treated separately since in the first case there is a specific wire to check, whereas in the second all wires need checking. The constraint is enforced by creating a new tube to hold the wires which have no tube.

The rule dealing with modification of wires is as follows:

```
RULE AllWiresInTube_1
WHEN Wires <== [ALL W | put_to(T)@W:wire OR put_from(F)@W]
IF Ends <== [ALL <To, From> | W1 in !Wires,
                              links(To, From)@W1:wire,
                              ~tube_linked(To)@From:tube]
DO
foreach pair in Ends do
begin
    var t := new tube();
    put_to(get_to@pair)@t;
    put_from(get_from@pair)@t;
end
END_RULE
```

```
COUPLING AllWiresInTube_1 CONDITION Deferred ACTION Immediate END_COUPLING
```

The rule for deletion or modification of a tube is similar but requires exploration of the extension of class wire:

```
RULE AllWiresInTube_2
WHEN [ANY | delete T:tube OR put_to(To)@T:tube OR put_from(From)@T:tube]
IF Ends <== [ALL <To, From> | links(To, From)@W:wire,
                              ~tube_linked(To)@From:tube]
DO
foreach pair in Ends do
begin
    var t := new tube();
    put_to(get_to@pair)@t;
    put_from(get_from@pair)@t;
end
END_RULE
```

```
COUPLING AllWiresInTube_2 CONDITION Deferred ACTION Immediate END_COUPLING
```

Note that in this rule any event instance will do to trigger the rule since there is no parameter required from the event, and one evaluation of the condition can identify all cases where the constraint has been broken.

**Example 2:** *If a tube contains any high voltage wires then it must be protected.* This constraint can only be violated when the end point of a tube or wire is changed, or when the voltage of a wire is modified. It can be fixed by making the tube protected. The cases involving a wire must be handled separately from those involving a tube.

The rule for tubes needs to check the wires in the tube for one with voltage greater than 5000 volts.

```
RULE HighVoltageWires_1
WHEN Tube <== [EACH T | put_to@T:tube OR put_from@T:tube]
IF [ | get_protected@!Tube == false, links(To, From)@!Tube,
     links(To,From)@W, get_voltage@W > 5000]
```

```
DO
begin
    put_protected(true)@Tube;
end
END_RULE
```

```
COUPLING HighVoltageWires_1 CONDITION Deferred ACTION Immediate END_COUPLING
```

The condition is merely a boolean since the action is only parameterised by the event variable. The action is executed once per event binding irrespective of the number of wires found by the condition (so long as at least one wire is found).

The rule for wires is as follows:

```
RULE HighVoltageWires_2
WHEN Wires <== [ALL W | put_to@W:wire OR put_from@W:wire OR
                        put_voltage(V)@W]
IF Tube <== [EACH T | W1 in !Wires, get_voltage@W1 > 5000,
                      links(To,From)@W1, links(To, From)@T,
                      get_protected@T == false]
DO
begin
    put_protected(true)@Tube;
end
END_RULE
```

```
COUPLING HighVoltageWires_2 CONDITION Deferred ACTION Immediate END_COUPLING
```

# 7 Distinctive Features

This section outlines some distinctive features relating to the development of the ROCK & ROLL active rule system, and some significant consequences which derive from the way the system has been designed.

## 7.1 Specification

This paper has taken the approach of describing the languages used by the user to define active applications in ROCK & ROLL in an informal manner. The complete system has, however, been formally specified. The semantics of the condition and action languages are the semantics of the passive languages ROCK and ROLL, as described in [5] and [14] respectively. The active rule extension has two additional components which must be described, namely:

1. *Event Definition Language:* This has been described by way of a mapping onto deductive rules over an event history described using the event calculus of [20]. As an example, the event for the rule:

    ```
    RULE R1
    WHEN aWire <= [EACH W | put_max_voltage(0)@W]
    IF ...

    COUPLING R1 CONDITION Immediate ...
    ```

gives rise to the following event rules:

starts(EId, trigger('R1', EId, W)) ←
      event(EId),
      happened(EId, completed(put_max_voltage, W, wire, 0)).

ends(EId, trigger('R1', _, W)) ←
      event(EId),
      happened(EId, completed(delete, W, wire)).

ends(EId, trigger('R1', EId, _)) ←
      event(EId),
      happened(EId, fired('R1', EId)).

The first rule indicates that it becomes true that the rule $R1$ is triggered when a *put_max_voltage* method has been sent to a wire $W$ with argument *0*. The rule can then be untriggered in one of two ways: as a result of the wire $W$ being deleted, or as a result of the rule being fired by the rule processor, in which case the fact that $R1$ has been *fired* is explicitly asserted. This description is necessarily rather superficial; the approach adopted is described fully in [15].

2. *Execution Model:* This has been defined formally using an operational style, which describes the algorithms and data structures used to record triggered rules and to schedule rule components for execution. The approach is described in [15].

Developing a formal specification of the active rule system has proved very useful to the development process, particularly in making explicit issues which require decisions to be made by designers at an early stage in the development process.

## 7.2 Analysis

The analysis of active rule bases involves the automatic detection of certain properties which are often felt to be desirable in rule bases. The two features most commonly searched for are *termination* (is rule processing guaranteed to terminate after any set of changes to the database in any state?) and *confluence* (is rule processing guaranteed to reach a unique final state for every valid and complete rule execution sequence starting at any database state?). Probably the most complete and broadly applicable framework for rule analysis is provided by [2], where there are two principal aspects in the development of a rule analyser:

1. *Trigger Graph Construction:* This involves identifying which pairs of rules are able to trigger each other. This analysis has often been done in a very conservative manner, which means that terminating or confluent rule bases are not always detected as such. In ROCK & ROLL, the presence of literals and unification in the event language combined with the constraint based techniques applied in the optimiser (for conditions described in [13]) makes it possible to build less conservative trigger graphs than in other systems.

This is an important benefit which derives from the retention of a declarative condition language.

2. *Trigger Graph Analysis:* This builds upon the triggering relationships mentioned above, and searches for patterns which guarantee terminating and confluent rule bases; the algorithms of [2] are applicable to ROCK & ROLL.

## 7.3 Optimisation

Active rule optimisation has received surprisingly little attention, but is important to the overall performance and uptake of active database systems. There are two principal aspects:

1. *Optimising Single Rules:* In ROCK & ROLL, the condition of each rule is optimised using the ROLL optimiser of [13], which often allows highly constrained searches to be carried out, given knowledge about literals and bindings extracted from events.

2. *Optimising Multiple Rules:* It is common for multiple rules to be triggered at the same time, which potentially allows multiple query optimisation to be applied to their conditions. In practice, multiple query optimisation can only be carried out when the order in which the rules are chosen for processing is known to have no effect on the results of evaluating their conditions. However, this property is exactly what is tested for when rule analysis searches for confluent rule sets, and the rule optimiser for ROCK & ROLL will exploit knowledge about confluence to support multiple query optimisation.

## 8  Conclusions

This paper has described the active rule language for the ROCK & ROLL DOOD system. The work is novel in a number of respects:

1. It is shown how a DOOD system can be extended with active features, indicating where existing functionality can be reused, and where new languages and features are required.

2. It is shown how a comprehension based syntax for event detection and condition expression can be employed to support a range of coupling modes and transition granularities.

3. It is shown how the filtering capabilities of events can be increased by the introduction of literals and unification, and how more flexible parameter passing can be obtained between events, conditions and actions.

4. It is shown how declarative features can be used for describing events and conditions (with benefits for analysis and optimisation), while comprehensive imperative programming facilities are provided for action execution. It is anticipated that future commercial active systems will have a similar balance of declarative and procedural features.

5. It has been indicated how the approach described can be formally specified, and how it lends itself to comprehensive analysis and optimisation of rules.

**Availability:** The ROCK & ROLL system is available over the WWW from http://www.cee.hw.ac.uk/Databases. The active rule language is currently being implemented, and is scheduled for inclusion in the public release from September 1996.

**Acknowledgement:** This research is supported by the UK EPSRC (grant GR/H43847) and the EU Human Capital and Mobility Network ACT-NET.

# References

1. A.I. Abdelmoty, N.W. Paton, M.H. Williams, A.A.A. Fernandes, M.L. Barja, and A. Dinn. Geographic Data Handling in a Deductive Object-Oriented Database. In D. Karagiannis, editor, *Proc. 5th Int. Conf. on Databases and Expert Systems Applications (DEXA)*, pages 445–454. Springer-Verlag, 1994.

2. A. Aiken, J.M. Hellerstein, and J. Widom. Static Analysis Techniqies for Predicting the Behaviour of Active Database Rules. *ACM TODS*, 20(1):3–41, 1995.

3. M.L. Barja, A.A.A. Fernandes, N.W. Paton, M.H. Williams, A. Dinn, and A.I. Abdelmoty. Design and Implementation of ROCK & ROLL: A Deductive Object-Oriented Database System. *Information Systems*, 20:185–211, 1995.

4. M.L. Barja, N.W. Paton, A.A.A. Fernandes, M.H. Williams, and A. Dinn. An Effective Deductive Object-Oriented Database Through Language Integration. In J. Bocca, M. Jarke, and C. Zaniolo, editors, *Proc. 20th Int. Conf. on Very Large Data Bases (VLDB)*, pages 463–474. Morgan-Kaufmann, 1994.

5. M.L. Barja, N.W. Paton, and M.H. Williams. Semantics Based Implementation of a Deductive Object-Oriented Database Programming Language. *J. Programming Languages*, 2(2):93–108, 1994.

6. H. Branding, A. Buchmann, T. Kudrass, and J. Zimmermann. Rules in an Open System: The REACH Rule System. In N.W. Paton and M.H. Williams, editors, *Rules in Database Systems*, pages 111–126. Springer-Verlag, 1994.

7. M. Carey, D. DeWitt, G. Graefe, D. Haight, J. Richardson, D. Schuh, E. Shekita, and S. Vandenberg. The EXODUS Extensible DBMS Project: An Overview. In S. Zdonik and D. Maier, editors, *Readings in Object-Oriented Databases*, CA 94303-9953, 1990. Morgan Kaufman Publishers, Inc.

8. R.G.G. Cattell. *The Object Database Standard: ODMG-93*. Morgan Kaufmann, 1993.

9. S. Ceri, G. Gottlob, and L. Tanca. *Logic Programming and Databases*. Springer-Verlag, Berlin, 1990.

10. S. Ceri and J. Widom. Deriving production rules for constraint maintenance. In *16th Intl. Conf. in Very Large Data Bases, Brisbane*, pages 567–577. Morgan Kaufman, 1990.

11. S. Chakravarthy, E. Anwar, L. Maugis, and D. Mishra. Design of Sentinel: an object-oriented DBMS with event-based rules. *Information and Software Technology*, 36(9):555–568, 1994.

12. O. Diaz, N. Paton, and P.M.D. Gray. Rule management in object oriented databases: a uniform approach. In G.M. Lohman, A. Sernadas, and R. Camps, editors, *17th Intl. Conf. on Very Large Data Bases, Barcelona*, pages 317–326. Morgan Kaufmann, 1991.

13. A. Dinn, N.W. Paton, M.H. Williams, A.A.A. Fernandes, and M.L. Barja. The Implementation of a Deductive Query Language Over an Object-Oriented Database.

In T.W. Ling, A.O. Mendelzon, and L. Vieille, editors, *Proc. 4th Intl. Conf. on Deductive Object-Oriented Databases*, pages 143–160. Springer-Verlag, 1995.

14. A.A.A. Fernandes, M.H. Williams, and N.W. Paton. A Logical Query Language for an Object-Oriented Data Model. In N.W. Paton and M.H. Williams, editors, *Proc. 1st Int. Workshop on Rules in Database Systems*, pages 234–250. Springer-Verlag, 1994.

15. A.A.A. Fernandes, M.H. Williams, and N.W. Paton. A Logic-Based Integration of Active and Deductive Databases, 1996. to be published in *New Generation Computing*.

16. S. Gatziu and K.R. Dittrich. Events in an active object-oriented database. In N.W. Paton and M.H. Williams, editors, *Proc. 1st Int. Workshop on Rules in Database Systems*, pages 23–39. Springer-Verlag, 1994.

17. S. Gatziu, A. Geppert, and K. Dittrich. Integrating active concepts into an object-oriented database system. In P. Kanellakis and J.W. Schmidt, editors, *Proc. $3^{rd}$ Workshop on Database Programming Languages*. Morgan-Kaufmann, 1991.

18. N.H. Gehani and H.V. Jagadish. ODE as an Active Database: Constraints and Triggers. In R. Camps G.M. Lohman, A. Sernadas, editor, *17th Intl. Conf. on Very Large Data Bases, Barcelona*, pages 327–336. Morgan Kaufmann, 1991.

19. G. Koch and K. Loney. *ORACLE: The Complete Reference (3rd Edition)*. Osborne McGraw-Hill, 1995.

20. R. Kowalski. Database updates in the event calculus. *Journal of Logic Programming*, 12:121–146, 1992.

21. N.W. Paton, O. Diaz, M.H. Williams, J. Campin, A. Dinn, and A. Jaime. Dimensions of active behaviour. In N.W. Paton and M.H. Williams, editors, *Proc. 1st Int. Workshop on Rules In Database Systems*, pages 40–57. Springer-Verlag, 1994.

22. R. Ramakrishnan, D. Srivastava, and S. Sudarshan. CORAL-Control, Relations and Logic. In Li-Yan Yuan, editor, *Proceedings of the 18th International Conference on Very Large Databases*, pages 239–250. Morgan Kaufman, 1992.

23. S. Reddi, A. Poulovassilis, and C. Small. Extending a Functional DBPL With ECA-Rules. In T. Sellis, editor, *Proc. 2nd Int. Wshp. on Rules in Database Systems*, pages 101–115. Springer-Verlag, 1995.

24. M. Stonebraker, A. Jhingran, J. Goh, and S. Potamianos. On rules, procedures, caching and views in database systems. In *Proc. ACM SIGMOD*, pages 281–290, 1990.

25. J. Widom and S. Ceri. *Active Database Systems*. Morgan Kaufmann, 1996.

26. J. Widom, R.J. Cochrane, and B.G. Lindsay. Implementing Set-Oriented Production Rules as an Extension to Starburst. In R. Camps G.M. Lohman, A. Sernadas, editor, *17th Intl. Conf. on Very Large Data Bases, Barcelona*, pages 275–286. Morgan Kaufmann (ISBN 1-55860-150-3), 1991.

# Integrity Constraints in Multiversion Databases

Anne Doucet[†], Stéphane Gançarski[‡], Geneviève Jomier[‡], Sophie Monties[†]

† LAFORIA - Université P. & M. Curie    ‡ LAMSADE - Université Paris Dauphine
Case 169, 4 place Jussieu              Place du M[al] de Lattre de Tassigny
75252 Paris cedex 5, France        75775 Paris cedex 16, France
{doucet,monties}@laforia.ibp.fr     {gancarski, jomier}@lamsade.dauphine.fr

**Abstract.** This paper analyses the extension of integrity constraint mechanisms in order to maintain consistency in multiversion databases is studied. Unlike monoversion databases, a multiversion database represents several states of the modeled universe. Thus, both the notion of consistency and the means to maintain it have to be extended. To this aim, we consider new integrity constraints induced by versioning. Constraints are characterized according to several criteria, and a general framework for optimizing their checking in the context of ACID transactions is given. The database versions model [CJ90] is used as it offers a sound basis for the definition of consistency.

**Keywords** : database, versions, consistency, integrity constraints.

## Introduction

Maintaining consistency in databases is an important need in applications. The classical way to manage consistency is to define *integrity constraints*, which are assertions that must be verified at the end of each transaction. Integrity constraints can concern single entities as well as several entities. A database is consistent if and only if all constraints are satisfied. [GA93] gives a survey of the various approaches used to manage integrity constraints.

Versioning is also a major need in a growing number of applications. For instance, in design applications (e.g. CAD, CASE, etc.), designers need to create and handle versions in order to cope with the "trial and error" nature of the design process. They need to manipulate *object versions*, in order to keep tracks of different experimentations, revisions and alternatives, made over design objects. Here the term object is used in its common sense of entity. As design objects are grouped to form a final product, or project, designers need also to manage *project versions*, often called *configurations* [KA91, EC94]. In order to support such activities, several version models have been proposed [Zdo86, Atw86, AJ89, KBG89, Kat90, KS92, TOC93, AHLZ95]. As well version mechanisms are now beginning to appear in commercial DBMSs, particularly in OODBMSs, e.g. [O2T95], for handling *multiversion databases* which are databases able to manage versions.

In order to support new applications, both integrity mechanisms and versioning have to be used. Constraints must be defined and checked according to the new dimension introduced by versioning. Consider for example a software development application where *software objects* (e.g. programs, libraries, modules) are developed and maintained. The whole software may be seen as a collection of programs, libraries and modules, where configurations are composed of versions of different objects (programs, libraries or modules). Usually, a new configuration is created by *deriving* (copying followed by updating) an existing one. Constraints must be defined to express consistency of configurations. A constraint might be: "for each function call $f(x, y, \ldots)$ appearing in a configuration $C$, there must exist a program version in $C$, where $f$ is implemented with a signature corresponding to the call". Consistency *across* configurations must also be maintained, because modifications addressed to a configuration may be inconsistent with the content of other configurations. Constraints may also be defined to enforce a versioning policy. Examples of such constraints are : "a configuration must have less listed bugs than the configuration it is derived from", "the total number of configurations cannot decrease" and others.

As new applications aim at using DBMS as efficient repositories, maintaining consistency in multiversion databases is a crucial issue. The integrity mechanism must be coordinated with the versioning policy, according to application semantics. In conventional DBMSs, the state of a database models a possible representation of the real world, and transactions transform the database from a representation to another, if all constraints are checked at the end of the transaction. In a multiversion DBMS, the state of a database models many possible representations (e.g. configurations) of the real world, and transactions transform the database from a set of representations to another set of representations. Thus, not only the definition of constraints must be extended, but also the mechanism to check them efficiently. This makes the problem of maintaining consistency in multiversion databases a new and difficult issue. Consider for instance a constraint stating that "a configuration must have less listed bugs than the configuration it is derived from". Checking this constraint requires not only to read, for each configuration, all the program versions it contains and to aggregate their number of bugs, but also to pairwise compare the results obtained for each couple of configurations bound by a derivation link. This simple example shows that the complexity of checking integrity constraints would be greater in databases with versions than in conventional monoversion databases. Thus, integrity constraints have to be defined in a clear and sound version model to be handled with good performance.

To provide a general integrity mechanism for multiversion databases, a theoretical framework is required, in order to systematically explore the consistency issue in presence of versions and to provide a sound foundation for defining and checking constraints in such a context. The aim of this paper is to show the first steps in the definition of such a framework. Its main contributions are:

- An analysis of the requirements for integrating version management and integrity control mechanisms.
- A study of the features of constraints for multiversion databases, leading to an operational classification of those constraints.
- A global overview of an integrity mechanism allowing to manage those constraints efficiently.

As this paper focuses on integrity constraints, we do not address the problem of defining a new transaction model. We consider a conventional model, with flat transactions having well known ACID properties, consistency being checked just before the commit phase [GR93]. We present our work in the context of object databases. However, the results presented are general and independent from the data model. The term object denotes an entity, without referring to particular object-oriented features other than object identification and complex object representation through object references.

This paper is organized as follows. Section 1 explains the problem of consistency in databases with versions and states the difficulty of integrating versions and constraints. Section 2 presents the DataBase Versions (DBV) model, which allows to manage efficiently multiversion databases. Criteria used to characterize integrity constraints on such multiversion databases are studied in section 3 and used to determine an operational classification. Section 4 gives the general organization of the integrity mechanism. Then, section 5 concludes.

# 1 Related work

The integration of integrity constraints and versions appears a crucial issue, which raises the following question: when there are so many papers on each subject, versions and integrity constraints, why are there so few papers dealing with both subjects together ? The answer is very straightforward. The basis of integrity constraints is consistency. They are centred on the idea of "consistent database states" at beginning and end of transactions. However, as shown in [CJ90], in most version models, defining consistent database states is a problem. More precisely, in monoversion databases, the consistency of a database state is defined in reference to a state of the real world modeled by the state of the database. The specificity of a database with versions is that it contains the description of several states of the real world. To be able to define consistency of such a database, the version model must provide users with means of expressing which sets of versions are "consistent" (i.e. object versions inside such a set are "mutually consistent"), as it is pointed out in [BG80, Zdo86, Atw86] with the notions of *layer*, *slice* and *partial consistency*. Moreover, the version model must allow defining the concept of consistency of a state of the whole database, when it is built from such sets of object versions. Clearly, this point is essential to use the concept of transaction in a sound way.

However, if the problem of consistency in databases with versions has been largely perceived, practically very few version models offer a way to define consistency so that this concept may be efficiently handled by a version manager. Actually, consistency may be soundly defined in the following cases:

- in temporal databases (using versions),
- in systems including a configuration manager, if a configuration is defined as a set of object versions with at most one version of each object per configuration,
- in multiversion databases using the database version approach.

As the work presented in this paper is based on the database version approach, in the introduction, we only comment the work related to temporal databases and to configuration managers, on the double point of view of versions and integrity constraints.

Temporal databases [Sarda90, TCG+93] use different dimensions of time (e.g. valid time, transaction time etc.). If only one dimension of time is used, for instance valid time, the database represents as many states of the real world as there are different valid states present in the database. These states are totally ordered. As a consequence, integrity constraints may be specified using temporal logic. This is a first step toward the integration of integrity constraints and versions. However, the total order imposed by the semantics of time on the versions induces a strong limitation on the extension of this method to other domains, like design applications (e.g. CAD, CASE) where generally versions are organized in a tree or a DAG.

In configuration management [KA91, EC94, Reich.89], it rarely appears that integrity constraints are evoked in order to ensure the quality of a configuration. A conventional example of such a constraint in the CASE area is "the parameters of a program call must be compatible with the signature (declared parameters) of the called program". This kind of constraint may be considered inside some or all the configurations of a "repository". From a multiversion database point of view, as these constraints operate inside each configuration separately from the others, they are quite similar to constraints defined in monoversion DBMSs (even if often the configuration is not built on top of a DBMS but on top of a file management system, where the notion of transaction is not well defined). As far as we know, in that kind of application, integrity constraints involving some configurations simultaneously have not been defined, even if their usefulness appears clear.

Finally, properties required for a version model to be a good candidate at the integration of integrity constraints in general purpose DBMS are (1) the multiversion database consistency must be well defined and (2) the organization of versions coming from the derivation must not be limited to a sequential order. Those properties are fulfilled by the database version (DBV) model, presented in the next section. The interest of the DBV approach for integrity constraints had previously been pointed out in [BMCJ93].

## 2 The DBV approach

In this section, the DBV approach is briefly presented, restricted to the characteristics relevant to this paper. Then, the main issues related to consistency are formulated within this model.

### 2.1 Presentation

One of the main features of the DBV approach, which distinguishes it from other approaches, is the distinction between the logical level, "what the user sees", and the physical level, "what is managed by the system".

At the logical level, the multiversion database is seen as a set of *DataBase Versions*, or DBV, identified by a database version identifier and composed of object versions. Each DBV represents a possible state, or version, of the modeled world, and thus is a natural way to store *configurations*. As an object version may have the same value in several database versions, the conventional concept of "object version" is split in two new concepts: a *logical object version* represents the object version as it is seen by users in a given database version; a *physical object version* is used by the system to store the value of all the logical versions of this object having the same value. A database version is composed of one logical version of each object, identified by a pair (object identifier, database version identifier). If object $o$ does not exist in DBV $d$, the value of its logical version $(o, d)$ is $\perp$. DBVs are created by logical copying, called *derivation*, and may evolve independently from each other. This means that a DBV may be updated or deleted without side effect on other DBVs. In order to represent application semantics, DBVs may be characterized by labels, using *DBV attributes*, and the DBV set may be organized according to users needs, for instance into a graph [GJZ95].

At the physical level, the version mechanism, described in [CJ90], allows to manage efficiently as many DBVs as needed.

Figure 1 gives a very simplified example of a multiversion database for software development. Software objects are described by the following two classes:

```
class Program type tuple (          class Function type tuple(
  name: string,                       name: string,
  role: string,                       input: set(Arg),
  nb_bug: integer,                    output: Arg,
  nb_funct: integer,                  exec_duration: integer,
  creation: date,                     body:...);
  last_modif: date,
  exec_duration: integer,
  declare: set(Function)
  body:...);
```

where names of the attributes clearly state their semantics. For instance nb_funct, exec_duration, nb_bug respectively represent the number of functions, the average execution duration and the number of listed bugs of a program, input and output represent the signature of a function. Both Program and Function bodies may contain function calls. Other classes may exist, in order to describe other software components, or to refine existing classes via inheritance links (e.g. Public_Program and Draft_Program may be subclasses of class Program). For this paper's purpose, we assume that the whole software may be seen as a collection of Program objects $p_1, p_2, \ldots$ and Function objects $f_1, f_2, \ldots$. In order to simplify the presentation, attribute name is assumed to be used as a user-defined object identifier: two different objects cannot have the same name. Thus, in the following, object names are used as object identifiers.

The database is composed of six database versions, d1, d2, d3, d4, d5, d6, plus the root DBV (the root DBV is not represented because it is hidden from users),

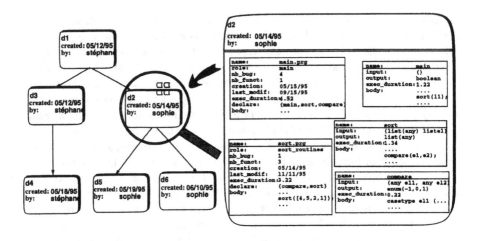

**Fig. 1.** A multiversion database. Focus on DBV $d_2$

labeled by the date and the designer of their creation. Each DBV contains one configuration. A partial order organizes the DBV set, materialized by arrows: it represents the derivation order among configurations, i.e. $d_1 < d_2$ means that $d_2$ has been derived from $d_1$. The right side of the figure focuses on DBV $d_2$. It shows its content: the logical object versions belonging to $d_2$ and their respective values. For instance, the logical object version $(main.prg, d_2)$ has four listed bugs and calls three functions $(main, sort, compare)$.

## 2.2 Issues in maintaining consistency

The DBV model offers a sound framework for the introduction of an integrity mechanism into multiversion databases. As each DBV models a possible representation of the real world, it is similar to a conventional monoversion database. Thus, the consistency of a DBV may be defined exactly in the same manner as the consistency of a monoversion database [GR93], in reference to a consistent state of the modeled universe. As shown above, there are two ways of evolution of a multiversion database: updating a DBV, in a way similar to the updating of a monoversion database, and logically copying (deriving) a new DBV from an existing one, or logically deleting an existing DBV. The DBV model does not impose any restriction to database evolution inside this framework. As a consequence, each DBV may evolve independently from the others. The consistency of the multiversion database is defined as the consistency of its set of DBVs. When each DBV evolves independently from the others, the consistency of the multiversion database is reduced to the consistency of each DBV. Finally [CJ90], a transaction takes a multiversion database from a consistent state to a consistent state. This definition is a generalization of the definition of transaction for monoversion databases in the sense that a multiversion database represents several states of the modeled universe.

However, in most applications, the application semantics imposes relationships, links between DBVs, so that a DBV cannot evolve without taking into account some others. Such links have to be expressed by integrity constraints *over* the DBV set. As transactions take into account the additional dimension introduced by versioning, the constraint mechanism has to be extended in the same way to control transaction execution. For instance, the constraint stating that "a configuration must have less listed bugs than the configuration it has been derived from" involves all the versions of all the objects of the class Program in all the DBVs and requires to compare the content of each DBV with its predecessor's content. When that kind of integrity constraint which may involve several DBVs is considered, the previous definition of multiversion consistency is still valid. However, in that case, it is not sufficient to check if each DBV is consistent (internal consistency of the DBV), the mutual consistency of DBVs must be checked as well.

Due to the complexity of this issue, a systematic study is required, in order to precisely know (1) which kinds of constraint may be defined on a multiversion database (2) how to check them efficiently. Both points are developed in the two following sections.

## 3 Classification criteria

Like in monoversion databases, integrity constraints are used to define and maintain consistency in multiversion databases. In monoversion databases, constraints are classified and grouped according to their checking methods. Those methods depend on the nature of the constraints, i.e which elements are involved by a constraint and how they are related by it. Constraints for multiversion databases, denoted *mv-constraints* in the following, involve not only classes and objects, but also database versions. Thus they have more expressive power and their checking is more complex. In this section, we study the nature of mv-constraints, in order to classify them according to their checking method. We define several criteria relevant to this goal and use them to deduce different categories of mv-constraints.

### 3.1 Scope

The scope criterion allows to restrict the checking area of the constraint. There are three domains: database version, class and object. Constraint checking requires the reading of one object (mono-object) or several objects (multi-object), belonging to one class (mono-class) or several classes (multi-class), in one database version (mono-DBV) or several database versions (multi-DBV). The eight categories obtained are illustrated on Figure 2. Here are some examples:

- mono-object, mono-class, mono-DBV mv-constraint:
  $C_1$ : *The role of object main.prg of class Program is "main" in DBV $d_1$.*

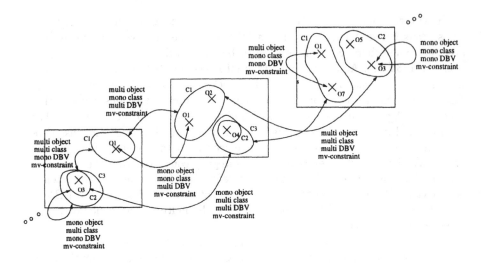

**Fig. 2.** The scope criterion

- mono-object, mono-class and multi-DBV mv-constraint:
  $C_2$ : *The object main.prg belonging to the class Program always has at least one function call in its body.*
- multi-object, mono-class, multi-DBV mv-constraint:
  $C_3$ : *For each program, from a DBV to the next one, either the number of functions has grown or the number of listed bugs has decreased.*
- multi-object, multi-class, multi-DBV mv-constraint:
  $C_4$ : *In each database version, the number of program versions of program is less than 30 and the number of function versions is less than 200.*

$C_2$ is applied to one object belonging to one class, in each database version: it is a mono-object, mono-class and multi-DBV constraint. Since $C_3$ is multi-object, mono-class and multi-DBV, its checking requires the reading of the number of listed bugs and of the number of functions of each program across all the database versions. The scope criterion is used to adapt the checking to each case: for instance, constraints on one object across several database versions are not going to be checked in the same way as constraints involving all the objects of one class in one database version.

## 3.2 Binding

Like the scope criterion, the binding criterion has three domains, object, class and DBV, and allows to restrict constraint checkings. A constraint may involve one element of a domain at once (intra-domain) or several elements simultaneously (inter-domain). As a consequence, mono-domain constraints are intra-domain, whereas multi-domain constraints may be intra or inter-domain.

Inter-domain mv-constraints are relating versions of objects belonging to different elements of the same domain: for instance comparing them or making some computations on them. For example mv-constraint $C_5$ is inter-object, inter-class and intra-DBV, since it compares object versions of class Function with object versions of class Program in each DBV.

– $C_5$ :*If a function is called in a program, the signature (input and output parameters) of the function must match the signature of the function declaration in the header of the program*

On the other hand, $C_4$ is an intra-class and intra-DBV because there is no relationships between versions of Program objects and versions of Function objects or between DBVs.

The scope criterion selects the object versions involved in the multiversion constraint, whereas the binding criterion focuses on dependencies between these object versions. This criterion is used to split the set of multi-domain mv-constraints into intra-domain and inter-domain subsets, for each domain, the checking being different from one subset to another. The checking of a multi-intra-domain mv-constraint consists in checking a mono-domain mv-constraint on several (possibly all) elements of the domain, whereas several elements of the domain must be considered simultaneously for the checking of a multi-inter-domain mv-constraint.

As for each of the three domains, three cases (mono, multi-intra, multi-inter) may be deduced from binding and scope criteria, 27 ($3^3$) categories of mv-constraints appear. Three of them are illustrated below, considering the three possible cases for the DBV domain:

– Multi-intra-object, multi-intra-class, mono-DBV:
$C_6$ : *The size of object versions in database version $d_1$ must always be less than 1 Mbyte.*
– Multi-inter-object, multi-inter-class, multi-intra-DBV:
$C_7$ : *A program execution duration is longer than its called functions execution duration.*
This constraint has to be checked in all database versions (multi-DBV), however, it doesn't generate any link between object versions in different databases versions (intra-DBV).
– Multi-intra-object, mono-class, multi-inter-DBV: $C_3$

## 3.3 Static versus dynamic

Like static monoversion constraints, static mv-constraints are applied to a multiversion database state, even if they involve several database versions, i.e. several states of the modeled universe. For instance, $C_3$ is a static mv-constraint: at the end of the transaction, the number of listed bugs and the number of versions of Function object are computed and compared from one DBV to the following one.

As generalization of dynamic constraints for monoversion databases, dynamic mv-constraints control multiversion database state transitions. Both initial and final states of transactions must be considered for their checking, as for $C_8$ or $C_9$.

- $C_8$ : *The number of database versions cannot decrease.*
- $C_9$ : *For each program version, fixing a bug should not increase its execution duration by more than 10 %.*

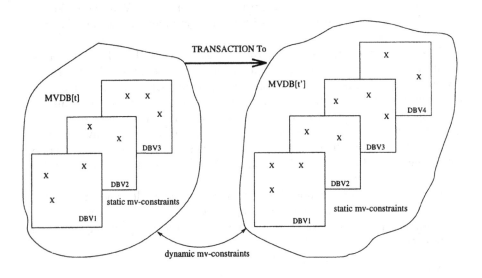

**Fig. 3.** The static vs dynamic criterion

Checking $C_9$ requires comparison, for each database version, of the list of bugs and execution duration at the beginning and at the end of the transaction.

Figure 3 illustrates the difference between static and dynamic mv-constraints. Since each category defined in 3.2 can be divided into static and dynamic subcategories, mv-constraints are classified into 54 categories, according to the three criteria (scope, binding, static/dynamic). Below are two examples of classified mv-constraints.

- $C_{10}$ : *Within a database version, the last-modification date of each program can only increase.*
  dynamic, multi-intra-object, mono-class, multi-intra-DBV.
- $C_{11}$ : *The last-modification date of a program version in a DBV must be greater than the last-modification date of a version of the same program in the preceding DBV.*
  static, multi-intra-object, mono-class, multi-inter-DBV.

## 3.4 Validity

In some applications, it may be useful to avoid the checking of all the constraints at each transaction. For instance, constraint $C_3$ is too restrictive for someone who would like to develop a new configuration using temporarily programs that have been found to contain bugs. Similarly, during the integration of different program versions, or during the testing of an application, it may be useful to accept some temporary inconsistencies. Some mv-constraints are to be checked only after some steps in the multiversion database life. Thus, mv-constraints which are to be checked only in specific situations must be set apart from the others, which are to be checked at the end of each transaction, and users must be provided with tools for describing these situations. One solution is to use a user-defined context. This context may be represented by a flag stating whether the constraint is active or not. It may also be a formula stating after what events or operations the constraint is to be checked, or after (before) which date the constraint is active. More generally, the context allows to specify the conditions of activity/inactivity of an mv-constraint. A constraint must only be checked when it is active: validity does not modify the way of checking constraints, but only the time of checking. Thus, we will not go further on that point.

# 4    Management of consistency in multiversion databases

The consistency of a multiversion database must be checked at the end of each transaction. Transactions are sequences of operations which transform an initial state of a multiversion database into a final state. We consider only ACID and flat transactions.

As seen above, the static/dynamic criterion allows to determine if both the initial and final states of a multiversion database have to be checked or if it is sufficient to consider the final state. The scope criterion allows defining if one or several elements are concerned by the mv-constraint for each domain (object, class or DBV). When several elements of a same domain appear in an mv-constraint, the presence of relationships between them implies that these elements have to be tested simultaneously; otherwise, they can be tested separately. The binding criterion detects these relationships. These three criteria allow to obtain an operational classification: a checking method is associated to each mv-constraint nature.

A general description of the mv-constraint checking methods is given in Section 4.1 and the consistency checking mechanism is sketched in Section 4.2.

## 4.1    Mv-constraint checking

Because of the wide range of mv-constraints, it is impossible to elaborate a unique and efficient checking method, well adapted to all kinds of mv-constraint. Thus, we propose to define several checking methods, according to the classification presented in Section 3. Each checking algorithm takes into account the specific

nature of the mv-constraint. Below the main principles of these checking methods
are presented. A major concern is efficiency. To this aim, it is crucial to reduce
the set of elements implied in the checking process.

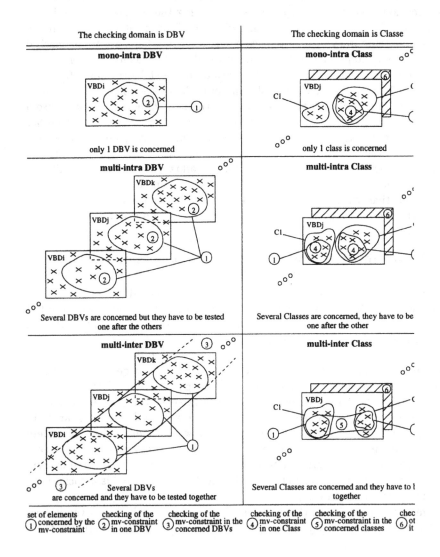

**Fig. 4.** Checking of static mv-constraints for the DBV and class domains

Figure 4 illustrates the methods defined for static mv-constraints. For these
constraints, consistency must only be checked at the final state. Let us consider
the following cases :

– Mono-domain mv-constraint.

The constraint might only be violated by the element of the domain appearing in it. If this element is updated by a transaction, the mv-constraint is checked for this element only.

– Multi-intra-domain mv-constraint.

Although several elements of the domain appear in the mv-constraint, there are no dependencies between them. Thus, only the objects modified by a transaction might violate the mv-constraint. The mv-constraint does not have to be completely checked. Only the part restricted to the elements that have been modified is checked, for those modified objects. The checking method is similar to the previous one (mono domain). It is successively repeated for each modified element. If no element violates the mv-constraint, it is maintained. Otherwise, the mv-constraint is violated by the transaction, which is aborted.

Let us consider for instance mv-constraint $C_{12}$.

- $C_{12}$ : *The number of bugs of a public program is less than 3 and the number of bugs of a draft program is less than 10.*

This is a multi-intra-class mv-constraint, concerning classes Public_Program and Draft_Program. Let a transaction T update the number of bugs of some elements of class Public_Program, but no element of class Draft_Program. Only the part of the mv-constraint concerning Public_Program is to be checked, with the objects modified by transaction T.

– Multi-inter-domain mv-constraint.

The checking method for multi-inter-domain mv-constraint is rather different. Indeed, the elements of the domain implied in the mv-constraint are related, and it is no longer possible to check the mv-constraint by considering the modified elements successively and independently. In addition to the modified elements, we must now take into account the elements related to them. The mv-constraint is checked using the modified elements together with their bounded elements. This operation is repeated for each element modified by the transaction. The mv-constraint is maintained if all checks succeed. Otherwise, it is violated, and the transaction is aborted.

Let us consider, for example, a multi-inter-class mv-constraint stating that the value of a given object of class $Cl_1$ implies the value of a given object of class $Cl_2$. Suppose that transaction T modifies the value of some objects of class $Cl_1$. In order to check this mv-constraint after the execution of transaction T, it must be tested against all objects of class $Cl_1$ modified by T, and against all objects of class $Cl_2$, which are related to the former.

When checking dynamic mv-constraints, two states of the multiversion database must be considered, the initial and the final state of the transaction. It is not necessary to consider all elements of these two states. Thus, only the elements of the initial state which are relevant to check the dynamic mv-constraints are kept. Figure 5 illustrates the various checking methods for dynamic mv-constraints.

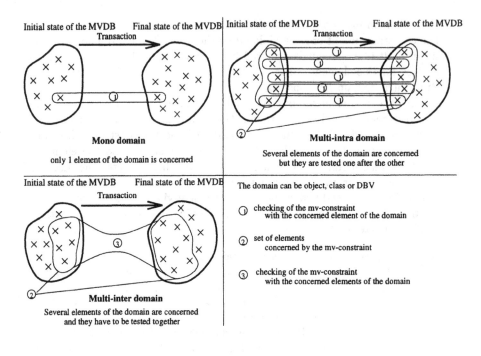

**Fig. 5.** Checking of dynamic mv-constraints

All these checking methods are contained in a library of checking methods. The next section describes the checking process of the consistency of a transaction.

## 4.2 Checking consistency at the end of a transaction

A transaction is a sequence of elementary statements, each of them updating, inserting or deleting an element of the multiversion database. In order to ensure atomicity and consistency of a transaction, the mv-constraints must be checked at the end of each transaction. If all mv-constraints are checked, the transaction is committed. Otherwise, it is aborted. It is essential to elaborate efficient checking methods to determine if a transaction is accepted or not, and to restrict the number of mv-constraints to be checked as well as the elements of the multiversion database implied in the checking process.

To reduce the field of checking, only the set of mv-constraints that might be violated by a transaction T, denoted by C(T), has to be checked against only the elements of the multiversion database which might violate these mv-constraints. To this aim, a syntactic analysis of the transaction is performed, providing the set of elements updated by T and the kind of each modification for each updated element. The syntactic analysis of a mv-constraint establishes its nature and the set of elements concerned by this mv-constraint. The comparison between these sets allows to build C(T) and to determine the set of elements against which the mv-constraints of C(T) will be tested. T is executed and the relevant checking method is selected in the library with respect to the nature of the mv-constraint in order to check each mv-constraint of C(T). Figure 6 illustrates the checking process of the transaction.

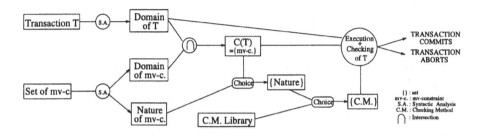

**Fig. 6.** Checking process

The syntactic analysis of a transaction T detects all the elements of a multi-version database which are updated by T (classes, DBV, objects and attributes) and the kind of each update (insertion, deletion, modification, derivation, etc.). To this aim, each elementary instruction of T is analyzed. All these elementary analyses are grouped at the end of the transaction and form the *domain of T*.

For example, let transaction $T_1$, which inserts an object in the class Program, modify the declaration and the date of the last modification of another object of the same class in a given version. The analysis of the first instruction of $T_1$ states that an object is inserted in the class Program. The analysis of the second and the third instructions respectively state that attributes `declare` and `last_modif` of an object of the class Program are modified in a given DBV. Then, the syntactic analysis of $T_1$ returns " object insertion, modification of attributes `declare` and `last_modif` in class Program in a given DBV".

The syntactic analysis of an mv-constraint $C$ returns the *domain of C*, the set of elements (DBV, classes and their sub-classes and objects) of the multiver-sion database related to the mv-constraint. For each DBV or class returned by this syntactic analysis, if an attribute is specified, then it is also taken into account. This allows knowing exactly what elements of the multiversion database are restricted by the mv-constraint.

For example, the domain of $C_{12}$ is the set of all DBVs, classes Public_Program and Draft_Program (these classes have no subclass) and the attribute nb_bug. The domain of $C_{13}$ is the set of all DBVs, the class Program and its subclasses, Public_Program, Draft_Program and the attributes `creation` and `last_modif`.

– $C_{13}$ : *A program's creation date happens before its last modification date.*

All the elements of a multiversion database concerned by an mv-constraint appear in its domain. Then, if a transaction T updates some elements belonging to the domain of an mv-constraint, this mv-constraint is inserted in C(T): the intersection of the mv-constraint domain and of T domain is non empty. Otherwise, this mv-constraint need not to be checked because it cannot be violated by T.

For transaction $T_1$, only mv-constraint $C_{13}$ has to be tested. The result of the syntactic analysis of $T_1$ contains the attribute last_modif of the class Program, then the mv-constraints concerning this attribute have to be tested. Since attribute nb_bug does not belong to this result, $C_{12}$ cannot be violated and is not tested.

The second objective of the syntactic analysis of an mv-constraint is to determine its nature, which allows selecting the relevant checking method in the checking library. The result of the syntactic analysis of each mv-constraint is used at the compilation of each transaction, so throughout the whole life of the multiversion database. Thus, this result must be stored in the database, since computing it at each compilation would be expensive in time.

The checking algorithm of a transaction T is generated at the compilation of T to reduce its execution time. It is elaborated with C(T), the relevant checking method for each mv-constraint of C(T), and all the concerned elements of the multiversion database. When the transaction is executed, the identity of the elements concerned by the transaction is known. Then the mv-constraint can be checked with just the updated elements by instantiating the algorithm and executing it. If no mv-constraint is violated by T, then T commits, otherwise T aborts.

## 5 Conclusion

This paper studied the extension of integrity constraint mechanisms for maintaining consistency in multiversion databases. The issue of describing and classifying such constraints and the issue of checking them efficiently are both addressed: constraints are characterized according to several criteria, and a general framework for optimizing their checking in the context of ACID transactions is given. This work is original because it addresses a new problem: the control of versions, inside and across database versions (or configurations), using integrity constraints. To this end, it benefits from the DBV approach on which it is based. Indeed, unlike previous version models, the DBV approach allows a clear definition of consistency: the multiversion database is consistent iff (1) each DBV is consistent and (2) DBVs are mutually consistent. Thus it offers a sound basis for defining constraints across versions with clear semantics.

Work is in progress at the Laforia and Lamsade laboratories in order to integrate consistency and version management mechanisms into DBMS. A *formalism* is being defined, based on logic, that will be used to express the constraints described in this paper. Different *checking methods*, corresponding to the checking of different kinds of constraint, are being specified and designed. A *constraint parser* is under study. It will use efficient data structures and indexes to store constraints, to easily retrieve a constraint and the corresponding checking method at transaction compilation time. At last, a *transaction compiler* will be developed, according to the description of section 4.2. Implementation will be realized on the top of the $O_2$ DMBS, by integrating two prototypes: *Modesty*, developed at Lamsade, which implements version management and manipulation, and $O_2$Integrity, developed first at LRI (University Paris Sud) and now at Laforia, which allows to handle integrity constraints in $O_2$.

Further extensions will be considered. They consist in further exploring the potential of the DBV approach. As the unit of versioning is the DBV, it is possible to consider together versions of classes, versions of objects, and versions of instantiation relationship links inside a DBV, as shown in [CJK91]. Thus, a multiversion database may track both schema evolution and object migration, which, at their turn, may be controled by extending integrity constraints. Last, constraints themselves may have versions, as suggested in [BMCJ93]. This allows a constraint to have different semantics according to the DBV it is applied to, but requires specific definitions and mechanisms in order to be managed properly.

# References

[AHLZ95]  E. Andonoff, G. Hubert, A. Le Parc and G. Zurfluh. Modeling inheritance, composition and relationship links between objects, object versions and class versions. Proc. CAISE'95, 1995.

[AJ89]  R. Agrawal and H. V. Jagadish. On correctly configuring versioned objects. *Proc. VLDB*, pages 367–374, Amsterdam, August 1989.

[Atw86]  T.M. Atwood. An object-oriented DBMS for design support applications. *Proc. COMPINT*, pages 299–307, Montréal, September 1986.

[BG80]  D. Bobrow and I. Goldstein. Representing design alternatives. *In : Proceedings of the Conference on Artificial Intelligence and the Simulation of Behavior.* – Amsterdam (Netherlands), July 1980.

[BD95]  V. Benzaken and A. Doucet. Thémis: A database Programming Language Handling Integrity Constraints *In : VLDB Journal* – Vol. 4 – Nr. 3 – 1995.

[BMCJ93]  C.M. Bauzer-Medeiros, W. Cellary and G. Jomier. Maintaining Integrity Constraints across Versions in a Database. *Proc. 8th Brazilian Database Conference*, Campina Grande, Brazil, 1993.

[CJ90]  W. Cellary and G. Jomier. Consistency of versions in object-oriented databases. *Proc. 16th VLDB*, Brisbane (Australia), 1990.

[CJK91]  W. Cellary, G. Jomier, and T. Koszlajda. Formal model of an object-oriented database with versioned objects and schema. *Proc. DEXA'91.*

[EC94]  J. Estublier and R. Casallas. The Adele Configuration Manager. – *In : Configuration Management*, ed. by W. Tichy, Wiley and son, in Software Trend Serie, 1994.

[GR93]  J. Gray and A. Reuter. Transaction Processing: concepts and techniques. Morgan and Kaufmann Publishers, ISBN 1-55860-190-2 – 1070 pages, 1993.

[GA93]  P. Grefen and P. Apers. Integrity control in relational database systems - an overview. *Data & Knowledge Engineering*, 10(2):187–223, 1993.

[GJZ95]  S. Gançarski, G. Jomier and M. Zamfiroïu. A Framework for the Manipulation of a Multiversion Database *In : DEXA'95 International Conference, Workshop Proc.*, ISBN 3-901653-00-7, pp. 247–256. London (U.K.), 1995.

[KA91]      J. Kimball and L. Aaron (L.). Epochs, configuration schema, and version cursors in the KBSA framework CCM model. *In: Proc. Third International Wshp. on Softw. Configuration Mgt.*, pp. 33–42, Trondheim (Norway), 1991.

[Kat90]     R. H. Katz. Toward a unified framework for version modeling in engineering databases. *ACM Computing Surveys*, 22(4):375–408, December 1990.

[KBG89]     W. Kim, E. Bertino, and J.F. Garza. Composite objects revisited. *ACM SIGMOD Record*, 18(2):337–347, June 1989.

[KS92]      W. Käfer and H. Schöning. Mapping a version model to a complex-object data model. *Proc. IEEE Data Engineering*, Tempe (Arizona), 1992.

[O2T95]     O2Technology. The $O_2$ user's manual, version 4.6. Technical report, Versailles, France, 1995.

[Reich.89]  Reichenberger (C.). Orthogonal version management. *In: Proceedings of the Third International Workshop on Software Configuration Management*, pp. 137–140, Princeton, New Jersey (USA), 1989.

[Sarda90]   N. Sarda. Extensions to SQL for historical databases. *IEEE Transactions on Knowledge and DataEngineering*, vol. 2, Nr. 2, pp. 220–230, June 1990.

[TCG+93]    A.U. Tansel, J. Clifford, S. Gadia, S. Jajodia, A. Segev and R. Snodgrass. *Temporal Databases: Theory, Design, and Implementation.* – Benjamin / Cummings, *Database Systems and Applications*, 1993.

[TOC93]     G. Talens, C. Oussalah, and M.F. Colinas. Versions of simple and composite objects. In *Proc. 19th VLDB*, Dublin, 1993.

[Zdo86]     S. Zdonik. Version management in an object-oriented database. *Proc. International Workshop on Advanced Programming Environments*, pages 138–200, Trondheim (Norway), 1986.

# The Development of a Semantic Integrity Constraint Subsystem for a Distributed Database (SICSDD)

H.Ibrahim*        W.A.Gray        N.J.Fiddian

Department of Computer Science, UWCC, Cardiff, UK
*Department of Computer Science, University of Agriculture Malaysia, Malaysia
h.ibrahim@cs.cf.ac.uk

**Abstract.** This paper presents a strategy for validating the semantic integrity constraints of a distributed database. The general method detects inconsistency by performing integrity tests against the database whenever an update occurs. The integrity test is much cheaper and easier to validate than the initial constraint. We use a two level approach where constraint validation can be performed before or after an update is made. We adopt the algorithm proposed by [NIC82] to generate post-tests and modify it to generate pre-tests which allow the initial constraints to be checked locally. This strategy has been implemented in a prototype system called SICSDD.

## 1  Introduction

A database contains assorted data and, together with its associated applications, models a real world enterprise. A relational database can be regarded as consisting of two distinct parts, namely: an intensional part (the schema or integrity constraints); and an extensional part (the data that populates the schema). **Integrity constraints** are metadata that specify the conditions that a database state (sequence of states) must satisfy in order to be consistent. Any update operation (insert, delete or modify) or transaction (sequence of updates) that occurs must not violate these constraints. Thus, a fundamental issue concerning integrity constraints is constraint validation, i.e. the process of ensuring that the integrity constraints are satisfied after the database has been updated. Today's DBMS technology offers only limited support for the automated verification of constraint satisfaction and enforcement. It is also recognized that constraint validation is extremely difficult to implement and can lead to prohibitive processing costs particularly in a distributed environment [QIA89]. In the database literature, most of the approaches proposed for improving the efficiency of constraint validation are not tailored for distributed database environments [GUP93].

Many researchers have studied the problem of maintaining the consistency of a database and have concluded that evaluating integrity constraints in their initial form is time-consuming. This evaluation can be reduced by taking advantage of the fact that the database is consistent prior to an update, so that the number of constraints to be validated at the database state transition is reduced. Another approach is to transform constraints into simplified forms (integrity tests) that are cheaper to enforce [NIC82, HEN84, QIA88, McC89] and can reduce the amount of data accessed, particularly in distributed databases as in [SIM86, QIA89, GRE90, GRE91, BAR92, GUP93, MAZ93, McC94]. Our work exploits both the above approaches.

In this paper, a method for constraint validation in a distributed database environment where data distribution is transparent to the application domain is proposed. By database distribution we mean that a collection of data which belongs logically to the same system is physically spread over the sites (nodes) of a computer network where intersite data communication is a critical factor affecting the system's performance. The technique that we propose allows the initial integrity constraints to be validated by localising constraint checking where data at a target site (local site) is accessed, hence eliminating the cost of accessing remote data. The motivation of this method derives from the fact that the information required to verify a global test can often be accessed at the target site. If no local testing can be performed, then global testing is required. Our method has been implemented in a prototype system called the SEMANTIC INTEGRITY CONSTRAINT SUBSYSTEM for a DISTRIBUTED DATABASE (SICSDD). The development and operation of SICSDD is divided into two phases: concerned with (i) processing that is performed at compile-time and is carried out by the COMPILE-TIME MODULE; and (ii) processing that is performed at run-time and is carried out by the RUN-TIME MODULE.

The structure of this paper is as follows. The following section briefly cites related work that has been carried out previously. In section 3, the architecture of SICSDD is overviewed. Section 4 discusses the COMPILE-TIME MODULE and explains the techniques that are applied to achieve its function, whilst section 5 briefly discusses the RUN-TIME MODULE. Conclusions and further research are presented in the final section, 6.


## 2  Related Work

[NIC82] presents a simplification method yielding simplified forms for integrity constraints. These simplified forms depend on the nature of the updating operation which is the cause of a state change. The method is based on syntactic criteria and is validated through first order logic. Our work is closely related to this approach.

[HSU85] provides a simplification rule based method. Constraints expressed in prenex normal form are transformed into AND-OR combinations of simpler constraints. The analysis of certain patterns in the prefixes of constraints enables the method to conclude when for a given type of update no simplification is possible at all, and when a significant improvement can be achieved.

[SIM86] constructs a simplification method for integrity constraints expressed in terms of assertions and extends it to distributed databases. The method produces at assertion definition time differential pre-tests called compile assertions, that can be used to prevent the introduction of inconsistencies in the database. The aim of the work is to reduce the amount of data that needs to be transferred across the network for the purposes of integrity checking.

[McC89] proposes a method that takes a constraint expressed in first order logic and a class of updates, and either proves that an update in the class cannot violate the constraint or produces a necessary and sufficient test (C') and a possibly sufficient test (D) that are used to accept or reject updates in the class. This method, which relies upon a theorem prover, defines "transaction axioms" which represent the relationship of the states of the database before and after an update. The method is proved correct and the tests generated can always be performed before the update is attempted.

[GRE90] has developed an integrity constraint handling subsystem for fragmented relations in a relational database system. The workload imposed by integrity checking is reduced by localising constraint testing. The method introduces a two-way approach to constraint enforcement, namely implicit and explicit constraint enforcement. If no local testing can be carried out, the explicit enforcement is invoked.

[GUP93] presents an algorithm to generate a parameterized local test that checks whether an update operation violates a constraint. The algorithm uses the initial consistency assumption, an integrity constraint assertion that is expressed in a subset of first order logic, and the target relation to produce the local test. The optimization technique allows a global constraint to be verified by accessing data locally at a single database where the modifications are made.

[McC94] uses the theorem proving approach, which is closely related to that of [McC89], for deriving a range of possible sufficient or necessary tests as well as complete tests for transaction safety with respect to a constraint. The novel feature of the method is the automatic division of integrity tests into Sub Tests, which independently investigate the safety of changes to disjoint sections of the database. In order to generate these tests, a set of integrity constraints, the transaction being considered and the partitioning strategy adopted in the database are used.

# 3   An Overview of SICSDD

## 3.1   Preliminaries

SICSDD has been developed in the context of relational databases. A database schema, $D$, is a set of relation schemas, $<R_1, R_2, ..., R_m>$. A relation schema is denoted by $R(A_1, A_2, ..., A_n)$ where R is the name of the relation (predicate) with n arity and the $A_i$'s are the attributes of R. Let $dom(A_i)$ be the domain of values for attribute $A_i$. Then, an instance of R is a relation $R$ which is a finite subset of the cartesian product $dom(A_1)$ x...x $dom(A_n)$. A database instance is a collection of instances for its relation schemas. A relational database schema in a distributed database system is a quadruple $(D, IC, FR, AS)$ where IC is a finite set of integrity constraints, FR is a finite set of fragmentation rules and AS is a finite set of allocation schemas.

Using the same style adopted by [ZHA94], a conjunct (literal) is an atomic formula of the form $R(u_1,...,u_k)$ where R is a k-ary relation name and each $u_i$ is either a variable or a constant. A positive atomic formula (positive literal) is denoted by $R(u_1,...,u_k)$ whilst a negative atomic formula (negative literal) is prefixed with $\rceil$. An (in)equality is a formula of the form $u_1$ op $u_2$ (prefixed with $\rceil$ for inequality) where both $u_1$ and $u_2$ can be constants or variables, and op $\varepsilon$ {<, <=, >, >=, =, <>} if the domain is real numbers or op $\varepsilon$ {=, <>} if the domain is the set of strings over the English alphabet.

Each integrity constraint in the set IC is expressed in prenex conjunctive normal form with the range restricted property [NIC82, McC89]. A formula is prenex iff it is of the form:

$$(Q_1V_1, Q_2V_2, ..., Q_tV_t)\ F$$

where $Q_i$ is the quantifier $\forall$ (denotes universal) or $\exists$ (denotes existential) and F is a well formed formula (wff) whose variables $V_1, ..., V_t$ are the only free variables in F.

A set of fragmentation rules, **FR**, specifies the set of restrictions, $C_i$, that must be satisfied by each fragment relation, F_i, indicated by those rules. These rules introduce a new set of integrity constraints and therefore have the same notation as **IC**. For simplicity purposes, we will consider horizontal fragmentation only. An allocation schema, **AS**, locates a fragment relation, F_i, to one or more sites. We will use the following employee-department relation which is taken from [GUP93] as an example throughout this paper. The letters at the beginning of the alphabet (eg. a,b,c) and the letters at the end of the alphabet (eg. x,y,z) denote lists of generic constants and variables respectively.

Schema:

emp(E,D,S)  % employee number E in department D has salary S
dept(D,MS)  % some manager in department D has salary MS

Integrity Constraints (Global Constraints):

*Key constraint*
"Every employee has a unique employee number"
GC1:  $\forall x \forall y \forall z \forall u \forall v$ (emp(x,y,z) $\wedge$ emp(x,u,v) --> (y=u) $\wedge$ (z=v))
*Referential integrity constraint*
"The department number of every tuple in the emp relation exists in the dept relation"
GC2:  $\forall x \forall y \forall z \exists u$ (emp(x,y,z) --> dept(y,u))
*User-defined constraint*
"Every employee earns less than or equal to every manager in the same department"
GC3:  $\forall x \forall y \forall z \forall u$ (emp(x,y,z) $\wedge$ dept(y,u) --> (u >= z))

Assume that the emp and dept relations are horizontally fragmented into 2 fragments {emp_1, emp_2} and {dept_1, dept_2} respectively, based on the conditions: department, D = D1; and department, D = D2. The fragmentation rules produced by the above conditions are as follows:

FR1:        $\forall x \forall y \forall z$ (emp_1(x,y,z) --> y="D1")
FR2:        $\forall x \forall y \forall z$ (emp_2(x,y,z) --> y="D2")
FR3:        $\forall x \forall y$ (dept_1(x,y) --> x="D1")
FR4:        $\forall x \forall y$ (dept_2(x,y) --> x="D2")

## 3.2  An Architectural Overview of SICSDD

Figure 1 presents an overview of the architecture of the SICSDD. The following components can be identified:

*Specific Knowledge Builder (SKB)*: responsible for building the specific knowledge base of a database application. It is applied only once for each database application. In this submodule the following tasks are performed:

i.    parse and convert the database schema into its internal form and store it in the Knowledge Base;

ii.   parse the fragmentation rules and convert them into AND/OR sub-trees; transform each leaf in each sub-tree into an equivalent clausal form and store it as an integrity constraint in the Knowledge Base;

iii.  parse the integrity constraints and convert them into equivalent clausal form; store them in the Knowledge Base.

*Constraint Compiler (CC)*: transforms the constraints specification at the relational level into a constraints specification at the fragment level. It uses knowledge about data distribution in order to achieve optimal fragment constraints. CC is also responsible for detecting redundancy and eliminating any fragment constraints that contradict the initial constraints. The fragment constraints derived by this module are stored in the Knowledge Base.

*Constraint Distributor (CD)*: responsible for distributing the fragment constraints to the appropriate sites. It refers to the allocation schema and uses the strategy proposed in [QIA89] in order to achieve optimal distribution.

*Constraint Analyser (CA)*: analyses each fragment constraint and, based on the syntax, derives all possible update templates. It employs the well-known theorem used by [NIC82, McC89]. The update templates are then stored in the Knowledge Base.

*Constraint Optimizer (CO)*: CO uses the information stored in the Knowledge Base (fragment constraints, update templates) and generates global and local tests. These tests are stored in the form of rules in the Constraint Base to be used later by the RUN-TIME MODULE.

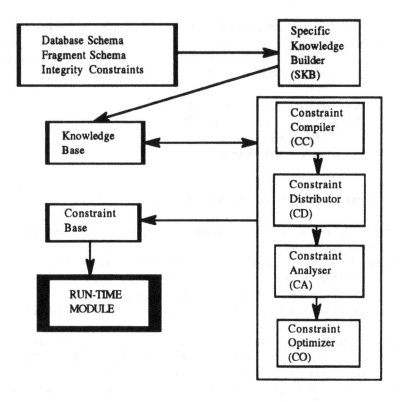

**Figure 1: SICSDD architecture**

## 4 Compile-Time Module

There are two main problems in designing an integrity subsystem for a DDBMS [SIM86], which are i. the definition and storage of constraints and ii. the enforcement of these constraints. The problems are concerned with the definition of the constraints being global but their enforcement being at a local fragment level. This means that the global constraints must be transformed into local fragment constraints that are effective in maintaining the consistency of the global distributed database. In this transformation the aim is to create fragment constraints that are held at the local sites where they will be enforced, which maintain the global consistency, minimise the use of data held at the other sites, and remove operations redundant to the local constraint enforcement, which occur in global constraint enforcement. This will overcome the problems identified by [SIM86] which are concerned with global constraints being enforced at the local level. The SICSDD aims to transform global constraints into fragment constraints meeting the transformation aims above by exploiting semantic knowledge of the application domain.

The SICSDD compile-time module, which consists of the five components discussed in the previous section, is responsible for the definition and storage of constraints. Briefly, there are four main tasks performed at compile-time. They are:

i.      transform global constraints into fragment constraints (definition)
ii.     distribute fragment constraints (storage)
iii.    generate update templates
iv.     generate integrity tests

These tasks are explained in the following sub-sections. The enforcement of constraints is briefly discussed later, in Section 5.

## 4.1    Transform Global Constraints into Fragment Constraints

In a distributed database, integrity constraints specified by the user are expressed in terms of global relations. In this paper, these constraints are called global constraints. Transforming a global constraint specified at the relational level into a set of logically equivalent fragment constraints is necessary since enforcement of these constraints takes place at the fragment level at the local site holding a fragment [GRE90]. A fragment constraint is a constraint which is specified over fragments of global relations. [QIA89] has stated that each global constraint has a corresponding fragment constraint.

Given a global integrity constraint, GIC, an equivalent fragment constraint is derived by replacing each occurrence of a global relation, R, with its m fragment relations, $F\_i$. A formula of the form $(\forall x1 \forall x2...\forall xn) R(x1,x2,...,xn)$ is transformed to $\bigwedge^m_{i=1} (\forall x1 \forall x2...\forall xn) F\_i(x1,x2,...,xn)$, and a formula of the form $(\forall x1...\forall xn \exists y1...\exists yn) R(x1,...,xn,y1,...,yn)$ is transformed to $\bigvee^m_{i=1} (\forall x1...\forall xn \exists y1...\exists yn) F\_i(x1,...,xn,y1,...,yn)$. For simplicity, a fragment constraint of the form $\bigwedge^m_{i=1} F\_i$ is rewritten into $m$ fragment constraints $F\_i$ where i $\varepsilon$ $\{1,2,...,m\}$.

**Example 4.1.1** The following fragment constraints are constructed for the example database.

FC1ij:    $(\forall x \forall y \forall z \forall u \forall v)$ (emp_i(x,y,z) $\wedge$ emp_j(x,u,v) --> (y=u) $\wedge$ (z=v))

         for i $\varepsilon$ {1,2} and j $\varepsilon$ {1,2}

FC2i:    $\bigvee^2_{j=1} (\forall x \forall y \forall z \exists u)$ (emp_i(x,y,z) --> dept_j(y,u)) for i $\varepsilon$ {1,2}

FC3ij:   $(\forall x \forall y \forall z \forall u)$ (emp_i(x,y,z) $\wedge$ dept_j(y,u) --> (u >= z))

         for i $\varepsilon$ {1,2} and j $\varepsilon$ {1,2}

The fragment constraints above can be further simplified if knowledge about the fragmentation of relations is used. In [OSZ91] and [SIM86], set-oriented assertions (single-relation multivariable constraints and multirelation multivariable constraints) can be simplified if the relations involved in the constraints are fragmented on a join attribute. Instead of deriving all combinations of fragment constraints, only compatible fragment constraints are constructed.

**Example 4.1.2** The fragment constraints FC2i and FC3ij above can be simplified into the following fragment constraints since both relations emp and dept are fragmented on the join attribute.

FC2i': $(\forall x \forall y \forall z \exists u)$ (emp_i(x,y,z) --> dept_i(y,u)) for i $\varepsilon$ {1,2}

FC3i: $(\forall x \forall y \forall z \forall u)$ (emp_i(x,y,z) $\wedge$ dept_i(y,u) --> (u >= z)) for i $\varepsilon$ {1,2}

Eliminating redundant constraints is essential even though a redundant set of constraints is semantically correct. A redundant constraint is a constraint that can be implied by other existing constraints. Excluding redundant constraints can improve the enforcement time.

**Example 4.1.3** The above fragment constraints FC112 and FC121 are redundant. Eliminating FC121 will produce the following set of fragment constraints.

FC1i: $(\forall x \forall y \forall z \forall u \forall v)$ (emp_i(x,y,z) $\wedge$ emp_i(x,u,v) --> (y=u) $\wedge$ (z=v))

                for i $\varepsilon$ {1,2}

FC112: $(\forall x \forall y \forall z \forall u \forall v)$ (emp_1(x,y,z) $\wedge$ emp_2(x,u,v) --> (y=u) $\wedge$ (z=v))

Further optimization can be achieved by reformulating the constraints into ones which are syntactically different but semantically equivalent. This approach which exploits knowledge of the application domain and the database implementation can reduce the execution cost of constraint validation as reported in [QIA86, QIA87]. [MAZ93] has addressed the issue of how constraints can be reformulated into ones that are more local, and at best are entirely local.

**Example 4.1.4** The fragment constraint FC112 above can be reformulated using the fragmentation rules FR1 and FR2, and the key constraints FC11 and FC12, into the following fragment constraint.

FC112': $(\forall x \forall y \forall z \forall u \forall v)$ ($\overline{\text{emp}}$_1(x,y,z) V $\overline{\text{emp}}$_2(x,u,v))

## 4.2 Distribute Fragment Constraints

The fragment constraints produced above can involve data stored at different network sites. These constraints need to be distributed so that validation can be done locally hence minimising the cost of integrity checking. A fragment constraint is *local* to a site if each fragment relation mentioned in the constraint has a copy physically stored at that site. Distributing the whole set of fragment constraints to every site is not cost-effective since not all fragment constraints are affected by an update. Finding an optimal distribution is the main objective so that whenever an update occurs at a site, the validation of the fragment constraints at that site implies the global validity of the update. This distribution is performed by the CD, which uses the proven strategies suggested by [QIA89].

Initially, a fragment constraint, FC, is allocated to a site s if and only if there is a fragment relation at site s which is mentioned in FC. If there is more than one site, say sites s and t, which store some of the fragment relations mentioned in FC, but all of the s fragment relations of FC are also contained in t, then it is sufficient to allocate FC to site t only. An update that occurs at site s that may invalidate FC implies that the update will also invalidate FC at site t. Furthermore, the cost of validating FC at site t is less than that at site s since t has more local fragments than s. In [SIM86], the storage of these constraints is based on a constraint taxonomy.

**Example 4.2.1** Assume that emp_1 and dept_1 are allocated to site S_1 and emp_2 and dept_2 are allocated to site S_2. FCi(local) denotes a local fragment constraint, and FCi(non-local) otherwise.

FC11(local): {S_1}    FC112'(non-local): {S_1,S_2}    FC12(local): {S_2}
FC21'(local): {S_1}    FC22'(local): {S_2}
FC31(local): {S_1}    FC32(local): {S_2}

In order to validate FC112' against an update operation, eg. insert(emp_1(a,b,c)) into emp_1 at site S_1, we check the fragmentation rule FR1, and the integrity test $(\forall u \forall v) \neg$emp_2(a,u,v). The test states that FC112' is not violated if there is no employee with employee number "a" in the fragment relation emp_2. This is achieved by sending a query to the remote site, S_2. It is clear that the cost of checking a local fragment constraint is cheaper than that of checking a non-local fragment constraint, since all the information required to verify the constraint can be accessed at a single site. Later, we will show how the cost of validating non-local fragment constraints can often be reduced by enforcing local tests.

### 4.3  Generate Update Templates

Update templates are generated automatically by the CA from the fragment constraint definitions. The following theorems are applied in order to produce the necessary update templates. The proofs of these theorems can be found in [NIC82, McC89].

*Theorem 1:* Whenever an update operation is dealing with the extension of a relation R, integrity constraints in which R does not occur are unaffected. For example, consider the constraint $\neg R(x)$ and an insert operation S(a).

*Theorem 2:* Integrity constraints (considered in prenex conjunctive normal form) which do not contain R in a negated atomic formula (respectively, a nonnegated atomic formula) are unaffected when a tuple is inserted (respectively, deleted) into (from) the extension of R.

*Theorem 3:* The case where the above two theorems are not applicable. This occurs when the conditions imposed by the constraint contradict the actual updated tuple. For example, an attempt to insert P(a,b) will falsify the constraint $(\forall x \forall y)$ $((\neg P(x,y) \; V \; (y = \text{"a"}))$.

**Example 4.3.1** Refer to the column Update Template in Example 4.4.1 below.

### 4.4 Generate Integrity Tests

Enforcing the above fragment constraints is not very efficient since these constraints can be simplified by applying various techniques; based on syntactic criteria [NIC82], rule-based processing [HSU85], differential pre-tests [SIM86] and theorem proving [McC89]. The simplified forms of these constraints are also known as integrity tests. An integrity test can either be a post-test (evaluated after the update is performed) or a pre-test (evaluated before the update is performed).

We use the algorithm proposed by [NIC82] to generate post-tests and this is referred to as Algorithm-A. These post-tests are obtained by applying the substitution, subsumption and absorption rules. The definition of these terms can be found in [NIC82], also the generation steps and examples, which are therefore omitted here. A local fragment constraint is always simplified to a local post-test while a non-local fragment constraint is always simplified to a global post-test.

The essential steps for generating a pre-test, referred to as Algorithm-B, uses the same approach as Algorithm-A but with some modification. Pre-tests are always local to a site regardless of whether the fragment constraint is local or non-local. Therefore in the rest of this paper, the term pre-test is used instead of local pre-test. Figure 2 summarizes the various alternatives succinctly. Before the steps are illustrated, we would like to highlight the following notations and their intended meaning which are important to the subsequent discussion.

*TR*: A *target relation* is a relation referred to by an elementary update operation. For an insert operation (example insert(R(b,c))), TR is a negated atomic formula (example ⌉R(x,y)) in FC. A FC which consists of more than one atomic formula whose predicate is equivalent to TR but with different variables is rewritten so that each insert operation affects at most one atomic formula of FC.

*OR*: Other relations in FC which are not TR are denoted as OR.

*ETR*: (In)equality that imposes domain comparison on the target relation TR only.

*EOR*: (In)equality that imposes domain comparison on relations other than TR.

*ETO*: (In)equality that imposes domain comparison between TR and OR.

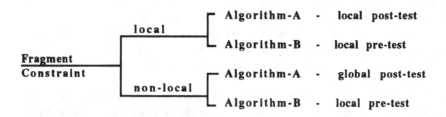

**Figure 2:   The integrity tests generated by Algorithm A and B**

A pre-test is derived by applying the substitution and absorption rules to a fragment constraint, FC. The test makes reference only to the target relation, TR. We assume that all tuples in TR before the update satisfy the FC. Let $\{A_{TR1}, A_{TR2}, ..., A_{TRm}\}$ be the set of attributes in TR, $\{A_{OR1}, A_{OR2}, ..., A_{ORn}\}$ be the set of attributes in OR. Let Ci be the conditions (restrictions) imposed in FC on attribute $A_{TRi}$, where $A_{TRi}$ is not a key of TR and Ci can be C1 $\land$ C2 $\land$...$\land$ Cm. Let Ri be the range allowed by Ci on attribute $A_{TRi}$. Let <f1, f2, ..., fn> be a tuple in TR and <e1, e2, ..., en> be the inserted tuple. Based on the assumption made earlier, <f1, f2, ..., fn> satisfies FC and therefore satisfies Ci, i.e. the actual value of fi is in the allowed range Ri. If the value of ei is in the range of the value of fi then by the transitive rule, the value of ei is also in the allowed range, Ri, and therefore the inserted tuple <e1, e2, ..., en> satisfies Ci, which also implies that inserting the tuple <e1, e2, ..., en> will not violate the FC.

Table 4.4.1 below shows the steps required to generate a pre-test for an insert operation and table 4.4.2 shows the steps required to generate a pre-test for a delete operation. Modify operations are considered as a sequence of a delete followed by an insert operation.

---

**Table 4.4.1 Algorithm for generating pre-test for an insert operation**

Step 1: Construct the set of substitutions $\theta$ according to the occurrences of TR (target relation) in FC and the inserted tuple <e1, ..., en>. Construct the set of substitutions $\alpha_i$ according to the occurrences of OR (other relations) in FC and the substitutions $\theta$. If $\theta$ is an empty set then the inserted tuple does not affect the FC, STOP. If $\alpha_i$ is an empty set and there is no other relation than TR then STOP. (Algorithm-A is used to derive the integrity test).

Step 2: Let $\sigma^+$ be the set of substitutions obtained as the intersection of $\theta$ and $\alpha_i$. If $\sigma^+$ is an empty set or if $\sigma^+$ is identical to $\theta$ then STOP. $\sigma^+$ is a set of attributes that denotes join attributes in FC.

Step 3: Let $\lambda^+$ be the set of substitutions obtained by applying $\theta$ to ETR in FC. If $\alpha_i$ U $\lambda^+$ is equivalent to $\theta$ then STOP.

Step 4: Let $\eta^+$ be the set of substitutions obtained by applying $\theta$ to ETO in FC. If $\alpha_i$ U $\eta^+$ is equivalent to $\theta$ then eliminate Step 6.

Step 5: Apply $\sigma^+$ and $\eta^+$ to FC. Replace each pre-valued literal by its truth value and apply as much as possible, the absorption rules. All OR and EOR are eliminated by assuming that they are false in the FC. Let W be the obtained formula.

Step 6: Negate W.

---

---

**Table 4.4.2 Algorithm for generating pre-test for a delete operation**

Step 1: Construct the set of substitutions $\theta$ according to the occurrences of TR (target relation) in FC and the deleted tuple <e1, ..., en>. Construct the set of substitutions $\alpha_i$ according to the occurrences of OR (other relations) in FC and the substitutions $\theta$. If $\theta$ is an empty set then the deleted tuple does not affect the FC, STOP. If $\alpha_i$ is an empty set and there is no other relation than TR then STOP. (Algorithm-A is used to derive the integrity test).

Step 2: Let $\sigma^-$ be the set of substitutions obtained as the intersection of $\theta$ and $\alpha_i$. If $\sigma^-$ is an empty set or if $\sigma^-$ is identical to $\theta$ then STOP. $\sigma^-$ is a set of attributes that denotes join attributes in FC.

Step 3: Let $\lambda^-$ be the set of substitutions obtained by applying $\theta$ to ETR in FC. If $\alpha_i$ U $\lambda^-$ is equivalent to $\theta$ then STOP.

Step 4: Let $\eta^-$ be the set of substitutions obtained by applying $\theta$ to ETO in FC.

Step 5: Apply $\sigma^-$ and $\eta^-$ to FC. Replace each pre-valued literal by its truth value and apply as much as possible, the absorption rules. All OR and EOR are eliminated by assuming that they are true in the FC. Let W be the obtained formula.

---

To illustrate these algorithms, consider FC2i' and an attempt to insert emp_i(a,b,c), followed by an attempt to delete dept_i(a,b).

> Update: insert(emp_i(a,b,c))
> Target Relation: emp_i
> Other Relation: dept_i
> Test-FC2i' (Algorithm-A): $(\exists u)$ (dept_i(b,u))
>
> Step 1: $\theta$ (emp_i) = {x/a,y/b,z/c}, $\alpha$ (dept_i) = {y/b}
> Step 2: $\sigma^+ = \theta \cap \alpha = \{y/b\}$
> Step 3: $\lambda^+ = \{\}$, $\alpha$ U $\lambda^+ = \{y/b\}$
> Step 4: $\eta^+ = \{\}$, $\alpha$ U $\eta^+ = \{y/b\}$
> Step 5: Apply $\sigma^+$ and $\eta^+$ to FC2i,
> $(\forall x \forall z \exists u)$ ($\lceil$emp_i(x,b,z) V dept_i(b,u))
> Apply the absorption rules, /* dept_i(b,u) = F (false)*/
> $(\forall x \forall z)$ ($\lceil$emp_i(x,b,z) V F)
> W = $(\forall x \forall z)$ ($\lceil$emp_i(x,b,z))
> Step 6: Negate W, Test-FC2i' (Algorithm-B): $(\exists x \exists z)$ (emp_i(x,b,z))
>
> Update: delete(dept_i(a,b))
> Target Relation: dept_i
> Other Relation: emp_i
> Test-FC2i' (Algorithm-A): $(\forall y \forall z)$ ($\lceil$emp_i(x,a,z))

Step 1: $\theta$ (dept_i) = {y/a,u/b}, $\alpha$ (emp_i) = {y/a}

Step 2: $\sigma^- = \theta \cap \alpha = \{y/a\}$,

Step 3: $\lambda^- = \{\}$, $\alpha \cup \lambda^- = \{y/a\}$

Step 4: $\eta^- = \{\}$, $a \cup \eta^- = \{y/a\}$

Step 5: Apply $\sigma^-$ and $\eta^-$ to FC2i,

$(\forall x \forall z \exists u)$ ($\bar{}$emp_i(x,a,z) V dept_i(a,u))

Apply the absorption rules, /* emp_i(x,a,z) = T (true) */

$(\exists u)$ ( F V dept_i(a,u))

$(\exists u)$ (dept_i(a,u))

W, Test-FC2i' (Algorithm-B): $(\exists u)$ (dept_i(a,u))

A pre-test generated by the above algorithms specifies the information required to verify if an update operation violates a global constraint, and is applied to the current database state as a query *before* the update is made. The result of the test is a boolean value true(TEST) which indicates that there is such information in the database or false(TEST) which indicates that there is no such information. The result of these tests will generate different trigger actions based on the type of information required and the type of update. This is summarized in Table 4.4.3 below. Only the rules used in our examples are presented here. In presenting the tests, we use the notation $(\exists X)$ (resp. $\forall X$) as an abbreviation for $(\exists x_1, \exists x_2, ..., \exists x_n)$ (resp. $\forall x_1, \forall x_2, ..., \forall x_n$). If a pre-test is not applicable (no pre-test can be derived for a given update and constraint, or the pre-test fails to show that an update does not violate a constraint) then a post-test is selected and is performed after the update is made.

| **Table 4.4.3: The trigger action performed as a result of pre-test evaluation** | | |
|---|---|---|
| TYPE OF INFORMATION (embedded in pre-test) | UPDATE OPERATION | TRIGGER ACTION |
| | | {domain comparison} |
| rule_1 $(\exists X \vert \forall X)$ (a op X) $\Lambda$ | INSERT | true(TEST) :- INSERT |
| (key(a) V $\bar{}$key(a)) | DELETE | true(TEST) :- DELETE |
| | | false(TEST) :- ABORT |
| rule_2 $(\exists X)R(a,...,X) \Lambda$ key(a) | INSERT | true(TEST) :- ABORT |
| | | false(TEST) :- invoke(postTEST) |
| rule_3 $(\exists X)R(a,...,X) \Lambda$ $\bar{}$key(a) | INSERT | true(TEST) :- INSERT |
| | | false(TEST) :- invoke(postTEST) |
| rule_4 $(\forall X)\bar{}R(a,...,b,X) \Lambda$ | INSERT | true(TEST) :- invoke(postTEST) |
| (key(a) $\Lambda$ $\bar{}$key(b)) | | false(TEST) :- ABORT |

**Table 4.4.3: The trigger action performed as a result of pre-test evaluation (Continued)**

| TYPE OF INFORMATION (embedded in pre-test) | UPDATE OPERATION | TRIGGER ACTION |
|---|---|---|
| rule_5 $(\exists X)R(a,...,X) \wedge key(a)$ $(\exists X)R(a,...,b,X) \wedge$ $(key(a) \wedge \bar{}key(b))$ | DELETE | true(TEST) :- DELETE, invoke(postTEST) false(TEST) :- ABORT |
| rule_6 $(\exists X)R(a,...,X) \wedge \bar{}key(a)$ | DELETE | true(TEST) :- DELETE false(TEST) :- invoke(postTEST) |

Notes: $\bar{}key(a)$ (resp. $\bar{}key(b)$) denotes that a (resp. b) is not a key or a subset of a key; key(a) denotes that a is a key.

**Example 4.4.1** The following tests are generated for the fragment constraints derived in section 4.1. Assume the worst case where each fragment relation is distributed to different sites of the network. The tests generated by Algorithm-A are global post-tests except FC1i which is a local post-test.

| Update Template | Algorithm-A | Algorithm-B | Trigger Action |
|---|---|---|---|
| FC1i: insert(emp_i(a,b,c)) | $(\forall u \forall v)$ $(\bar{}emp\_i(a,u,v) \vee$ $((u=b) \wedge (v=c)))$ | $(\forall y \forall z)$ $(\bar{}emp\_i(a,y,z) \vee$ $((y=b) \wedge (z=c)))$ | rule_4 |
| FC112': insert(emp_1(a,b,c)) | $(\forall u \forall v)$ $(\bar{}emp\_2(a,u,v))$ | $(\exists y \exists z)$ $(emp\_1(a,y,z))$ | rule_2 |
| insert(emp_2(a,b,c)) | $(\forall y \forall z)$ $(\bar{}emp\_1(a,y,z)$ | $(\exists u \exists v)$ $(emp\_2(a,u,v))$ | rule_2 |
| FC2i': insert(emp_i(a,b,c)) | $(\exists u)\ dept\_i(b,u)$ | $(\exists x \exists y)$ $emp\_i(x,b,z)$ | rule_3 |
| delete(dept_i(a,b)) FC3i: | $(\forall x \forall y)(\bar{}emp\_i(x,a,z)$ | $(\exists u)\ dept\_i(a,u)$ | rule_5 |
| insert(emp_i(a,b,c)) | $(\forall u)(\bar{}dept\_i(b,u)$ $\vee (u>=c))$ | $(\exists x \exists y)$ $(emp\_i(x,b,z) \wedge (c<z))$ | rule_3 |
| insert(dept_i(a,b)) | $(\forall x \forall y)(\bar{}emp\_i(x,a,z)$ $\vee (b>=z))$ | $(\exists u)\ (dept\_i(a,u)$ $\wedge (u<b))$ | rule_3 |

Note: $i \in \{1,2\}$.

# 5 Run-Time Module

The structure of the RUN-TIME MODULE is shown in Figure 3 below. We assume distribution transparency, that is details of data distribution are hidden from the user. Any update request is written as a global update as though the database were centralized without having to specify the sites at which the data referenced in the update resides. At run time, when a user requests an update, the actual update is mapped into equivalent "fragment updates" by using the knowledge about data distribution so that sites which are not affected by the update will not be considered at all. This is achieved by the Update Mapping (UM) component. For example, insert(emp(100,d1,5400)) is mapped into insert(emp_1(100,d1,5400)). The fragment update is then compared with the update templates in the Constraint Base. If they are compatible, the integrity test (post-test and pre-test) together with their trigger actions generated earlier are sent to Update Optimizer (UO), i.e. only those constraints that may be violated by an update are selected for further evaluation. For example, insert(emp_1(100,d1,5400)) is compatible with update templates for FC11, FC112', FC21' and FC31. If there is more than one fragment constraint affected by the update (as in the example above) then UO will have to decide which test should be enforced first, i.e. it reschedules the execution of the integrity tests, thereby enabling early update abortion in the case of constraint violation. For the example above, pre-test FC11 is preferred to the other pre-tests since violation of pre-test FC11 implies that no insertion should be made at all. FC31 is preferred to FC21' since the truth of test FC31 implies the truth of test FC21' (but the truth of test FC21' does not imply the truth of FC31). In such situations, heuristic rules are used. UO is also responsible for substituting generic variables in the tests with the actual values as specified in the update request.

As shown in Table 4.4.3, the appropriate trigger action is performed based on the type of information required and also the type of update. For example, insert(emp_1(100,d1,5400)) and FC31 will generate the local pre-test $(\exists x \exists y)$ $(emp\_1(x,d1,z)) \wedge (5400 < z))$. The local pre-test is then evaluated by performing a query at the target site. This is accomplished by the Constraint Enforcer (CE). Since the information required is not a key of the relation emp and the update operation is an insert, therefore rule_3 is applied. If the result from the query indicates that there exists an employee who works in department d1 and whose salary is greater than 5400, then we can conclude that the insert operation will not violate fragment constraint FC31 and global constraint GC3. But if the result from the query is false then a post-test is performed.

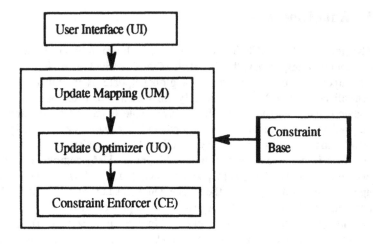

**Figure 3: Run-Time Module**

## 6 Summary

In this paper, we have proposed a technique for constraint validation in a distributed database. The technique is embedded in our prototype system called SICSDD which has been implemented in Quintus Prolog. The system has been developed in a modular way in which several existing techniques are applied and modified to fit into the underlying framework of SICSDD.

The technique proposed by [NIC82] is extended so that global constraints can be validated by localising constraint checking. We have used a two stage approach where constraint validation can be performed *before* or *after* the update is made. Our method generates local pre-tests and post-tests at compile-time. When an update request is to be executed, local pre-tests are selected in order to minimise the amount of data accessed during the integrity enforcement activity. These tests, which are evaluated before the update is performed, avoid the need to undo (rollback and recover from) an update in the event of constraint violation, and thus reduce the overhead cost of checking integrity. If a pre-test is not applicable (no pre-test can be derived for a given update and constraint, or the pre-test fails to show that an update does not violate a constraint) then a post-test is selected and is performed after the update is made.

The major contribution of this work is a new, promising approach to efficient constraint validation for a distributed database system. Currently, we are extending our prototype system with integrity enforcement facilities and it is hoped to incorporate aggregate constraints into the system in the future. Also we are looking at ways to extend the algorithms proposed in this paper so that they can be applied to transactions with multiple updates. Further, we would like to evaluate the performance of the above approaches in quantitative terms.

# References

[BAR92]  Barbard, D. and Garcia-Molina, H. The Demarcation Protocol: A Technique for Maintaining Linear Arithmetic Constraints in Distributed Database Systems. *Extending Database Technology Conference*, LNCS 580, March 1992, pp. 373-397.

[GRE90]  Grefen, W.P.J., Flokstra, J. and Apers, P.M.G. Parallel Handling of Integrity Constraints. *Proceedings of the Prisma Workshop*, 1990, pp. 242-258.

[GRE91]  Grefen, P.W.P.J. and Apers, P.M.G. Parallel Handling of Integrity Constraints On Fragment Relations. *Proceedings of the 2nd DEXA Conference*, Germany, August 1991.

[GUP93]  Gupta, A. and Widom, J. Local Verification of Global Integrity Constraints in Distributed Databases. *ACM SIGMOD*, 1993, pp. 49-58.

[HEN84]  Henschen, L.J., McCune, W.W. and Naqvi, S.A. Compiling Constraint-Checking Programs from First-Order Formulas. *Advances in Database Theory*, Vol. 2, Gallaire, H., Minker, J. and Nicolas, J.M., Eds. Plenum Press, 1984, pp. 145-170.

[HSU85]  Hsu, A. Integrity Checking for Multiple Updates. *Proceedings of the ACM SIGMOD International Conference on the Management of Data*, 1985, pp. 152-168.

[MAZ93]  Mazumdar, S. Optimizing Distributed Integrity Constraints. *Proceedings of the 3rd International Symposium on Database Systems for Advanced Applications*, Korea, April 1993, pp. 327-334.

[McC94]  McCarroll, N. and Kerridge, J. A Strategy for Semantic Integrity Enforcement in a Parallel Database Machine. *Proceedings of the 12th British National Conference on Databases*, July 1994, pp. 137-152.

[McC89]  McCune, W.W. and Henschen, L.J. Maintaining State Constraints in Relational Databases: A Proof Theoretic Basis. *Journal of the Association for Computing Machinery*, Vol. 36, No. 1, January 1989, pp. 46-68.

[NIC82]  Nicolas, J.M. Logic for Improving Integrity Checking in Relational Data Bases. *Acta Informatica*, Vol. 8, No. 3, 1982, pp. 227-253.

[OSZ91]  Oszu, T.M. and Valduriez, P. *Principles of Distributed Database Systems*. Prentice-Hall, Englewood Cliffs, New Jersey, 1991.

[QIA86]  Qian, X. and Wiederhold, G. Knowledge-based Integrity Constraint Validation. *Proceedings of the 12th International Conference on Very Large Data Bases*, Kyoto, August 1986, pp. 3-12.

[QIA87]  Qian, X. and Smith, D. R. Integrity Constraint Reformulation for Efficient Validation. *Proceedings of the 13th International Conference on Very Large Data Bases*, Brighton, 1987, pp. 417-425.

[QIA88]  Qian, X. An Effective Method for Integrity Constraint Simplification. *IEEE DE 4*, 1988, pp. 338-345.

[QIA89]    Qian, X. Distribution Design of Integrity Constraints. *Proceedings of the 2nd International Conference on Expert Database Systems*, 1989, pp. 205-226.

[SIM86]    Simon, E. and Valduriez, P.   Integrity Control in Distributed Database Systems. *Proceedings of the 19th Hawaii International Conference on System Science*, 1986, pp. 622-632.

[ZHA94]    Zhang, X. and Ozsoyoglu, Z.M. Reasoning with Implication and Referential Constraints in Semantic Query Optimization. *Proceedings of POST-ILPS'94 Workshop on Constraints and Databases*, USA, November 1994.

# Understanding the Tension Between Transition Rules and Confidentiality

X. C. Delannoy

Laboratoire TIMC-IMAG

Faculté de Médecine de Grenoble

38706 La Tronche Cedex - France

Xavier.Delannoy@imag.fr

http://curie.imag.fr/~delannoy

**Abstract** - This paper presents formally how the covert channel unavoidably opened by checking integrity constraints is exploitable to unveil unreadable data and is thus the source of tension between confidentiality and integrity. Only discretionary confidentiality models which independantly grant the READ and the UPDATE privileges on data items and transition rules (a special case of transition integrity constraints) are considered here. Because of a relational representation of transition rules and the introduction of the concept of saturation, unveiling is simply a relational query. Unveiling is exact or partial - several possible values are returned - depending on the mathematical properties of the transition rules.

**Keywords** - Relational Model, Discretionary Models of Confidentiality, Transition Integrity Constraints, Covert Channel.

## 1. Introduction

The database design process defines consistency rules for a database. They are expressed by integrity constraints [DELA94]. A few papers have noted that these constraints can be exploited by users of the database to reduce the uncertainty on the value of data items for which they do not have read privilege. The functionalities of confidentiality and consistency are therefore not independant since the second can be used to circumvent the first. [MAZU88] refers to the *tension* between confidentiality and consistency.

Formalizing this concept is difficult because of the wide variety of integrity constraints. Wihin the relational framework, we formally present the tension for a subclass of transition integrity constraints [GREF93] that we call transition rules. To our knowledge no other paper adresses the problem of tension for transition rules and more generally for transition integrity constraints.

The general form of a transition constraint is a predicate P(S1,S2) where S1 and S2 are two states of the database. If P(S1,S2) holds, then S2 is a possible consecutive state for S1. When the only difference between S1 and S2 concerns a single data item, we call the constraint a transition rule. A simple example would be: *"the age of a person can only increase"*. We will show that any data item is in fact constrained by a *unique* transition rule.

From the definition, a transition rule is therefore a characterization of what the admissible next values of a data item are, given its current value. It can be represented by a binary relation which associates all its next possible values to any possible value of the data item.

We assume that transition rules are checked by a dedicated part of the consistency rule checker of the database named the Transition Rule Checker (TRC). The TRC is called at the end of transactions to make sure that the transition is valid. In that case, the TRC returns either a message of acceptance, or a message of refusal and the transaction is aborted.

Consider the generic transaction which updates a given data item, refered as the update-transaction of the data item. The nature of the message returned by the TRC for an instance of this update-transaction depends only on whether or not the suggested value for the data item belongs to the set of its possible values in the next state of the database. If so, an acceptance message is returned. If not a refusal message is returned. Thus the TRC, when applied to an instance of update-transaction, formally corresponds to the characteristic function[1] of the set of the possible values of the data item in the next database state. Consequently it constitutes a channel of communication between the next database state and the user. This channel is clearly not intended for communication, and is therefore called a *covert channel* [WISE88] .

Although this channel is of limited bandwidth, we argue that it enables a user who has update, but not read privilege, on a given data item, to reduce uncertainty on its the current value [DELA96].

Indeed, the covert channel makes it possible for a user with only update priviledge on a data item to compute the set of all its possible values in the next state by successively submitting the TRC all the instances of the update-transaction of the data item. There is one instance for each value of the domain of the data item.

In the example of the age of a person, a user with update privilege on attribute *age* will try to update it to 0, then to 1, 2, ... , 200, assuming that the possible values of age belong to [0,200]. Some values will be rejected by the TRC. Others will compose the set that we call *saturation* associated with the data at the current state. If the age is 35, saturation is *{35, ..., 200}*. Notice that each time a value is accepted, the value of the data item is changed. A rollback operation must be performed to return it to its original state.

---

[1] Given a set E, the characteristic function $f: E \rightarrow \{0,1\}$ of a subset F of E is: $\forall x \in E$, if $x \in F$ then $f(x) = 1$ else $f(x) = 0$.

Once saturation is obtained, we consider the set of all the possible values of the unreadable data item which can exacly evolve to saturation. This set contains the actual value of the unreadable data and is therefore an unveiling of it. We show that it can be computed by a relational query on the binary relation associated with the transition rule. The cardinality of the set is dependant on the mathematical properties of the transition rule. If the cardinality is one, we say that unveiling is *exact*. Otherwise it is *partial*.

In our example, only 35 can evolve exactly to saturation. Indeed, 36 evolves to *{36, ..., 200}*, 34 to *{34, ..., 200}* and so on. Consequently, 35 is the value of the age. The age has been exactly unveiled.

Using transition rules it is thus possible to circumvent some confidential specifications, using the covert channel opened by the TRC. There is consequently a tension between transition rules and confidentiality .

In this paper this tension is formally presented. We first define which confidential scheme is required, and then give a formal definiton of transition rules. The covert channel raised by the TRC is discussed in section 4, whereas the Theorem of Unveiling is reported in section 5. Section 6 studies those factors which influence the quality, exact or partial, of the unveiling. Section 7 details how the tension can be exploited under the Oracle Data Base Management System (DBMS). Finally we present related works based on other kinds of consistency rules.

## 2. Confidential Scheme

According to [BANC77] a confidentiality scheme is defined by the answers to the following questions : (i) What is protected ? (ii) Against whom is there a protection ? (iii) How is protection maintained ? (iv) What does "to protect" mean ?

In this paper, we are concerned with (i) data of a relational database, (ii) protected against properly identified users, (iii) by acceptance or rejection of interactions of the user with the database, (iv) where "to protect" means to limit, via privileges, the ways a user can access the content of a relation.

The answer (iv) situates our confidentiality scheme in the framework of discretionary models of security. This is the type of confidentiality of most interest where general purpose DBMS are concerned and is unsurprisingly the one implemented by commercial DBMS. For our purposes we only retain two basic privileges[2] defined by the SQL-2 [SQL92] standard :

*READ* or *SELECT*: ability to read tuples from the relation. These tuples can be used anywhere in queries by the user. The READ ability may be restricted to a subset of attributes. If this privilege is not granted to a user on an attribute, this attribute is *unreadable* for the user.

*UPDATE* : ability to modify existing data in the relation. This ability may be restricted to a subset of attributes.

---

[2] Other privileges are required for inserting, deleting, etc., but we do not need them.

For example, a user, e.g., a data capture operator, with UPDATE but not READ privilege on the attribute *age* of the relation *Employee(ssn, name, age)*, can perform the SQL command *UPDATE Employee SET age=30 WHERE ssn=127;* whereas *SELECT age FROM Employee;* and *SELECT \* FROM Employee WHERE age > 25;* will be rejected. By default users have all privileges on the table they create, and no privilege on those created by others. They can grant privileges to other users on their relations.

Some theoretical discretionary models of security for databases such as the Action Entity Model [BUSS83] [FUGI84] [CAST94] or [BERT94] in the framework of object oriented databases, impose dependence between privileges. In particular the UPDATE privilege cannot usually be granted on an attribute if the READ privilege has not already been granted. We suppose no dependence at all : the UPDATE privilege can be granted independently of the READ privilege.

Although surprising, this hypothesis corresponds to actual needs [MELT95] that justify its appearence in SQL-2 [SQL92] and its maintenance in SQL-3 [SQL94]. The DBMS's System R [GRIF76], Oracle [ORAC95], and Ingres [INGR93] ensure this independance too.

*Definition* - An *unveiling* of an unreadable attribute of a given tuple is a set of values including the exact value of this attribute. The unveiling is *exact* when it has only one element. Otherwise it is *partial*.

Accuracy of partial unveiling is proportional to the smallness of the cardinality of the set. The domain of the attribute is the least accurate partial unveiling.

## 3. Transition Rules

A transition rule applies to an attribute of a relation. For any tuple of this relation it states all the possible values of this attribute in the next database state according to its value in the current state. Consider, e.g., the database *schema ORDER(Order_Nb, Status)* where $Dom^3(Order\_Nb)=INTEGER$ and $Dom(Status)=\{In\_Process,Delivered,Paid\}$. A transition rule on the attribute *Status* of relation *ORDER* might be :

TR_1: *If the status of an order is "In_Process" then it can only evolve to "delivered" or remain "In_Process" and if it is "Delivered" then it can only evolve to "Paid" or remain "Delivered".*

Transition rules can be expressed in first order temporal logic. A temporal logic formula is constructed from state formulae to which temporal operators, boolean connectives and quantifiers are applied [MANN91]. In the case of transition rules only the temporal operator noted by • is required. For a predicate P, the semantics

---

[3] *Dom* is the domain of the attribute.

of •P is informally « P holds in the next state ». See [MANN91] for details. It follows that TR_1 can be rewritten in temporal logic as :

TR_1 : $\forall x,y$ ( $ORDER(x, In\_Process) \wedge \bullet ORDER(x,y) \rightarrow y=In\_Process \vee y=Delivered$ ) $\wedge$ ( $ORDER(x, Delivered) \wedge \bullet ORDER(x,y) \rightarrow y=Delivered \vee y=Paid$ )

The correspondance between the current and next possible values of an attribute $A$ can be expressed inside a binary relation $Tr_A$ on $Dom(A)$ of attribute *Current* and *Next*. Each tuple of this relation is of the form *(Current_Value, Next_Value)* where *Current_Value* is a possible value for the attribute in the current state of the database, and *Next_Value*, a possible value of this attribute in the next state.

| Current | Next |
|---------|------|
| In Process | Delivered |
| In Process | In Process |
| Delivered | Paid |
| Delivered | Delivered |
| Paid | Paid |

**Fig. 1** Relation $Tr_{Status}$

The binary relation $Tr_{Status}$ associated with TR_1 is shown opposite in figure 1. Notice that the relation is reflexive due to the fact that TR_1 allows orders to remain in their current state. Using $Tr_{Status}$, TR_1 can be rewritten :

TR_1 : $\forall x,y,z\ ORDER(x,y) \wedge \bullet ORDER(x,z) \rightarrow Tr_{Status}(y,z)$

Specifying valid transitions with a binary relation allows the following syntactical definition of a transition rule :

*Definition*[4] - Given a relation R of key $X$[5] and with attribute $A$, $A \notin X$, a transition rule on attribute A is a first order temporal logic formula T of the form :

$$\forall x, a^{current}, a^{next}\ R(x,...,a^{current},...) \wedge \bullet R(x,...,a^{next},...) \rightarrow Tr_A(a^{current}, a^{next})$$

where $Tr_A$ is binary relation on $Dom(A)$. We note $r(T)=Tr_A$ .

It must be emphasised that, according to the definition, $X$ must be the key of the relation R, and $A$ does not belong to the key. The importance of this restriction on $X$ has been noted in [GREF93]. It implies that no transition rule can be defined on a key. In a forthcoming paper in collaboration it will be shown that our formal presentation of the tension can be extended to the case where $X$ is not a key attribute.

*Property* - If $T_1$ and $T_2$ are two transition rules on the same attribute $A$ of a relation $R$, then $T_1 \wedge T_2$ and $T_1 \vee T_2$ are transition rules on the attribute $A$. In addition, $r(T_1 \wedge T_2) = r(T_1) \cap r(T_2)$ and $r(T_1 \vee T_2) = r(T_1) \cup r(T_2)$.

---

[4] Transition rules existentially quantified ($\exists$) are not adressed here.
[5] X is a mono or a multi attribute key. This remark also applies through out.

*Proof* - The binary relation associated with a conjunction (resp. disjunction) of transition rules is the intersect (resp. union) of the binary relations of these transition rules. □

In other words, this property states that the definition of a conjunction (resp. disjunction) of transition rules on an attribute is equivalent to the definition of a unique transition rule on this attribute.

Any non-key attribute *A* of a relation is constrained by its *free transition rule*, i.e., the transition rule T where $r(T)=Dom(A)\times Dom(A)$. Since any conjunction and/or disjunction of transition rules on the same attribute can be reduced to one transition rule (see property below), any attribute is constrained by *only one* transition rule.

We have seen in the introduction that transition rules are checked by the TRC. In practice, databases do not implement a TRC. To our knowledge the only exception is the commercial database SABRINA [GARD89]. However, the TRC can be emulated through the use of triggers or by an ad hoc dedicated process running with database administrator privilege.

Having presented the required confidentiality model and transition rules, we formally present the tension between these two notions which originates in the covert channel opened by the TRC. This is formally presented below.

# 4. Covert Channel Identification

## 4.1 Definition

Covert channels are introduced in [WISE88] and discussed in [WISE89], [WISE90a] and [WISE90b]. A covert channel is an unexpected means of communication which appears as a side effect of another scheme. For example, a protection mechanism always open a new communication channel, namely the mechanism itself. Indeed, the protection mechanism can be seen as a blackboard shared by the database and the user. When a user performs an operation on some data, the result is written on the blackboard. If there is no answer, an empty set is returned. If the user is not cleared for the operation on the data, "*No_Access*" is written on the blackboard. In this last case, although no data are returned, the user knows that the information exists, which is a security leak.

The channel of communication opened by the security mechanism is clearly not intended to be used for communication and is therefore called a covert channel.

## 4.2 Covert Channel Opened by the TRC

*Definition* - Let relation $R$ of key $X$ and with attribute $A$, $A \notin X$. The *update-transaction* for attribute $A$ is :     BEGIN TRANSACTION
                                    UPDATE  R  SET A=a WHERE $X=x$ ;
                                    COMMIT ;
                                    END TRANSACTION
where $x$ is the key of the tuple of $R$ to be updated and $a$ the suggested value for $A$.

We denote by $\underline{U}(R,x,A = a)$ an instance of the update-transaction for attribute $A$ of relation $R$ for a given $x$ and $a$.

The nature of the message returned by the TRC at the execution of $\underline{U}(R,x,A = a)$ only depends on whether or not the new suggested value for the attribute belongs to the set of possible values for that attribute in the next state of the database. If so, an acceptance message is returned. If not, a refusal message is returned. Thus the TRC when applied to $\underline{U}(R,x,A = a)$ behaves like the characteristic function of the set of all possible values for the attribute in the next database state. In other words, it constitutes a channel of communication between the next database state and the user. This channel is clearly not intended for communication, and is therefore a *covert channel.*

Although this channel is of limited bandwidth it can enable a user to partially or exactly unveil the current value of an attribute on which a transition rule is defined and is thus the source of the tension between transition rules and confidentiality. To exploit this channel, we introduce the concept of *saturation.*

# 5. Exploitation of the Covert Channel

## 5.1 Concept of Saturation

*Definition* - Given a relation $R$ of key $X$ and with attribute $A$, $A \notin X$, the *saturation*, in the *current state* of the database, for attribute $A$ of a tuple of key $x$ of $R$, is the mono-attribute relation $\underline{R}(x,A) = \prod_{Next} ( \sigma_{Current=a} Tr_A )$ on $Dom(A)$, where $a$ is the value of $A$ in the current state of the database.

Less formally, the saturation is the set of all the possible values for $A$ in the tuple of key $x$ in the next database state. The relational expression defining the saturation is made of a selection followed by a projection. The selection $\sigma_{Current=a} Tr_A$ has to identify the value $a$ of the attribute $A$ in the tuple of key $x$. Without the READ privilege granted on $A$, the value $a$ is unreadable, making the saturation not directly computable.

However, it is possible to compute it indirectly when the UPDATE privilege is granted on $A$. Since the TRC answers "*Accepted*" or "*Refused*" to any update of the attribute $A$ (covert channel), this answer is in fact the value of the characteristic function of the saturation. If the updating transaction $\underline{U}(R,x,A = a)$ for any $a \in Dom(A)$ is accepted then the value $a$ belongs to the saturation. If it is refused it does not. Thus, one can compute $\underline{R}(x,A)$ by successively submiting the TRC all the possible update-transactions $\underline{U}(R,x,A = a)$, $a \in Dom(A)$. Each time an update is accepted, the data item is changed. Therefore, a rollback operation must be performed to return it to its original state.

The search space $Dom(A)$ of the above iterative algorithm can be reduced if one remarks that the saturation is, by definition, a subset of the values appearing in the attribute *Next* of the relation $Tr_A$. Consequently, the computation of the saturation can be done by successively submiting all the possible $\underline{U}(R,x,A = a)$ with $a \in \prod_{Next} Tr_A$ to the TRC.

*Property* - If $\prod_{Next} Tr_A$ is finite, the saturation $\underline{R}(x,A)$ can be computed by successively issuing all the $\underline{U}(R,x,A = a)$ with $a \in \prod_{Next} Tr_A$ and keeping all the $a$ for which the update-transaction is accepted by the TRC. This computation requires only the update privilege on $A$. $\square$

### 5.2 Theorem of Unveiling

*Theorem of Unveiling* - Given a relation $R$ of key $X$ and with attribute $A$, $A \notin X$, and a tuple of key $x$ of $R$, the set $Un = \{a \in Dom(A) \mid \forall b \in Dom(A) : (a,b) \in Tr_A \Leftrightarrow b \in \underline{R}(x,A)\}$ of all the values of attribute *Current* of $Tr_A$ exactly associated with $\underline{R}(x,A)$ is an unveiling of attribute A of the tuple of key $x$.$\square$

The set $Un$ can be computed by the following relational query, refered to as the Unveiling Query:

$$Un = (Tr_A \div \underline{R}(x,A)) - (\prod_{Current} (Tr_A - \prod_{Current} Tr_A \times \underline{R}(x,A))).$$

The division of the formula determines the set of all the values of attribute *Current* of $Tr_A$ associated with the saturation, including those associated with extra other values. The second part of the query suppresses these indesirable values.

The privileges required to compute the Unveiling Query are those required to access or compute $Tr_A$ and $\underline{R}(x,A)$.

As usual in works on the tension between integrity constraints and confidentiality, cf. [MAZU88], we assume that transition rules are known to all users. Consequently $Tr_A$ is accessible to any user. If this table is not stored in the database, the user can construct it from the logical expression of the transition rule as shown in section 3. The computation of the saturation $\underline{R}(x,A)$ on the other hand, requires that READ privilege be granted on $A$. However, using the property found in section 5.1, the UPDATE privilege is in fact sufficient to compute it.

To conclude, *the computation of the Unveiling Query only requires the UPDATE privilege on A*. Thus users with that privilege can unveil data for which they do not have the READ privilege. As this result originates from the checking of transition rules, it reveals the tension between transition rules and confidentiality.

### 5.3 Application of the Theorem of Unveiling

The Theorem of Unveiling can be exploited by data capture operators. Consider the database schema and the transition rule TR_1 defined in section 3 (the extension of relation *ORDER* is shown opposite in figure 2). Data capture operators in charge of updating the status of each order are granted the UPDATE privilege on the attribute *Status* of the relation *ORDER*. However they are not granted the READ privilege due to the sensitive nature of the information.

| Order_Nb | Status |
|----------|--------------|
| 126 | Delivered |
| 127 | In_Process |
| 128 | Paid |

☐ READ and UPDATE
▨ UPDATE only

**Fig. 2**   Relation ORDER

To unveil the current status of order 127 for example, an operator can first compute the saturation

$ORDER(127, Status) = \{(In\_Process, Delivered)\}$

using the property found in 5.1. Then the operator computes the Unveiling Query which returns *{(In_Process)}*. Therefore the status of order 127 in the current state of the database is *In_Process*. The unveiling is exact.

Notice that if $Tr_{ORDER}$ would have contained tuple *(Delivered, In_Process)*, the Unveiling Query would have lead to the partial unveiling *{(In_Process, Delivered)}*. Conditions for exact unveiling are discussed in the next section.

# 6. Quality (Exact/Partial) of the Unveiling

## 6.1 One Condition for Exact Unveiling

For R a binary relation on a set E we note: $\forall x \in E \ R(x) = \{ y \in E \mid R(x,y) \}$.

*Theorem* - If the binary relation $Tr_A$ satisfies $\forall x,y \in Dom(A) \ x \neq y \rightarrow Tr_A(x) \neq Tr_A(y)$, then the unveiling given by the Theorem of Unveiling is exact.

*Proof* - The set which is refered to in the Theorem of Unveiling contains all the values of attribute *Current* of relation $Tr_A$ exactly associated with $\underline{R}(x,A)$. Since

$Tr_A(x) \neq Tr_A(y)$, two different values of *Current* are associated with two different sets of values. Therefore, there is only one value of *Current* which is exactly associated with $\underline{R}(x,A)$ and the unveiling is exact. $\square$

## 6.2 Desirable Properties of Transition Rules

The hypothesis of the preceding theorem is validated using the mathematical properties on $Tr_A$. Before expressing these properties, we first recall some usual definitions on binary relations.

For R a binary relation on a set E, we note $R^{-1}$ the inverse of R and I the identity on E, i.e., the binary relation $\{ (x,x) \mid x \in E \}$. For R and S two relations on E, we note RoS the composition of R and S, i.e., the binary relation $\{ (x,y) \mid x \in E \; y \in E \; \exists z \in E : (x,z) \in R \wedge (z,y) \in S \}$.

*Definitions* -
— R is reflexive iff $R \cap I = I$.
— R is areflexive iff $R \cap I = \varnothing$.
— R is asymmetrical iff $R \cap R^{-1} = \varnothing$.
— R is antisymmetrical iff $R \cap R^{-1} \subseteq I$.

— R is transitive iff $R \subseteq R \text{o} R$
— R is total iff $R \cup R^{-1} \cup I = E \times E$.
— R is an order relation if and only if is antisymmetrical and transitive and reflexive.

*Properties* - Given a binary relation R on E,
If R is total and areflexive
If R verifies the properties of reflexivity and antisymmetry $\Big\}$ then $\forall x,y \in E \; x \neq y \rightarrow R(x) \neq R(y)$.
If R is an ordered relation

*Proof (first property)* - Let $x \in E$, $y \in E$ et $x \neq y$. Since the relation R is areflexive, (*i*) $x \notin R(x) \wedge y \notin R(y)$. Moreover, R is total and $x \neq y$, therefore $(x,y) \in R \vee (y,x) \in R$, in other words, (*ii*) $y \in R(x) \vee x \in R(y)$. The conjonction of (*i*) and (*ii*) implies that $[y \notin R(y) \wedge y \in R(x)] \vee [x \notin R(x) \wedge x \in R(y)]$. Therefore $R(x) \neq R(y)$. $\square$

According to the theorem found in 6.1, these properties, if they apply to $Tr_A$, ensure that the unveiling given by the Theorem of Unveiling is exact.

In the example of section 5.3, $Tr_{ORDER}$ satisfies the properties of reflexivity and antisymmetry, which justifies that the unveiling is exact.

## 6.3 Free Transition Rules

*Property* - If the transition rule defined on an attribute $A$ is equivalent to its free transition rule (see section 3), then the unveiling given by the Theorem of Unveiling is the entire domain of $A$ and therefore the least accurate possible unveiling. $\square$

## 7. Exploiting the Tension Under Oracle

The Theorem of Unveiling can be applied on Oracle. Let the relation *EMPLOYEE(Employee_nb, Age)* with *Dom(Employee_nb) = INTEGER* and *Dom(Age) = [0, 200]* and the transition rule : *"The age of an employee can only increase"*. The Theorem of Unveiling reveals that it is possible for a user with only the UPDATE privilege on *Age* to unveil the value of this attribute for any tuple of *EMPLOYEE*.

Using the Oracle embedded programming language PL/SQL we sucessively give : (i) the trigger which enforces the transition rule (it plays the role of the TRC), (ii) the code of the update-transaction for attribute *Age*, and (iii) the code to compute *EMPLOYEE*(127, Age). Since the Unveiling Query is a simple formulae of relational algebra, its translation in SQL is let to the reader.

```
(i) — CREATE TRIGGER TRC_Age    -- // Trigger to enforce the transition rule
                                 -- // « The age of an employee can  only increase ».
          AFTER UPDATE OF Age ON EMPLOYEE
              FOR EACH ROW
                  BEGIN
                      IF :OLD.Age >  :NEW.Age
                          THEN INSERT INTO FOO VALUES (0);
                          END IF
                  END;
```

FOO is a mono-attribute relation defined to generate a *Check_Constraint_Violated* message when the value 0 is inserted. The built in binary relation ' > ' implements $Tr_{Age}$ .

```
(ii) — FUNCTION UPDATE_TRANSACTION (key NUMBER, value NUMBER)
                                         RETURN BOOLEAN IS
       BEGIN                      -- // Computes U (EMPLOYEE, 127, Age = value)
           UPDATE EMPLOYEE SET Age=value WHERE Employee_nb=key;
           RETURN TRUE;
       EXCEPTION
           WHEN Check_Constraint_Violated THEN RETURN FALSE;
       END UPDATE_TRANSACTION;
```

The EXCEPTION clause is performed if the trigger above generates a *Check_Constraint_Violated* message.

```
(iii) —  PROCEDURE  SATURATION ( ) IS          -- // Computation of the Saturation
         COMMIT; key := 127 ;
         FOR value IN 0..200  LOOP               -- // Domain of attribute Age
            IF TRANSACTION(key, value) = TRUE
               THEN  ROLLBACK;
                  INSERT INTO R VALUES (value);   -- // R = EMPLOYEE(127, Age)
               COMMIT;
            END IF
         END LOOP
         END  SATURATION ;
```

## 8. Related Works

In our work we formally present the tension between transition rules and confidentiality. Other research is concerned with the same problem but consider other kinds of semantic information.

The work of [MAZU88] is the closest to ours since it considers static integrity constraints. This approach is original in that it mixes static integrity constraints and the expression of unreadability in the same logical formalism which allows them to rely on a theorem prover.

[MORG87] considers the semantic of the applications which use the database. This additional information applies to data in the application environment even though they are not explicitly stored in the database.

Finally, [CAST94] considers "sensitive statistics", i.e., statistics that can lead to identifying unreadable information, in their survey of inference protection techniques for statistical databases.

## 9. Conclusion

We have formally presented the tension between transition rules and discretionary confidentiality models where the UPDATE privilege can be granted independently of the READ privilege.

The source of the tension is the covert channel opened by the Transition Rule Checker when a transaction which only updates one data item is executed, since it allows unveiling of unreadable but updatable data. Depending on the mathematical properties of the transition rules, this unveiling is either partial or exact.

The formal presentation of the tension uses a relational representation of transition rules and introduces the concept of saturation. Both of which allow unveiling to be simply formalized as a relational query.

The work presented in this paper is still in progress. We are currently investigating the following directions :

— Extension of the formalisation by relaxing the constraint on the key which appears currently in all the definitions, properties and theorems.
— Compile time or runtime solutions to counter the covert channel.
— Extention of the approach to some classes of static constraints.

The formal simplicity of the relational model has been of great help in our formal approach. Nevertheless, we envisage to extend the formalisation of the tension between transition integrity constraints and confidentiality to the object oriented database landscape.

## Acknowledgements

I thank C. Del Vigna very much for our many fruitful discussions from the early stage of the paper. His contributions often helped to clarify some notions and many of his proposals have been included in this paper. I also thank A.&M. Simonet for their careful proofreading of the paper.

## References

[BANC77] Bancilhon, F., Spyratos, N., *Protection of Information in Relational Data Bases*, VLDB, 1977.

[BERT94] Bertino, E., Weigand, H. , *An Approach to Authorization Modeling in Object Oriented Database Systems*, Data &Knowledge Engineering, volume 12, Number 1, February 1994.

[BUSS83] Bussolati, U., Fugini, M.G, Martella, G., *A Conceptual Framework for Security System Design*, Proc. 9th IFIP World Conf., Paris, September 1983.

[CAST94] Castano, S., Fugini, M., Giancarlo, M., Pierangela, S., *Database Security*, Addison Wesley, 1994.

[DELA94] Delannoy, X., *La Cohérence dans les Bases de Données*, Research Report RR-936I, University of Grenoble (France), IMAG-TIMC Lab., November 1994.

[DELA96] Delannoy, X., *The Tension Between Transition Rules and Confidentiality* , Research Report, University of Grenoble (France), IMAG-TIMC Lab., January 1996.

[GARD89] Gardarin, G., Valduriez, P., *SGBD Relationels : Analyse et Compararaison des Bases de Données, Eyrolles*, 1989.

[GREF93] Greffen, P., Apers, P., *Integrity Control in Relational Database Systems - An Overview*, Data & Knowledge Engineering, 10 (1993), p187-223, North Holland, 1993.

[GRIF76] Griffiths, P., Bradford, W., *An Authorization Mechanism for a Relational Database System*, ACM Transactions on Database Systems, Vol. 1, No. 3, page 242-255, September 1976.

[FUGI84] Fugini, M.G., Martella, G., *ACTEN : A Conceptual Model for Security System Design*, Computers and Security, Elsevier (North Holland), 3(3),1984.

[INGR93] *Ingres manuals*, Release 4.55, Computer Associate ,1993.

[MANN91] Manna, Z., Pnueli, A., *The Temporal Logic of Reactive and Concurrent Systems -Specification -*, Springer-Verlag, 1991.

[MAZU88] Mazumdar, S., Stemple, D., Shread, T., *Resolving the Tension between Integrity and Security Using a Theorem Prover*, ACM SIGMOD, 1988.

[MELT95] Melton, J., Personal correspondance with Jim Melton, Senior Architect of Standards for Sybase Corp. and Editor of the ISO SQL-92 and emerging SQL-3 standards, December 1995.

[MORG87] Morgenstern, M., *Security and Inference in Multilevel Database and Knowledge-Based Systems*, Proceedings of Association for Computing Machinery Special Interest Group on Management of Data, 1987.

[ORAC95] *Oracle Manuals*, Release 7, Oracle Corp., 1995.

[SQL92] *Information Technology - Database Language SQL*, Third Edition, ISO/IEC 9075 (and 1994 addendum), 1992.

[SQL94] *Database Language SQL (SQL3)*, ISO-ANSI Working Draft, ANSI TC X3H2, ISO/IEC JTC 1/SC 21/WG 3, August 1994.

[WISE88] Wiseman, S., Terry, P., Wood, A., Harrold, C., *The Trusted Path between SMITE and the User*, IEEE Symposium on Security and Privacy, April 18-21, Oakland, 1988.

[WISE89] Wiseman, S., *The trouble with Secure Databases*, Procs. MILCOMP'89, London, September 1989.

[WISE90a] Wiseman, S., *On the Problem of Security in Data Bases*, Database Security III, Status and Prospects, Results of the IFIP WG 11.3 Workshop on Database Security, September 1989.

[WISE90b] Wiseman, S., *Control of Confidentiality in Databases*, Computers and Security, Vol. 9, No.6, October 1990.

# SPEAR: Extending ER
# for Dynamic Behaviour and Refinement

Simon Wiseman and Bryony Pomeroy

Defence Research Agency
Malvern, Worcestershire WR14 3PS
{wiseman,pomeroy}@hydra.dra.hmg.gb

**Abstract.** SPEAR is an Entity–Relationship approach to modelling database systems which not only captures static requirements, but also dynamic behaviour. The notation can be used to give high level abstract requirements, or more detailed implementation level designs, and an additional refinement notation can be used to describe how specifications at different levels relate to one another. Tools to support the use of the notation, through a natural language interface, have been developed and have been used to construct the examples given.

## 1 Introduction

The Entity-Relationship approach to modelling database systems was originally proposed by Chen in 1976 [1]. Since then numerous extensions and variations have been put forward. One of these, SPEAR [2], was defined in order to assist with the specification of secure databases.

The original design of SPEAR was driven by three motivations. The first was to produce a single notation that was capable of capturing both high and low level specifications for database states. The second was to produce a notation which was itself specified mathematically. The third was to avoid the awkward terminology that surrounds the distinction between what Chen termed "entities" and "entity sets".

The need to support high level specifications was seen to be important from a security point of view, because there is often a significant disparity between a security requirement and a security mechanism. For example, a requirement for purchases to be authorised by two people may need a mechanism that allows signatures to be collected on various forms. Thus a notation which can only describe low level specifications cannot help relay difficult security requirements.

The provision of a mathematical foundation to the model was seen as a way of ensuring that all details of the model were well understood by its designers. With hindsight, this was a very valuable strategy. Although design of the notation has seemed slower as a result, there have been many occasions where a construct whose meaning was thought to be intuitively understood turned out to have some awkward side effects when it came to define its semantics rigorously.

The importance of terminology cannot be over-emphasised. Existing E-R terminology can be very confusing, especially to the novice. Further, when it is used to state security requirements, serious misunderstanding can result. Hence the terminology used in SPEAR was carefully chosen, with some new terms, to allow individual entities and collections of entities to be distinguished easily.

Once the initial model had been defined, a graphical notation was developed [3]. The underlying model is defined using Z [4], but this is only readable by the mathematically inclined. The graphical notation essentially provides a readable syntax for the Z, making it a practical way of specifying databases.

To help produce the SPEAR diagrams, a simple tool was developed. To avoid the expense of developing a diagram editor, this tool was written in Prolog on a Macintosh and took simple sentence patterns as input and produced the diagram described by the sentence, which could then be cut and pasted into a document.

Once use was made of this primitive tool it became apparent that there was merit in the approach of using natural language to drive a CASE tool. As a result, a full prototype tool, called SABRE, was produced to support the development of SPEAR specifications. Microsoft Word is used to enter constrained-English descriptions of a specification and then SABRE is invoked from the Word menus. The text is extracted from Word, parsed by SABRE, the diagram is produced and automatically pasted into the document. A knowledge base containing a description of the specification is maintained and this is used to check for consistency and to generate schemas for relational databases.

Initially, like other E-R models, SPEAR was designed to express the static structure of a database. Though it did allow for constraints on how data was to be classified, it was apparent that many security requirements are constraints on the dynamic behaviour of a system.

While most methods for developing database systems include ways of describing dynamic behaviour, such as Entity Life Histories and Data Flow Diagrams [5], these are really specifications of orthogonal views of the system and not extensions to the E-R model used for the static structure. Relating these different views, and reconciling the differences in notation, is difficult, with the result that documentation often lacks consistency and completeness.

For SPEAR the aim was to ensure that security requirements could be stated precisely and unambiguously, hence a way of specifying dynamic behaviour which provides close integration between the description of static structure and dynamic behaviour was required. Fortunately it has proved possible to extend the existing SPEAR notation with constructs for describing dynamic behaviour, and include these in the SABRE tool [6], without any major reworking. The resulting notation is described in [7] and [8].

In the development of large databases, implementation level specifications alone do not provide adequate documentation for the maintenance of the database throughout its lifetime. In order to manage changing requirements it is necessary to produce a number of specifications, starting with one at a high level of abstraction which gives a high level view of the requirements. Further specifications then refine previous ones with additional detail, until an implementation level specification is produced.

However, in order to support maintenance effectively, it must also be possible to document how each specification relates to its refined specification.

To this end, a notation for refinement has been developed for SPEAR. This is not strictly part of the E-R model, but does use the same constraint notation and has a related graphical representation.

In this paper, an overview of the E-R state model of SPEAR is given in section 2, while the extensions for describing dynamic behaviour are described in section 3. Refinement is then discussed in section 4. A complete example of a simple database description is given in section 5 and some conclusions are drawn in section 6.

# 2 Defining the State

## 2.1 Entities and Classes

A specification is a model of some real or imaginary world. The things of interest in that world are modelled as entities. The things may be physical or abstract, so for example a particular ship or a particular request for action might be considered entities.

Entities may have observable properties, which are called attributes. Each attribute of a particular entity is associated with either a collection[1] or list[2] of values. So for example, a ship entity might have a name attribute which is the collection of one element, "Britannia", and a destination attribute which is the list having "London" in position 1, "New York" in position 3 and "London" in position 4. Note that attributes having just one simple value are modelled as a collection of one element.

Whilst attributes normally have values, it is also possible for them to have entities. This is a serious departure from conventional E-R modelling, but it provides a straightforward way to represent simple relationships, and is illustrated in section 2.3.

Entities need not possess attributes which uniquely identify them, because they may be referenced by "pointing at them". This is equivalent to the way things are referenced in the real world, where for example one may point to a hazy blur on the horizon and ask "what is the name of that ship?".

Where there is no unique attribute, it is not possible to ascertain statically whether two different references "point" at the same entity. For an example in the real world, consider pointing at stars in the heavens. Two stars in different places may have the same spectra and periodicity, but we cannot tell whether it is the same star observed twice due to gravitational lensing or in fact two different but remarkably similar stars.

---

[1]  A collection is a multi-set, in that the number of times something is included in a collection is significant.

[2]  A list is an ordered collection of things, though the positions need not be sequential.

However, dynamic changes can reveal differences. For example, if one star suddenly explodes, leaving the other intact, we can be sure that the stars were different.

A class is a collection of some entities (strictly, it is a collection of some "pointers" to entities). Each class places constraints on its members, in particular a class insists that its members possess certain attributes whose values meet specified criteria. Further general constraints can be imposed, using the SPEAR constraint notation, which is relatively readable despite having the expressive power of first order predicate calculus.

In general, an entity may belong to more than one class and may possess more attributes than are demanded by any class to which it belongs. Also, an entity need not belong to a class even though it meets the membership criteria. For example, the class of ships may insist that its members have name, destination and cargo attributes. Some ships may also possess additional attributes, such as top speed. Some entities may have similar attributes and yet not be ships, for example a delivery truck may meet the criteria for inclusion in the class of ships, but it would be inappropriate for it to be included.

## 2.2 Relationships and Families

Much information about the state of the world is conveyed by relationships between entities. In general, there may be many parties to a relationship, with each party associated with a collection or list of entities. Also a relationship may have some attributes. For example, a marriage relationship would typically involve three parties: a bride, a groom and a collection of witnesses, and have a date attribute.

A family is a collection of some relationships. Each family places constraints on its members; in particular a family insists that its members possess certain parties and attributes which meet specified criteria, in a similar way to classes of entities.

## 2.3 Simple Example

Consider the following simple example specification. The italicised text is the input to the SABRE CASE tool. This builds a knowledge base about the specification, interacting with the user to resolve any ambiguities in the text, and produces the graphical diagrams which precisely summarise the requirement.

*A person has a name, which is a string, and an age which is an integer between 1 and 120.*

```
Person
  name:   String
  age:    Integer

1 ≤ age ≤ 120
```

*A ship has a unique name, which is a string, and a destination.*

Note that attributes need not be constrained to particular domains and, in the graphical notation, unique attributes are underlined.

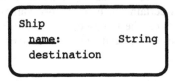

*A captain, who is a person, commands at most one vessel, which is a ship. All ships are vessels.*

In the graphical notation, parties have solid lines when each entity in the associated class must be included in the party of at least one relationship in the family. Also, party names are underlined to indicate that no two relationships can have the same collection of entities for that party.

This specification might be more naturally phrased using attributes which are associated with entities rather than values, as follows.

*A ship has a unique name, which is a string, a destination and a captain, who is a person.*

```
Ship
    name:          String
    destination
    captain:       Person
```

The knowledge base constructed for these two specifications are quite different, but SABRE will generate the same relational schemas for both.

## 2.4 Hierarchies

A class may be defined as a specialisation of another class. In such cases the entities that belong to the child class must also belong to the parent class.

A particular consequence of a specialisation is that all the entities in the child class must possess those attributes required by the parent class. Therefore, to simplify the specification any required attribute constraints in the parent are inherited by the child, without them having to be explicitly stated.

For example, suppose we add to the specification given above.

*Some people are drivers. A driver has a unique license number. The age of a driver is at least 17.*

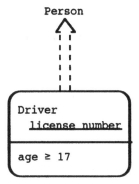

This diagram states that all entities in the class of drivers must have a license number, but also implicitly states that they have a name and an age, and these attributes can be mentioned in the general constraints of the class. In the graphical notation, the use of a dotted arrow here indicates that not all people need be drivers.

More generally, hierarchies are formed as constraints over a number of specialisations with a common child or parent. A hierarchy may be disjoint and may be mandatory.

With common-parent hierarchies, any entity in one of the child classes must also be in the parent class. If the hierarchy is mandatory, all entities in the parent must be in at least one of the children. If the hierarchy is disjoint, no entity may be in more than one child.

For example, *A ship is either a merchant ship or a naval ship.*

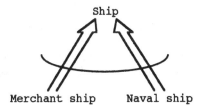

In the graphical notation, the use of solid arrows indicates that all ships are either merchant ships or naval ships or both, and the arc indicates that no entity is both a merchant ship and a naval ship, hence ships are partitioned into merchant and naval.

With common-child hierarchies, all entities in the child must also be in each of the parents. If the hierarchy is mandatory, any entity in one of the parent classes must be in the child class. If the hierarchy is disjoint, no entity may be in more than one of the parent classes.

For example, *Some assets are either ships or people.*

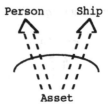

Hierarchies for families can be defined in a similar way to those for classes.

# 3 Dynamic Behaviour

## 3.1 Operations and Theatres

The state of a system is described in terms of classes of entities and families of relationships. The way in which a system may behave is described by all the possible state changes that can occur. The state is changed by applying an operation, which is something that relates a before-state, a collection of instigating entities and some parameters to an after-state and some outputs.

The set of operations that are valid for a system completely describe its behaviour. Some operations may take the same combination of before-state, instigators and parameters, but produce different after-states or outputs. This allows specifications to be non-deterministic.

A theatre is a set of operations[3]. A theatre will place constraints on its members in terms of their instigators, parameters, outputs, the parts of the state upon which their outcome depends and the parts of the state that they modify – the later two aspects are described in terms of operands.

A theatre can require that its members take various parameters and produce various results. In the graphical notation, a parameter is given by a name followed with a question mark, while an output is a name followed with an exclamation mark. It may also require various instigators, constrained to be from specified classes.

## 3.2 Operands

There are three kinds of operand: select, remove and add; and each is associated with some class or family. When an operation is applied some collection of entities or relationships are associated with each operand. These collections must meet any general constraints which are imposed by the theatre in addition to the following conditions:

---

[3] One definition of a theatre is "a place of action".

• Select operand: the associated collection must belong to the class or family in both the before-state and the after-state.

• Remove operand: the associated collection must belong to the class or family in the before-state, and must not belong in the after-state.

• Add operand: the associated collection must belong to the class or family in the after-state, but not in the before-state.

Each operand is also associated with three lists of attributes or parties that are required by the class or family. These are the identification, observation and modification lists which constrain each operation as follows:

• Identification: lists what attributes (parties) of any entity (relationship) in the class (family) associated with the operand may be 'inspected' in order to determine whether it should be included in the operand's collection.

• Observation: lists what attributes or parties of the things chosen for an operand may be 'inspected' in order to determine the outcome of the operation.

• Modification: lists what attributes or parties of the chosen things may be changed by the operation.

In the graphical notation, the lists are given following the name of the operand. The identification list is given first, enclosed in round brackets. The observation list is next, followed by a Δ and the modification list. If the identification list or observation list are omitted, a default of all attributes (and parties) is assumed, while if the modification list is omitted, a default of no attributes (or parties) is assumed.

The following example illustrates the use of operands.

*Qualifying takes a name which is a string, involves a candidate who is a person and a new driver who becomes a driver. The name of the candidate is the name. The candidate is the new driver.*

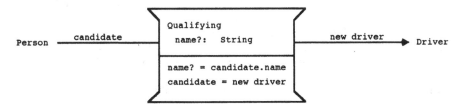

Note that this specification does not place any constraint on the value chosen for the license number. This means the implementation is free to choose any value, as long as it meets the uniqueness constraint specified for the attribute in the Driver class.

### 3.3 Instigators

It is often the case that some operations must only be invoked at the behest of some responsible person or organisation. To capture this idea the SPEAR model insists that, when an operation is invoked, the entities who are responsible for invoking it are identified. Theatres are then able to constrain the instigators of their operations, in order to specify what control is required over "who may do what".

A theatre may have any number of instigators and each is much like a select operand, except that they have no identification list and are drawn with a dashed line. When an operation is invoked, collections of instigating entities are associated with each instigator, such that all the instigating entities are assigned to at least one of· the theatre's instigators, and the theatre's constraints are satisfied. However, as a special case, if a theatre has no instigators, there is no constraint over who can invoke the operations.

Usually, the majority of operations can be invoked by just one individual. For example:

*Manoeuvring may be instigated by a captain who is a person. Manoeuvring involves a ship and modifies its destination. The captain is the captain of the ship.*

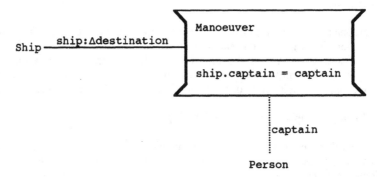

However, some more sensitive operations may only be permitted at the behest of more than one person, acting in agreement. For example, committing large sums of money may require the signature of two people. This "separation of duty" [9] is a powerful security mechanism and can be modelled in SPEAR at the abstract level. However, a more detailed specification would probably reveal that the signatures are collected independently, perhaps in any order. This too can be modelled in SPEAR, with separate operations each requiring just one instigating entity.

For example, suppose the earlier specification is extended and the owner of a ship is recorded and operations that allow ships to be bought and sold are introduced.

*A ship has an owner who is a person.*

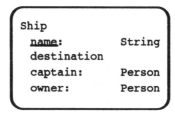

```
Ship
    name:           String
    destination
    captain:        Person
    owner:          Person
```

*Trading may be instigated by a seller who is a person and a buyer who is a person. Trading involves a ship. The owner of the ship is the seller. The owner of the ship, afterwards, is the buyer.*

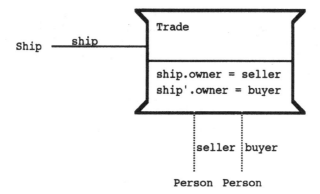

```
                            Trade
Ship ──── ship ────

                    ship.owner = seller
                    ship'.owner = buyer


                    seller  buyer

            Person  Person
```

When constraints are given for theatres, a name qualified by a tick refers to the state of an entity or relationship after the operation has completed. Hence in the above example, the ship's owner is the seller before the operation and the buyer afterwards.

# 4  Tightening and Refining Specifications

A high level specification may be loose, in that it does not precisely define the behaviour of a system. For example, when a ship is required to deliver a cargo, a high level specification may say that a cargo attribute can have any value by not giving a domain constraint. The implementation is then free to decide how to represent cargo values.

*A busy ship has a cargo.*

```
Busy ship
    cargo
```

A lower level specification may be more precise about the form of cargo, without introducing additional structures into the specification. For example, the cargo may be restricted to always be a single string value.

*The cargo of a busy ship is a string.*

```
Busy ship
   cargo:   String
```

When a low level specification is derived from a high level specification only by adding additional constraints, the specification is said to be tightened.

However, most high level specifications omit details of structure in order to make them clearer. A low level specification which includes this detail is a refinement of the high level specification. A refined specification does all that is required by the high level specification, but also does more, in the sense that the omitted detail means the system can be in many more states.

For example, the cargo attribute may be represented by a description of the type and quantity of items being carried. This would be reflected by the following refined specification (note this is a separate specification to that given above).

*A busy ship has a type which is a string and quantity which is an integer.*

```
Busy ship
   type:       String
   quantity:   Integer
```

Refinements in SPEAR are described as functions which map the elements of a low level specification onto the elements of a high level specification. This is achieved by stating how each class, family and theatre in the high level specification is constructed from the parts of the low level specification.

The high and low level specifications are defined using the static and dynamic elements of SPEAR, that is in terms of classes, families and theatres. However, the refinement specification is actually a third specification written using a separate specification language, although this is broadly similar to the graphical notation for the static and dynamic elements.

The refinement for each class defined in the high level specification is introduced using a class refinement construct. Like a class this appears as a soft cornered box, but with the class name offset to the left and the box has in general three sections: declarations, constraints and assignments.

The declarations section introduces names for collections or lists of entities, relationships or operations drawn from the classes, families and theatres of the low level specification. All possible combinations of these collections and lists which meet the constraint in the optional constraints section (the default is the condition 'true') are considered and for each valid combination there is an entity in the high level specification. The assignments section describes how the attributes of this entity are determined.

For example, one way in which the first specification in this section is refined by the second specification is described by the following third specification:

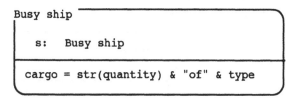

This says that a busy ship (name of the box) exists in the high level specification for each busy ship (name in declarations section) in the low level specification, and that the high level value of the cargo attribute is made up of the concatenation of the low level quantity (after it has been converted from an integer to a string) and type attributes.

The refinements for each family and theatre are defined in a similar way to those for classes.

# 5 An Example Specification and Refinement

In this section, a complete example is given to illustrate the use of SPEAR.

## 5.1 High Level Specification

This specification describes the requirement for a parcel delivery system.

*A package has a destination.*

```
Package
  destination
```

*Dispatching takes a dest and involves a consignment which becomes a package. The destination of the consignment , afterwards, is the dest.*

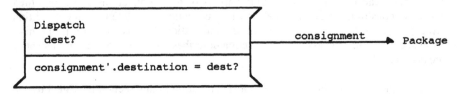

*Delivering takes a dest and involves a consignment which ceases to be a package. The destination of the consignment is the dest.*

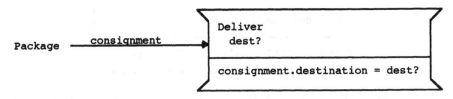

## 5.2 Low Level Specification

This specification gives more detail as to how the previous requirement is to be implemented.

*A package has a unique id.*

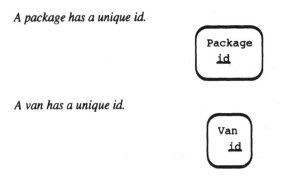

*A van has a unique id.*

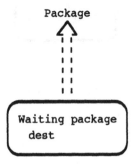

*A waiting package has a dest.*

*A busy van has a dest.*

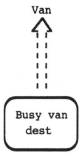

Van

Busy van
dest

Note that the destination of a package is not recorded directly with the package. The intuition is that each waiting package in the depot is placed in a bay which is marked with the destination, and each busy van has only one destination, which it knows. Therefore the destination of each package is always known implicitly.

*A van, which is busy, carries a load which is a collection of at least one package. Each van carries one collection of loads.*

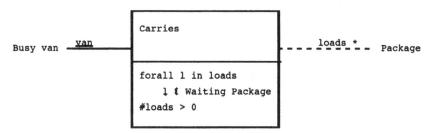

Busy van — van — Carries — loads * — Package

```
Carries

forall 1 in loads
    1 t Waiting Package
#loads > 0
```

Note that an extra constraint is included without being introduced in constrained-English.

*Arriving takes an id, involves a van which ceases to be a busy van and a collection of loads which cease to be packages. The van carries the loads but does not carry them afterwards. The id of the van is the id.*

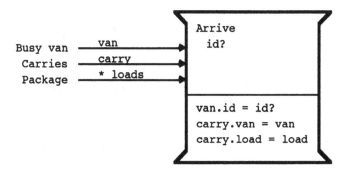

```
Arrive
id?

Busy van — van →
Carries — carry →
Package — * loads →

van.id = id?
carry.van = van
carry.load = load
```

*Dispatching takes a dest, involves a consignment which becomes a waiting package and returns an id. The dest of the consignment, afterwards, is the dest. The id is the id of the consignment, afterwards.*

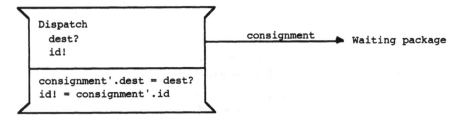

*Collecting takes a dest, involves a collection of loads which cease to be waiting packages, a van which becomes a busy van and an idle van which is a van. The van is the idle van. The van carries the loads but does not carry them afterwards.*

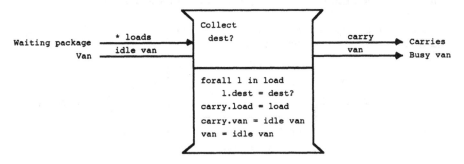

### 5.3 Refinement Specification

The refinement specification shows how the implementation level specification relates to the requirement level specification.

The notation is still under development and as yet support for constructing these specifications has not been included in the SABRE tool. In particular, no means of deriving the specification from natural language statements has been devised.

The refinement of the Package class is shown below. This essentially defines a function which maps elements of the low level specification onto the class of Packages in the high level specification. Which elements are mapped is shown in the declarations section; in this case simply the class Package.

Since there is no constraints section, a default of 'true' is used. This means that each package in the low level specification is mapped to a package in the high level specification.

Finally, the predicate in the assignments section dictates the relationship between the values of attributes in the low and high level specifications. In this case the predicate is complex. This is because the way the low level specification records the destination of packages is not a straightforward implementation of the requirement.

```
Package ─────────────────────────────────┐
                                          │
    p:   Package                          │
 ─────────────────────────────────────────
 if p Ɛ Waiting Package
 then
       destination = p.dest
 else
       destination -> (dest)Busy Van
                    -> Carries
                    -> p
```

The refinement of the Dispatch theatre is shown below. Here the assignments section uses the refinement function of the Package class (denoted by the package name enclosed in square brackets) to show that the entity which is the consignment in the low level specification maps to the high level consignment entity.

```
Dispatch ─────────────────────────────────┐
                                           │
    d:    Dispatch                         │
 ──────────────────────────────────────────
 dest? = d.dest?
 consignment = [Package](d.consignment)
```

The refinement of the Deliver theatre is shown below. In this case the refinement function maps a number of low level elements to each high level Deliver operation: an operation from the Collect theatre, an operation from the Arrive theatre and an entity from the Package class. However, not all combinations of these elements produce a high level operation, as the Collect and Arrive operations must be carrying the same load for them to constitute a high level Deliver operation.

```
Deliver ───────────────────────────────────┐
                                            │
    c:    Collect                           │
    a:    Arrive                            │
    p:    Package                           │
 ───────────────────────────────────────────
 c.carry = a.carry
 p Ɛ c.load
 ───────────────────────────────────────────
 dest? = c.dest
 consignment = [Package](p)
```

The high level specification deals with individual packages while the low level specification deals with collections of packages. For this reason it is necessary to include a package in the declarations section and constrain it to be part of the load. This package is then mapped to the high level consignment in the assignments section, using the Package refinement function.

# 6  Conclusions

The SPEAR notation had to support the specification of secure database systems. This meant it had to describe both the static structure and dynamic behaviour of a system in a consistent way, and in a style that meant it could be included in readable documentation. In addition, specifications of large systems have to be broken down into separate specifications with increasing levels of detail. For secure systems it is important that the relationships between these specifications are properly documented, hence the need for a refinement notation.

While SPEAR does include specific features for describing systems that handle sensitive government information these are non-intrusive, in that they are only visible if they are used. This means the benefits of SPEAR are equally applicable to commercial applications.

# 7  References

[1]     The Entity-Relationship Model – Toward a Unified View of Data, P.P.Chen, ACM Trans. Database Systems, Vol 1, Num 1, March 1976, pp9..36.

[2]     Abstract and Concrete Models for Secure Database Applications, S. Wiseman, Procs. IFIP WG11.3 Workshop on Database Security, Shepherdstown, WV, November 1991, pp 239..273, publ. North Holland.

[3]     The SPEAR Data Design Method, P.J.Sell, Procs. IFIP WG11.3 Workshop on Database Security, Vancouver, BC, August 1992, pp 55..72, North Holland.

[4]     The Z Notation – A Reference Manual, J.M.Spivey, Prentice-Hall, ISBN-0-13-983768-X, 1989.

[5]     Conceptual Database Design, C.Batini, S.Ceri & S.B.Navathe, Benjamin/Cummings, ISBN-0-8053-0244-1, 1992.

[6]     SABRE User Guide, E.R.Bilsby, S.R.Lewis & B.R.Pomeroy, February 1996.

[7]     SPEAR User Guide – Volume 1: Using SPEAR to Model the Information Structure of an Application, S.R.Lewis, E.R.Bilsby & B.R.Pomeroy, March 1996.

[8]     SPEAR User Guide – Volume 2: Using SPEAR to Model The Dynamic Behaviour of an Application, S.R.Lewis, E.R.Bilsby & B.R.Pomeroy, March 1996

[9]     A Comparison of Commercial and Military Computer Security Policies, D.D.Clark & D.R.Wilson, Procs. IEEE Symp. on Security and Privacy, Oakland CA, April 1987, pp184..194.

# Speeding up Knowledge Discovery in Large Relational Databases by Means of a New Discretization Algorithm

## Alex Alves Freitas and Simon H. Lavington

{freial,lavis}@essex.ac.uk
University of Essex, Dept. of Computer Science
Wivenhoe Park, Colchester, CO4 3SQ, UK

### Abstract

Most of the KDD (Knowledge Discovery in Databases) algorithms proposed in the literature have been applied to relatively small datasets and do not permit any integration with a DBMS. Hence, the application of these algorithms to the huge amounts of data found in current databases and data warehouses faces serious scalability problems, particularly the problem of excessive learning time. This paper investigates a way of improving the scalability of KDD algorithms, via discretization of ordinal or continuous attributes. This work has two novel aspects. First, we map a generic discretization primitive into an SQL query. Second, we propose a new discretization algorithm for classification tasks. We show how the new discretization algorithm can be implemented with good effect via the SQL primitive.

## 1 Introduction: the Problem

Current databases and data warehouses contain huge amounts of data. Clearly, there is a strong need for extracting interesting, useful information from such large datasets [Piatetsky-Shapiro & Frawley 91], [Fayyad et al. 96].

There are many hundreds of KDD algorithms which have emerged from research areas such as Machine Learning and Statistics, to which may be added more recent KDD activity in Neural Networks and Genetic Algorithms. However, there is no single KDD algorithm that is ideally satisfactory for all classes of database and all kinds of KDD task [Schaffer 94], [Michie et al. 94]. Therefore, any practical KDD system has to have a range of available techniques that cover classification, clustering, association and summarisation on data that is both categorical and numeric. Furthermore, any practical KDD system has to be able to deal efficiently with large quantities of data within a commercial-strength DBMS.

Despite the demands of large databases and data warehouses, "conventional" Machine Learning (ML) algorithms have been applied mainly to relatively small datasets (typically less than 10,000 tuples) and do not have any integration at all with RDBMS. Hence, the application of these algorithms to very large amounts of data faces serious scalability problems, particularly the problem of excessive learning time. For instance, [Catlett 91] estimated that C4.5 would take several months to learn from 1,000,000 tuples by using state-of-the-art hardware at that time. More recently, [Provost & Aronis 96] report that a standard version of the RL algorithm is impractical (i.e. take too long to run) on datasets of more than 70k tuples.

In this paper we address an important aspect of efficiency which relates to data that is numeric - i.e. data whose attributes are ordinal (integer-valued) or continuous (real-valued) variables. Some existing KDD algorithms (e.g. ITRULE [Smyth &

Goodman 91]) cannot handle such attributes unless the attributes are first converted into a small set of discrete values (or categories). Furthermore, for those ML algorithms that can handle ordinal/continuous attributes directly, the processing of these attributes is much slower than processing categorical attributes [Paliouras & Bree 95], [Catlett 91a]. Finally, discretization usually improves the comprehensibility of the discovered knowledge [Catlett 91a].

Therefore, on the grounds of speed and ease of use, there is much to be gained from developing efficient and generic discretization techniques which can be used by a range of KDD systems. However, there are two caveats. Firstly, an inherent disadvantage of discretization is that it may reduce the accuracy of the discovered knowledge since discretization, along with any kind of summarization process, may cause some relevant detailed information to be lost. Secondly, any new discretization technique should for preference be useable within a RDBMS environment so as to be compatible with current commercial data processing practice.

The challenge is therefore to develop a generic discretization technique that is SQL-compatible, improves KDD run-times, and does not unduly diminish the accuracy of the discovered knowledge.

By way of further justification for emphasizing SQL, we have shown in a recent paper [Freitas & Lavington 96] that other generic KDD activities may be mapped into SQL. In particular, we have implemented a decision-tree learner using generic KDD primitives expressed as SQL queries, and evaluated its performance on a parallel DB server. It is our belief that the use of suitable SQL primitives is a promising strategy for developing efficient KDD on large volumes of real-world data.

The rest of this paper is organized as follows. Section 2 presents our approach to the discretization process. Section 3 reviews other work on discretization algorithms. Then in Section 4 we propose a generic SQL-based primitive which underpins the discretization process. In Section 5 we show how this primitive may be used to implement a new class-driven, information-theoretic discretization algorithm. In Section 6 we give the results of running this new algorithm on test datasets, and finally Section 7 presents some conclusions.

## 2 Approach to Discretization

We follow a Machine Learning (ML) approach for KDD. However, many arguments of this paper also apply to a Statistics-based approach for KDD, since the core of ML and Statistics methods are often very similar. We focus on relational databases (RDBMS) and on classification tasks (also called supervised learning), where each tuple belongs to a class, among a pre-defined set of classes. Tuples consist of a set of predicting attributes and a class attribute. For instance, a tuple may represent an employee record, where the predicting attributes are the employee's age, gender, educational level, etc; and the class attribute is the managerial level of the employee. The goal of the classification algorithm is to find some relationship (e.g. in the form of a decision tree or a set of rules [Quinlan 93]) between the predicting attributes and the class one. Thus, the classification process can use this relationship to predict the class of a new, unknown-class tuple.

We present a class-driven discretization algorithm, i.e. an algorithm that takes into account the class of a tuple when carrying out the discretization procedure. Hence, this algorithm was designed particularly for classification tasks. Our work has two novel aspects. First, we map a generic primitive operation of discretization algorithms into an SQL query. Second, we propose a bottom-up, class-driven discretization algorithm based on information theory. This algorithm differs from other bottom-up, class-driven discretization algorithms, which are typically based on a statistical measure of association (or significance test) - see Section 3.

We favour a tight integration between the KDD system and the DB system. This allows the KDD system to benefit from several important database facilities, such as integrity maintenance, recovery, security and concurrency control. In addition, it helps to scale up KDD systems for very large data sets, by using efficiency-oriented database facilities such as automatic query optimization. See e.g. [Provost & Aronis 96] for an overview of the reasons why it is desirable that a ML algorithm learns from very large datasets. Here we briefly remark that increasing the size of a dataset may be seen as a *domain-independent* way of achieving higher accuracy. This is in contrast with most "improvements" of machine learning algorithms proposed in the literature, which in essence are a kind of bias, and so have a *domain-dependent* effectiveness [Schaffer 94], [Michie et al. 94].

The use of SQL offers the benefit of portability across a wide range of database systems and parallel database computers, from symmetric shared-memory multiprocessors to massively-parallel computers. Note that the use of parallel processing as one approach for improving the scalability of ML algorithms is complementary to the discretization approach investigated in this paper. Naturally, both approaches may be used together to improve the scalability of ML algorithms.

## 3 Related Work on Discretization of Continuous Attributes.

Discretization algorithms accept as input the values of an ordinal - i.e. integer-valued or possibly continous (real-valued) - attribute (henceforth the input attribute) and output a relatively small list of ordered intervals in the form $[X_{lower}-X_{upper}]$, where $X_{lower}$ and $X_{upper}$ are the lower and upper bounds associated to the input attribute's values within the interval.

Discretization algorithms can be classified in two broad groups: class-blind and class-driven algorithms. Class-blind algorithms discretize a given attribute without considering the value of the class (goal) attribute [Mannino et al. 88]. For instance, the equal-width method simply divides the range of values of an attribute into a pre-specified number of equal-width intervals, where width is computed as $X_{upper}$ minus $X_{lower}$.

Class-driven algorithms consider the class value when discretizing the input attribute. The input for this kind of algorithm is a relation with two attributes: the input attribute (to be discretized) and a class attribute, whose value indicates the class the tuple belongs to. It is well established that class-driven discretization algorithms work better when the output intervals will be used to pre-process a dataset to be used by a classification algorithm, which is the case in our research. In this paper, we are interested in discretization algorithms which work in two steps. First, the values of the input attribute are sorted. Second, a discretization procedure is applied to the sorted values to produce a set of ordered intervals. This kind of algorithm can be further divided into two groups: top-down and bottom-up algorithms.

An example of a top-down algorithm is D-2 [Catlett 91a]. After sorting the values, D-2 first chooses a threshold T to partition the set of values S into two subsets $S_1$ (with values $\leq$ T) and $S_2$ (with values > T). T is chosen in such a way to maximize the information gain after the binary partition, as in ID3/C4.5 [Quinlan 93]. Then D-2 recursively applies this method to choose thresholds for subsets $S_1$ and $S_2$, and so on, until a stopping criteria is satisfied. Hence, D-2 avoids the computationally expensive sort operation in all subsets, unlike ID3/C4.5, where the sort is done in all tree nodes.

An example of a bottom-up algorithm is ChiMerge [Kerber 92]. It first sorts the input attribute's values, and assigns each value to a (single-value) interval. Then ChiMerge iteratively computes the $\chi^2$ (Chi-squared) value - concerning the class frequency distribution - for every group of N adjacent intervals and merges the N adjacent intervals with the lowest $\chi^2$ value, where N is a user-specified parameter. The rationale behind this is that the lower the $\chi^2$ value, the higher the similarity in the class frequency distribution of the N intervals, and so the higher the motivation to merge those intervals. This iterative process continues until all groups of N adjacent intervals have a $\chi^2$ value above a given threshold. As an additional merging-stopping criterion, the user can specify the minimum and maximum number of intervals that can be created by the algorithm.

ChiMerge has two drawbacks. First, the $\chi^2$ significance test is not reliable when the number of values in the intervals being merged is very small. This is a serious problem for large datasets with a real-valued input attribute, where the number of distinct values of that attribute can be equal to the number of tuples in the input relation. In this case, the early iterations of the merging process will consider intervals with very few values, once each input attribute value will very likely be associated with just one class value. In one extremum, the first iteration will consider single-value intervals. [Kerber 92] partially alleviated this problem by modifying the $\chi^2$ formula so that the denominator of every term of the $\chi^2$ formula has a value of at least 0.5 (to avoid division by a very small number). Although this author reports that this (rather arbitrary) value works well, there is no statistically-sound justification for it. Actually, the statistics theory recommends to use another significance test rather than $\chi^2$, in these situations.

Second, statistical measures of association, such as $\chi^2$, were not designed for *classification*. Rather, they were designed for measuring the association (or dependency) between two attributes in a *symmetric* way, i.e. none of the two attributes being analyzed is given special treatment when computing the $\chi^2$ value. On the other hand, classification is an *assymetric* task with respect to the two attributes being analyzed. We want to predict the value of the class attribute given the input attribute, not the other way round.

Another bottom-up algorithm is StatDisc [Richeldi & Rossotto 95], which produces a hierarchy of intervals. First, the input attribute values are sorted. The initial intervals are assigned to leaf nodes of the interval hierarchy. Then StatDisc iteratively computes the $\Phi$ (Phi) value, a statistical measure of association, for every group of N adjacent intervals (where N is a user-specified parameter) and merges the N adjacent intervals with the lowest $\Phi$ value. When intervals are merged, a new internal node (parent of the merged intervals) is added to the interval hierarchy. The merging process continues until all groups of N adjacent intervals have a $\Phi$ value greater than a given threshold. When the discretization process is over, the interval hierarchy can be explored to select a suitable set of intervals according to specific characteristics of the target application and of the dataset.

Before considering primitives for discretization, we should briefly justify the claim that in general a reduction in discovered-knowledge accuracy due to discretization is more than compensated for by the improvements in KDD efficiency. This claim is supported by some empirical evidence. For instance, [Catlett 91a] applied a discretization algorithm to several datasets, as a pre-processing step for ID3. He reported that ID3 applied to the discretized data achieved a speed up (over ID3 applied to the raw, non-discretized data) of more than 10 in datasets with many continuous attributes, with little or no loss of accuracy. In one dataset (with 92 real-valued attributes) the speed up achieved was more than 50, without significant decrease in classification accuracy. Actually, in some datasets the discretization process even slightly increased the classification accuracy. One possible explanation for this is that the discretization process may reduce the amount of noise in the continuous attributes.

## 4 Mapping a Generic Discretization Primitive into SQL

A primitive should satisfy at least two requirements, viz generality (i.e. it should find use in several algorithms) and significant time saving (i.e. in a given algorithm, it should occur frequently and/or be computationally significant). The use of primitives is not very common in the area of AI, probably due to the great difficult of finding domain-independent primitives in AI (see e.g. [Stolfo et al. 95]). Fortunately, however, we have found a generic, domain-independent primitive for discretization algorithms. Developing generic primitives is important because no algorithm can be expected to perform well across all domains [Schaffer 94], [Michie et al. 94].

Our primitive was designed to perform the initialization step of class-driven discretization algorithms (see Section 3), where the algorithm needs to sort tuples according to the input attribute (to be discretized) and compute the class frequency distribution for each tuple (initial interval). Note that, although this procedure is an initialization step, it is a computationally expensive step, taking $O(n \log n)$, where n is the number of tuples. Actually, it is usually possible to implement an optimized version of the discretization process itself in time $O(n \log n)$ as well [Kerber 92], so that the time taken for performing the initialization step is very significant.

In essence, our primitive (which will be called Count by Ordered Group) counts the number of tuples in each partition of an *ordered group by* statement. The result of this primitive can be represented in the form of the two-dimensional matrix shown in Figure 1. This is an n x k matrix extended with totals of rows and columns, where n is the cardinality of the input attribute and k is the number of classes. Each cell $C_{ij}$ (i=1,..,n, j=1,..,k) of this matrix contains the number of tuples in the input relation with input attribute's value equal to $A_i$ and goal (class) attribute's value equal to $G_j$. The summation of the count values along the i-th row (i=1,..,n) is denoted $C_{i+}$, and the summation along the j-th column (j=1,..,k) is denoted $C_{+j}$. The total number of tuples is denoted by $C_{++}$. Count by Ordered Group is implemented in a declarative style by Query 1, followed by a trivial computation of rows and columns totals.

Note that in one extremum, if each tuple has a unique value of the input attribute (typically in the case of real-valued attributes rather than integer-valued ones), n is equal to the number of tuples in the input relation. In this case Query 1 degenerates into a relational projection on the input and class attributes, since the *group by* and the *count(\*)* clauses become irrelevant.

| | $G_1$ ..... $G_k$ | Total |
|---|---|---|
| $A_1$ | $C_{11}$ .... $C_{1k}$ | $C_{1+}$ |
| . | . . . . . . . | . |
| . | . . . . . . . | . |
| | . . . . . . . | |
| $A_n$ | $C_{n1}$ .... $C_{nk}$ | $C_{n+}$ |
| Total | $C_{+1}$ .... $C_{+k}$ | $C_{++}$ |

**Fig. 1**: Structure of the result of Count by Ordered Group.

```
SELECT input_attribute, class_attribute, COUNT(*)
FROM   relation_name
GROUP BY input_attribute, class_attribute
ORDER BY input_attribute
```

**Query 1**: SQL query underlying the Count by Ordered Group primitive.

## 5 A Class-Driven, Information-Theoretic Discretization Algorithm.

We propose a new discretization algorithm that we will call InfoMerge. First, the input attribute values are sorted and the class frequency distribution for each value of the input attribute is computed (via the SQL primitive shown in Query 1).

Second, InfoMerge iteratively computes a measure of the *damage* associated with the interval-merging process for every group of N adjacent intervals (where N is a user-specified parameter) and merges the N adjacent intervals with the *lowest* value of that measure, following the bottom-up paradigm of ChiMerge and StatDisc. The difference is that both ChiMerge and StatDisc use a statistical measure of class-frequency-distribution similarity, respectively $\chi^2$ and $\Phi$ values. In contrast, we use an information-theoretic approach as follows, in order to address the problems with statistical measures of association discussed in section 3.

In each iteration of the merging process, InfoMerge first computes the entropy of each interval by using the class frequency distribution within that interval. Then InfoMerge computes, for each group of N adjacent intervals, the information *loss* associated with the merging of the N intervals. The information loss is computed as:

$$\text{Info\_Loss} = \text{Info\_After\_Merge} - \text{Info\_Before\_Merge} \quad (1)$$

where Info_After_Merge is the amount of information necessary to identify the class of a tuple after merging, measured by the information-theoretic Equation (2); and Info_Before_Merge is the corresponding amount of information before merging, measured by Equation (3). In these equations, k denotes the number of classes, and N denotes the number of adjacent intervals considered for merging. $C_{ij}$, $C_{i+}$, $C_{+j}$ and $C_{++}$ have the meaning defined in Section 4, with the difference that here the row index i varies in the range 1..N rather than 1..n (where n is the cardinality of the input attribute). Thus, in Equations (2) and (3) $C_{++}$ is the total number of tuples in all the N intervals considered for merging.

$$\text{Info\_After\_Merge} = \sum_{j=1}^{k} - (C_{+j}/C_{++}) * \log(C_{+j}/C_{++}) \qquad (2)$$

$$\text{Info\_Before\_Merge} = \sum_{i=1}^{N} (C_{i+}/C_{++}) * \sum_{j=1}^{k} - (C_{ij}/C_{i+}) * \log(C_{ij}/C_{i+}) \qquad (3)$$

Note that the minimization of information *loss* when merging intervals can be thought of as the dual operation of maximizing the information *gain* when splitting a node of a decision tree [Quinlan 93]. Actually, decision-tree learners are top-down algorithms, where the splitting process aims at improving the separation of the classes as much as possible in the new "intervals" (branches of the tree). On the other hand, InfoMerge is a bottom up algorithm, where the merging process aims at getting larger intervals, loosing as little class separation as possible in this process.

However, when merging intervals we should consider not only the information loss, but also the size of the intervals to be merged. For instance, assume that the merging of intervals I1 and I2 results in an information loss smaller than the merging of intervals I3 and I4. Now assume that intervals I1 and I2 are much larger (have a higher frequency of tuples) than I3 and I4. Intuitively, it is better to merge I3 and I4, rather than I1 and I2, since this will tend to produce "less harm" (smaller information loss) in the dataset as a whole. Hence, we weight the information loss in Equation (1) with the interval's size (relative frequency of tuples within the interval, in relation to the whole dataset). The final formula for computing the Weighted_Info_Loss in the InfoMerge algorithm is shown in Equation (4), where Info_Loss is computed according to Equation (1) and n is the total number of tuples in the whole dataset. In each iteration, InfoMerge merges the group of N adjacent intervals with the minimum value of Weighted_Info_Loss.

$$\text{Weighted\_Info\_Loss} = (C_{++}/n) * \text{Info\_Loss} \qquad (4)$$

Note that this weighting criterion for the use of information loss in a interval-merging process has no counterpart in the use of information gain in a data subset-splitting process. In this latter case, the classification algorithm (e.g. a decision-tree learner) typically computes the information gain for each candidate attribute, but in each computation the number of tuples in the data subset to be split is the same. Hence, information gain is used in a local context (the current data subset to be split). There is no need to make global decisions involving comparison of information gain across different data subsets. In contrast, the discretization algorithm does need to compare the information loss for different groups of intervals, where the size of the intervals (i.e. the number of tuples contained in each interval) can be very different from each other.

# 6 Results

We evaluated the performance of InfoMerge and ChiMerge in large datasets. Each dataset was randomly partitioned into a training set, used for learning, and a test set, used to measure the classification accuracy of the discovered knowledge. We report results for a single partition of the dataset, following the methodology used in the Esprit project Statlog to measure classification accuracy in large datasets [Michie et al. 94].

In all the experiments, N (the number of adjacent intervals considered for merging) was set to 2 (following [Kerber 92]), both for InfoMerge and ChiMerge. In both algorithms, the stopping criterion of the merging process depends on user-specified maximum and minimum number of intervals to be produced and on a given threshold. In ChiMerge, this threshold was determined by looking up a $\chi^2$ table to find the $\chi^2$ value for a significance level of 95% (see [Kerber 92] for details). In InfoMerge this threshold was empirically determined as a Weighted_Info_Loss value of 0.001. Hence, InfoMerge halts if Weight_Info_Loss is greater than 0.001 and the current number of intervals is smaller than or equal to the maximum specified; or if the current number of intervals is equal to the minimum specified (remember that the number of intervals is reduced at each iteration, by the merging process). In all the experiments the minimum and maximum number of intervals to be produced was set to 5 and 12, for both InfoMerge and ChiMerge.

The Labour Force Survey (LFS) data is produced by the UK's Department of Employment. The LFS dataset used in our experiments has 11 predicting attributes: Sex, Age, Ethnic code, Full-time/Part-time job, Permanent/Temporary job, Training status, Time as Employee in the company (denoted by EmpTime), Educational level, Public/Private Job, Industry-Area code, and Number of Employees at workplace. Attributes Age and EmpTime are ordinal (integer-valued). The other attributes are categorical. The class attribute is the Managerial status of an employee, with two possible values (indicating whether or not the employee has some managerial status, e.g. manager or supervisor). This dataset has 84532 tuples. We used 74,532 randomly-selected tuples as the training set and the remaining 10,000 tuples as the test set.

The Shuttle data has 58,000 tuples and 9 ordinal (integer-valued) attributes. There are 7 classes. The attributes concern the position of radiators in a NASA space shuttle, and the classes are the appropriate actions to be taken during a space shuttle flight [Catlett 91]. We used the same training/test set partition used in the Esprit project Statlog, viz. 43,500 tuples in the training set and 14,500 tuples in the test set. Although the LFS and the Shuttle dataset are not huge, they are large enough for testing purposes.

In order to evaluate the effectiveness of InfoMerge, we compared the classification accuracy achieved and the time taken by C4.5 [Quinlan 93] on the raw data and on the discretized data. Note that there is no straightforward, "optimal" way of evaluating the performance of a discretization algorithm. This performance depends on the classification algorithm which will be applied to the discretized data. We chose C4.5 because it is a state-of-the-art decision-tree learner algorithm, and decision-tree learners are in general the most used kind of ML algorithm. We used all the default parameters of C4.5.

The results are shown in Table 1. The first column indicates the dataset used in the experiments. The second and third columns show the size of the produced decision tree (number of tree nodes) and its associated error rate (in %), when C4.5 learns from the raw (non-discretized) data. The fourth and fifth columns show the correspondingly tree size and error rate when C4.5 learns from the data discretized by the ChiMerge algorithm. The sixth column shows the speed up associated with the discretization performed by ChiMerge, i.e. the ratio of the time taken by C4.5 to learn from the raw data divided by the time to learn from the discretized data. The seventh, eigth and ninth columns show the corresponding tree size, error rate and speed up associated with the discretization performed by our new InfoMerge.

For the LFS dataset the discretization performed by both ChiMerge and InfoMerge increased the error rate a little (the increase was 1.8% for ChiMerge and 1.0% for InfoMerge). However, there was a great gain in computational efficiency, resulting in speed ups by a factor of about 30. There was also a gain in simplicity and comprehensibility of the discovered knowledge, since the trees produced from discretized data are much smaller than the tree produced from the raw data. The discretizaton performed by InfoMerge resulted in smaller tree size, smaller error rate and greater speed up than the discretization performed by ChiMerge.

For the Shuttle dataset the discretization process did not result in any significant increase in error rate. On the other hand, discretization resulted in increased tree size. However, discretization still results in a speed up by a factor of about 10. The discretization performed by InfoMerge resulted in smaller tree size and greater speed up than the discretization performed by ChiMerge.

**Table 1**: Results running C4.5 on raw data and discretized data.

| Dataset | Raw Data | | ChiMerge Discretization | | | InfoMerge Discretization | | |
|---------|------|-------|------|-------|------|------|-------|------|
| | Size | Error | Size | Error | Sp | Size | Error | Sp |
| LFS | 7501 | 27.3 | 1643 | 29.1 | 27.7 | 1096 | 28.3 | 31.0 |
| Shuttle | 45 | 0.0 | 253 | 0.0 | 8.9 | 164 | 0.0 | 9.9 |

# 7 Conclusion

This paper investigated a way of improving the scalability of KDD algorithms, viz. the discretization of ordinal or continuous attributes. This paper has two novel aspects. First, we mapped a generic primitive of discretization algorithms into an SQL query, which is another step towards the goal of integrating the areas of Machine Learning (ML) and RDBMS. See [Freitas & Lavington 96] for a discussion of how other KDD stages can be mapped into SQL and how the use of parallel SQL servers speeds up a KDD algorithm.

Second, we proposed a bottom-up, class-driven, information-theoretic discretization algorithm, called InfoMerge. This algorithm was compared to the ChiMerge algorithm, based on the $\chi^2$ significance test, and the former was shown to achieve better results (i.e. smaller decision tree sizes, smaller error rates and greater speed up associated with the discretized data) than the latter.

In our future work, we intend to apply InfoMerge to other large datasets and develop other SQL-based KDD primitives to integrate ML and RDBMS.

## Acknowledgments

The first author is supported by Brazilian government's CNPq, grant number 200384/93-7. We thank D.R. Thoen for his help in the experiments. We also thank N.E.J. Dewhurst and R.A. Gamble for their support in early phases of this research. Finally, we thank the anonymous referees for their valuable comments.

## References

[Catlett 91] J. Catlett. Megainduction: a test flight. Proc. 8th Int. Workshop on Machine Learning, 596-599. 1991.

[Catlett 91a] J. Catlett. On changing continuous attributes into ordered discrete attributes. Proc. European Working Session on Learning (EWSL-91). LNAI-482, 164-178.

[Fayyad et al. 96] U.M. Fayyad, G. Piatetsky-Shapiro, and P. Smyth R. Uthurusamy. (Eds.) Advances in Knowledge Discovery and Data Mining. AAAI/MIT, 1996.

[Freitas & Lavington 96] A.A. Freitas and S.H. Lavington. Using SQL primitives and parallel DB servers to speed up knowledge discovery in large relational databases. Accepted for Symposium on Knowledge Discovery in Databases, 13th European Meeting on Cybernetics and Systems Research (EMCSR'96). Vienna, Apr./96.

[Kerber 92] R. Kerber. ChiMerge: Discretization of numeric attributes. Proc. 1992 Conf. American Assoc. for AI (AAAI-92), 123-128.

[Mannino et al. 88] M.V. Mannino, P. Chu and T. Sager. Statistical profile estimation in database systems. ACM Computing Surveys, 20(3), Sep./88, 191-221.

[Michie et al. 94] D. Michie, D.J. Spiegelhalter and C.C. Taylor. Machine Learning, Neural and Statistical Classification. New York: Ellis Horwood, 1994.

[Paliouras & Bree 95] G. Paliouras and D.S. Bree. The effect of numeric features on the scalability of inductive learning programs. Proc. 8th European Conf. Machine Learning (ECML-95). LNAI-912, 218-231. 1995.

[Provost & Aronis 96] F.J. Provost and J.M. Aronis. Scaling up inductive learning with massive parallelism. To appear in Machine Learning, 1996.

[Piatetsky-Shapiro & Frawley 91] G. Piatetsky-Shapiro and W.J. Frawley. (Eds.) Knowledge Discovery in Databases. Menlo Park,CA: AAAI, 91.

[Quinlan 93] J.R. Quinlan. C4.5: Programs for Machine Learning. San Mateo, CA: Morgan Kaufmann, 1993.

[Richeldi & Rossotto 95] M. Richeldi and M. Rossotto. Class-driven statistical discretization of continuous attributes. (Extended Abstract) Proc. 8th European Conf. Machine Learning (ECML-95). LNAI-912, 335-338.

[Schaffer 94] C. Schaffer. A conservation law for generalization performance. Proc. 11th Int. Conf. Machine Learning, 259-265. 1994

[Smyth & Goodman 91] P. Smyth and R.M. Goodman. Rule induction using information theory. In G. Piatetsky-Shapiro and W.J. Frawley. (Eds.) Knowledge Discovery in Databases. Menlo Park, CA: AAAI Press, 1991.

[Stolfo et al. 95] S.J. Stolfo, H.M. Dewan, D.Ohsie and M.Hernandez. A parallel and distributed environment for database rule processing: open problems and future directions. In: M. Abdelguerfi & S. Lavington. (Ed.) Emerging Trends in Database and Knowledge-Based Machine, 225-253. IEEE, 1995.

# Integration of Load Measurement Parameters into the Cost Evaluation of Database Queries

Guntram Flach[†] and Holger Meyer

Dept. of Computer Science, Rostock University
18051 Rostock, Germany
{gflach,hme}@informatik.uni-rostock.de

**Abstract.** In distributed systems, performance is often poorer than possible and resources are wasted due to an unbalanced load of the computer nodes. Load balancing enables performance improvements by equalizing the load over the available computer nodes. In the project HEAD, methods of load sharing and load balancing are used to control the multiprogramming level. The allocation of free operators is used to achieve an optimal processing of complex queries in a distributed database management system.

Cost analysis and the development of corresponding cost models for a heterogeneous and distributed database system is the basis for an efficient query processing. In order to achieve load balancing and scheduling in the context of a static optimization it is necessary to take into account the current system state to allocate relational operations to computer nodes and to determine the degree of parallelism.

In this paper, we focus our attention on parallel processing (pipelining) and its effect on the cost evaluation. In contrast to previous studies on parallel query processing, we present a cost analysis involving the actual load of the CPUs, the memory capacity and the load shifts during the execution of the relational operation itself. The new idea of this paper is the cost evaluation technique that adjusts the cost parameters in response to the workload situation of the recent past.

## 1 Introduction

The development of a distributed relational DBMS prototype takes place in the context of the project HEAD (*H*eterogeneous *E*xtensible *a*nd *D*istributed Database Management System) [FlLM94]. Distributed database systems are the key to high performance transaction and database processing. These systems utilize the capacity of several computer nodes interconnected by a local area network. HEAD is based on a physical shared nothing architecture. HEAD is called heterogeneous because of different computer architectures and the integration of different relational database management systems.

---

† The research was supported by the DFG (German Research Association) under contract: Me 1346/1-2

Optimal parallel query processing in a heterogeneous environment is the aim of the project HE$_A$D. In the following, the most important characteristics are given:

- We consider several forms of parallel query processing, namely horizontal and vertical (pipelining) inter-operator and intra-operator parallelism.

- The aim is to minimize the response time and to increase throughput by involving lower loaded workstations into the execution of algebraic operations.

- Methods of load sharing and load balancing are used to control the multiprogramming level and the allocation of free operations to achieve an optimal parallel processing of complex database queries.

Cost estimations are the prerequisites to find the optimal query execution plan. Therefore, it is necessary to develop a correct cost model for all relational operations. The basis of a cost model is the estimation of the communication and local processing costs. A different aspect is the right estimation of the intermediate result size after the execution of relational operations (scan, selection, etc.) [SAC+79]. Another part of the cost model is the evaluation of algorithms and current implementations of operations such as hash, sort merge or nested loop join. In [Flac95] the basic cost evaluation strategy of HE$_A$D is described and the results of analyzing the computer specific parameters (e.g. I/O and communication costs) are given.

The architecture of a heterogeneous workstation environment enables other applications to run simultaneously to the database application and to increase the load on the nodes and in the network. The consequence of an unbalanced work load in a distributed system may be a non efficient exploitation of resources. Performance improvements are possible by means of load sharing in the distributed system.

A hard problem is the qualified determination and valuation of significant load information about the actual load situation in a distributed system. We believe, that one possibility is the periodic determination of the current load situation on each computer node in the network by means of a load measurement component.

*In this paper, we present a cost model taking into account the load information. This new cost model is more appropriate to a distributed system connected by a local area network than conventional ones.*

The remainder of this article is organized as follows: The next section contains a brief survey of related studies on cost evaluation and parallel query processing. In Section 3, we motivate the need for the integration of load information into the cost model. Furthermore, we describe and analyze some restrictions of the cost evaluator depending on the parallel query processing and the main storage utilization. Section 4 provides an overview of the load measurement, the load information exchange, and the evaluation of the CPU load. After that, a validation of our method is exhibited by presenting some experiments demonstrating, that the optimal choice of a query execution plan depends on the current load situation. Finally, we summarize the major results of this investigation and give an outlook on future activities.

## 2 Related Work

A substantial amount of research has been carried out in cost estimation in general distributed systems and especially distributed database systems [ApHY79, DuKS92, HFLP89]. The basis of many cost models described in various articles are the techniques of [SAC+79, CePe85]. However, these studies usually assume that each relational operation can be processed by any node and that each operation only requires CPU and memory resources. This is only valid in the context of sequential query processing.

Most of the early proposals for cost evaluation assume that the communication costs largely dominate the local processing costs (I/O and CPU cost) [BeCh81, GoDa81]. This assumption is based on very slow communication networks (e.g. wide area networks). In those environments, we have to focus our attention to the minimization of the size of intermediate relations. On the other hand, a recent research effort [EnGH95] in the context of a parallel database system NonStop SQL/MP shows that communication costs are still significant - they may exceed the costs of operators such as scan, grouping or join.

Today, distributed processing environments with multiprocessor machines and local area networks of workstations are available. Most of the recent research efforts consider a weighted combination of the cost components since these contribute to the total cost evaluation of a query with a varying significance. In this context, the cost estimation strategy has to consider those methods minimizing all cost components, like horizontal parallelism and pipelining. Examples for this are shown in [MiCS88, Bült89]

In some papers, e.g. [MaLo86] and [Fong86], we find relatively complex investigations, that query processing algorithms optimize I/O operations, cost of data transmissions and the use of CPU which is required to perform the query. Cost functions are used to find optimal schedules for the placement and the execution of query operations. However, these papers only consider communication costs and take into account only local processing, but do not address the load situation in the distributed system.

In [Mare95], the degree of parallelism was analyzed in the case of single user mode in a shared nothing multiprocessor environment. In the same context, [Bült89] considers the main storage deficiency. Here, in addition to conventional parameters, the evaluation strategy integrates the available memory. In contrast to our approach, modeling the response time of complex queries, [Mare95] restricts attention to an analytical model abstracting from the physical aspects of the query processing.

Algorithms for processing distributed queries require a priori estimation of the size of intermediate results. Most such algorithms use a static approach, in which the query processing strategy is completely determined before the processing starts. If the estimation of intermediate results is inaccurate at some intermediate stage, the estimation result may differ enormously from the real intermediate results. Adaptive query execution may be used to reduce the problem [CaKu87,Cybe89].

Parallel query processing combined with dynamic load balancing is much more complex, since the performance is influenced by additional factors like disk I/O, data dependency and communication frequency [RaMa95, DeGo93, LuTa94].

However, until now, the static optimization approaches and cost evaluation strategies *do not solve the problem of a qualified hardware employment dependent on the load of distributed resources to achieve an optimal query processing.*

We assume, that a parallel or distributed system with a balanced load distribution achieves a higher throughput and therefore a better resource utilization than a non-balanced system. Due to this assumption, the optimal distributed execution of a database query cannot ignore the current system load and the load produced by performing the database operations.

In this paper, we propose a cost-based approach to optimize complex queries in a distributed environment by integrating significant load parameters. By means of the cost model[†] introduced in the following, we can investigate the influence of significant system parameters on the efficiency of the query parallelism algorithm. The cost model can be used further for the determination of a qualified *load balancing*.

## 3 Parallel Query Processing

### 3.1 Fundamental Consideration

In the context of the HEAD system, a static optimization is finished before the query execution starts. The sizes of the intermediate relations of a execution strategy are not known until run time. Therefore, it has to be estimated using database statistics. Errors in these estimate can imply the choice of worse query execution plans. Further, load shifts during the optimization phase and during the execution of the operation itself produce inaccuracies in the cost evaluation result too.

In the following, we present the general strategy in the HEAD system.

We consider three forms of parallelism, namely horizontal, vertical (pipelining) and intra-operator parallelism. The distribution of the database (fragmentation and replication) results in dividing the *Query Execution Plan* into parallel QEP's. This leads to a parallelism considered as horizontal parallelism. *Pipelining* enables the concurrent execution of operation sequences. In general, this leads to a decreased execution time. With these special techniques, we control the level of parallelism, and the response time is diminished.

Due to a higher degree of processing parallelism to response time minimization, it is possible that the total costs in the distributed system can essentially increase (for example by increasing parallel network transmissions). Therefore it is necessary to achieve a well-balanced relationship between response time minimization and the resource utilization in the distributed system.

The propagation of intermediate results which are badly estimated is corrected by a *parameter adaptation*. This adaptation occurs in frequently appearing query patterns about the comparison of the estimation results with the real selectivities of

---

† This paper is restricted to those cost functions which refer to the integrative aspect of load balancing.

single operators. Furthermore, we propose an estimation interrupt mechanism to prevent wrong optimization decision by error-propagation.

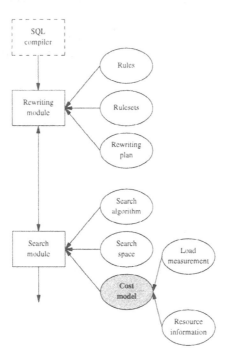

**Fig. 1**: HEAD Optimizer

Several studies [RaMa95, DeGo93, Cybe89] have already addressed dynamic load balancing issues for parallel query processing. However, load balancing was mainly considered for parallel multiprocessor DBMS. For distributed DBMS (shared nothing architecture), the physical database design aims at supporting a static form of load balancing for complex queries by declustering relations across many hosts to support a high degree of intra-query parallelism. Initial analyse [Link94, Flac95] have shown, that the aspect of *load balancing* could dominate the performance in a distributed system in comparison with the decision of a best level of static data distribution.

The *load measurement* component in HEAD (GRA: *G*lobal *R*esource *A*nalyzer) delivers static information on the capabilities of each network node and on the current load situation and tendency (Section 4). This information is presented as a load descriptor consisting of several parameters, e.g. memory utilization, number of CPU idle cycles and a static *resource information* descriptor.

Since many operator node mappings are possible, the mapping with the minimal costs should be chosen (*cost model*). The costs are represented by CPU-, I/O- and network costs. An optimal operator node mapping can be found by several optimization techniques. In HEAD, the optimization (Figure 1) is done in two steps. First, heuristics are used to limit the solution space. These include:

- **Rewriting module**: The algebra, the transformation rules and the set of rules are defined by an own specification language that has been developed based on regular grammars. Transformation rules can be comprised to rule sets. The application sequence is controlled by the set of rules.

- **Search module**: The search algorithm chooses a cost optimal plan from a set of equivalent plans. The search module spans the search space, generates a concrete solution (query execution plan) and uses the cost estimation of the chosen plan.

In the second step, an approximative technique (e.g. simulated annealing) is used to find the optimal solution. This technique compares the cost estimation results for different solutions.

**Description form: Petri net**

The query processing is based on a data-flow-controlled processing model. The algebra operations are not synchronized by special control structures. They are only controlled by the data stream. This results in a vertical parallelism. An advantage of this technique is the freedom from any central control structure which could become a bottleneck. In the following, we use *Petri nets* to describe parallel processing mechanisms like pipelining.

**Definition 1**:

A **Petri net** is a tuple $N = (S, T, F, m_0)$, where $S$ is the set of places, $T$ is the set of transitions, disjoint to $S$ $(S \cap T = \emptyset)$, $F$ is the flow relation $F = (S \times T) \cup (T \times S)$, and $m_0$ is the set of start marks.

In addition to the proposal in [MiCS88], we made some extensions. The model of the dynamic dataflow event control is possible by the initiation of start places (data sources) $S_i$ with a simultaneous valuation $m_0$ and stop places $S_e$ (Figure 2 (b)). Let us take an example to illustrate a *query petri net* (Figure 2 (a)) in correspondence to the above definition. Consider the following relational database with three relations where the key attributes are given in bold font:

```
CAR (PLATE, MODEL, COLOR)
OWNER (LICENCE, PLATE, DATE, CITY)
CHECK (PLATE, DATE)
```

**Query 1:**
```
select CAR.*, CHECK.DATE, OWNER.*
from CAR, CHECK, OWNER
where      CAR.PLATE=CHECK.PLATE and
           CAR.PLATE=OWNER.PLATE and
           CAR.COLOR='blue' and
           CHECK.DATE=121296 and
           OWNER.CITY='Berlin'
```

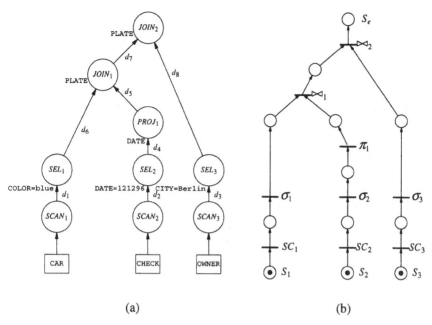

**Fig. 2**: (a) Operator Tree: Query 1 (b) Query Petri Net

The transitions shown in Figure 2 (b) can be interpreted as database events and as query operations. The places within a Petri net represent the conditions or the availability of the input data records needed for the execution of the query operations. Data transmissions are represented in a 'Query Petri Net' as edges from a transition to a place.

In Figure 2 (b) it is evident that a data flow (tuple stream) can be modeled as an acyclic path from the leaf nodes to the root. The leaf nodes are illustrated in the rule SCAN-operations; the root node is the mapping for the final operation of the considered subtree.

A transition (which corresponds to algebraic operations) has either one input path (selection) or two input paths (join). Multiple edges of a transition to several places represent the broadcast data transport to different algebraic operations.

The parallel query processing of HEAD can be derived from the Petri net representation (Figure 2 (b)) in the following way:

• Independent parts of the query graph can be executed in parallel.

• Tuple packages will be transmitted on the data flow edges instead of complete operands. In this matter, chains of operations (*pipelines*) simultaneously process the tuple packages of a relation.

## 3.2 Profile of Parallelism

To illustrate the valuation of parallel processing steps, we want to point out the effects of a sequence of parallel steps in a profile of parallelism (Figure 3). For simplification we do not consider any additional costs caused by the parallelism.

The start operations correspond to the SCAN-operations. The time axis of the diagram shows the duration of external storage access of the relations $R_i$. The other operations show the CPU processing time of the corresponding computer nodes $s_j$. This time duration depends on the size of the intermediate relation (data dependence) and the kind of the algebraic operation (instructions per tuple package).

The operations in a chain are in a waiting stack. When the first tuple packages arrive (point of time $t_1$), the following operations that are in the pipeline (e.g. $SCAN_1$ - $SEL_1$) are activated and the tuples are processed.

The attachment of pipelining to an edge of the operator graph essentially influences the processing time of the subquery:

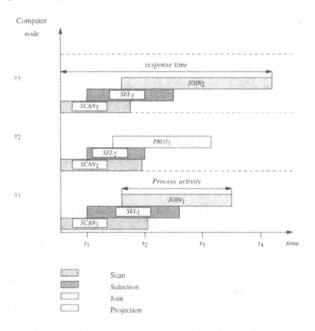

**Fig. 3**: Profile of Parallelism: Query 1

- increase of CPU-costs because a higher number of messages has to be sent and received,
- omission of the I/O-costs,
- avoidance of bottleneck situations within the communication net.

An overlap of the process activity (Figure 3) appears during the execution of an algebraic operation immediately after the arrival of a tuple package of the corresponding operator node.

### 3.3 Main Storage Access

The consequences of an unbalanced dataflow are not only waiting or idle processes but also the claim for larger memory capacity caused by data accumulation. In dependence on the current storage utilization, the data page overflow between main and external storage are very time intensive and are in opposition to minimization of response time. An efficient arrangement of the algebraic operations is possible by the following analyzing functions of the storage utilization and the cost model.

Let us consider the following declaration:

$\Psi_{s_j,n}(\Delta t)$ is the amount of the main storage requirement on computer node $s_j$ for the handling of the algebraic operations $\omega_i$; $n$ is the number of the operations $\omega_i$ which have to be processed on computer node $s_j$; $X_{s_j}(\omega_i)$ is the storage requirement (number of pages) generated as an intermediate result by the specific operation $\omega_i$; $max(\Psi_{s_j})(\Delta t)$ is the maximum of available storage on the computer node $s_j$ within the time interval $\Delta t$ and results from the parameters which are provided by the load measurement component (*freemem*, see also Section 4.1).

The following condition is valid:

$$\forall t \geq 0 \quad \forall s_j:$$

$$\Psi_{s_j,n}(\Delta t) \leq max(\Psi_{s_j}(\Delta t)) \ \wedge$$

$$\Psi_{s_j,n}(\Delta t) = \sum_{i=1}^{n} X_{s_j}(\omega_i)$$

Based on the second condition of the storage requirements, which are determined accumulatively for the operations processed on computer $s_j$, the calculated costs are increased by a fixed weighting factor $\zeta$, if the condition is not valid. The exact specification of the temporal effect of main storage restrictions is just in progress. Future studies will nevertheless intensively investigate these questions, so that some simplifications which are presently made, can be removed.

## 4 Load Measurement

The basic assumption of load sharing and balancing is that a distributed system with a balanced load distribution achieves a higher throughput and a better utilization of resources than a non-balanced system. Therefore, an optimal query processing cannot ignore the current system load and the load produced by executing the database operations.

In order to realize an efficient load balancing, it is necessary to get information about the current load of the system resources (CPU, I/O, network). It is necessary to measure the current load in order to make efficient load balancing decisions.

Therefore, a load component [Link94] has to periodically determine the current load situation on each node and on the network connecting different nodes.

## 4.1 Load Parameters

In the scope of load measurement, significant parameters are analyzed, as there are CPU run queue length, available main-memory, incoming and outgoing packets and the collision rate of the local area network. The load demon [Link94] reads these parameters periodically from the UNIX kernel.

The load information is represented as a load descriptor (*loadindex*):

```
loadindex {
time; // time of last actualization
host; // hostname
load_min1; // one minute load average
freemem; // count of free memory blocks
if_collisions;// collision rate
if_ipackets;// count of incoming packets
if_opackets;// count of outgoing packets
}
```

The count of waiting processes in CPU run queues reflects the load of the CPU [BaWa89, Zhou89, Zhou88]. The UNIX kernel variable *loadave[0]* represents the one minute load average (*load_min1*). The load demon gets the count of free memory blocks from the UNIX kernel variable *freemem*. These parameters do not include information about past or future to show tendencies of changes. Therefore, the load demon makes a regression analysis based on older and current values to calculate these tendencies.

## 4.2 Load Information Exchange

A frequent information exchange takes place to include load information from other computer nodes of the distributed system, where the load demons run. Access to information of the load descriptor is realized by requests. The load component periodically makes a regression analysis to calculate tendencies of the load change. On the other hand, with the regression analysis it is possible to reduce the frequencies of load measurements. Furthermore, the load information exchange takes place only after a significant change of the load parameters.

If a significant change of load parameters has happened, the information is transmitted by multicasting to all other computer nodes in the domain[†] (Figure 4).

In order to realize the load information exchange, the load demon has to be able to receive and transmit load information either to a computer node in the own domain or to computer nodes in other domains. If a request is addressed to a local computer or the local domain, it can be answered locally. In the case the load information is related to a computer node in the remote domain, the load demon tries to establish a connection to a dedicated computer node (gateway; $n_3$, $n_6$ in the above example).

---

† A group of computer nodes where the load information exchange is restricted to these nodes.

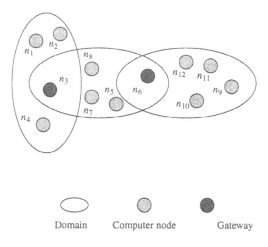

Domain     Computer node     Gateway

**Fig. 4**: Domain Concept

The whole concept of load measurement and information exchange in the HEAD-system is described in more detail in [Link94].

### 4.3 Evaluation of CPU load

HEAD is based on a physical shared nothing architecture and is called heterogeneous because of different types of computers with a UNIX-like operating system connected by a local area network. On the other hand, different relational database management systems are integrated in the distributed system. Due to the *non database applications* which are possible in heterogeneous environments, it is necessary to determine the current load and hardware power for an accurate cost evaluation.

The cost evaluation was often limited to static parameters such as communication traffic or local processing [MaLo86, MaLR90]. We assume that the static computer specific parameters such as CPU load are increasingly influenced for instance by multi media database applications.

Therefore, a load demon periodically reads parameters like CPU run queue length and others from the UNIX kernel. The number of waiting processes within CPU run queues (*load_min1*) reflects the load of the CPU.

A normalization results in a polishing of the absolute values. Furthermore, an adaptation of this normalized size is executed to determine a valid processor load factor $\Phi_{t_k}(s_j)$ with $(0 \leq \Phi_{t_k}(s_j) \leq 1)$.

For the determination of an upper bound value of the CPU load $\Upsilon(s_j)$, extreme application loads are produced in a time interval $(t_1 \leq t_k \leq t_m)$ and in the same time the CPU run queue length (*load_min1*) is read by the load measurement component.

The following target function of the current processor load factor is valid:

$$\Upsilon(s_j) = \max_{\Delta t}(\bigcup_{k=1}^{m} load\_min1_{s_j}(t_k))$$

$$\Phi_{t_k}(s_j) = \frac{load\_min1_{s_j}(t_k)}{\Upsilon(s_j)}$$

Figure 5 shows the relationship between the work load and the CPU run queue lengths. The computer nodes are low loaded until a workload of 40, i.e. until 50 processes within the run queue. The transition from a low to a middle state load causes a strong increase of the CPU run queue length.

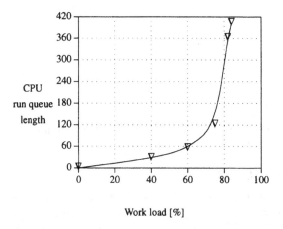

Work load [%]

**Fig. 5**: Correlation between work load and CPU run queue length

The evaluation of the local processing costs $C_{s_j,n}(P)$ of a subquery P depends on the kind of the algebraic operation $\omega_i$ (projection, selection, etc.). The size of the intermediate relation as an input factor of the operator can be estimated by specific calculating instructions [SAC+79]. The estimation of the profiles of the intermediate results is based on the assumptions of the independence and of uniform distribution of attribute values. The CPU rate $C_{cpu}(s_j)$ and the I/O rate $C_{io}(s_j)$ are computer node dependent variables of the cost function.

The number of data units that are transmitted between external and main memory $N_{io}(\omega_i)$ and the number of instructions depending on the algebraic operation (per tuple packet) $N_{inst}(\omega_i)$ represent further parameters. The target function for the local processing costs is represented as follows:

$$C_{s_j,n}(P) = \sum_{i=1}^{n}(N_{io}(\omega_i) * C_{io}(s_j) + N_{inst}(\omega_i) * C_{cpu}(s_j) * \frac{1}{1 - \Phi_{t_k}(s_j)})$$

Here, $n$ is the number of algebraic operations $\omega_i$, which have to be processed on computer node $s_j$, where the index $i$ denote a specific operation. The last term of the target function expands the CPU rate $C_{cpu}(s_j)$ by the normalized processor load factor $\Phi_{t_k}(s_j)$ $(0 \leq \Phi_{t_k}(s_j) \leq 1)$ with the remaining CPU performance $1 - \Phi_{t_k}(s_j)$.

## 4.4 Load Modification

If an optimized query graph is given with fixed operator sequence, a modification of the query graph can be reached by shifting of one or more operators to different computer nodes in the distributed system. Due to several load balancing aspects, a transfer of algebraic operations to low loaded computer nodes (e.g. CPU load, periphery load) can be taken into account to minimize the response time or total costs. Nevertheless, the load situation on a computer node can be dynamically changed by the algebraic operators themselves during the execution (pipelining) of these operators on a computer. Based on such a static cost estimation, it would come to a deviation of the estimated results (load variation) by a given basic load $\Phi_{t_k}(s_j)$ on a computer node.

This fact leads to an additional consideration of an *operator load* (overlap of operator activity, see also Figure 3) to a feasible exact approximation of the real load situation $\Phi_{t_k}{'}(s_j)$. The target function for the load variation is:

$$\Phi_{t_k}{'}(s_j) = \frac{\Phi_{t_k}(s_j) * \Delta t * C_{cpu}(s_j) + N_{inst}(\omega_i)}{\Delta t * C_{cpu}(s_j)}$$

**Example**:

$$C_{cpu}(s_1) = 28.5 \; MIPS; \quad \Delta t = 1 \; s;$$

$$\Phi_{t_k}(s_1) = 0.3; \quad N_{inst}(SEL_1) = 1330950$$

$$\Phi_{t_k}{'}(s_1) = \frac{0.3 * 28.5 \; MIPS * 1s + 1330950}{1s * 28.5 \; MIPS} = 0.347$$

Based on the example (Query 1), the processor loading factor $\Phi_{t_k}{'}(s_1) = 0.347$ is inserted into the target function $C_{s_j, \omega_i}(P)$ for the successor operation $JOIN_1$ within the processing chain $SEL_1 - JOIN_1$. Furthermore, the above target function is used to compute the resulting load change $\Phi_{t_k}{''}(s_1)$. This function takes into consideration $N_{inst}(JOIN_1)$.

## 4.5 Experimental Validation

The response time of a query mainly depends on the power of computer-specific resources which are used to process the operations of the query execution plan. Therefore, we developed a cost model describing the response time behavior of database queries. This depends on the respective computer-specific load profile.

By the means of this model, we can investigate fundamental tradeoffs of parallel query processing. Furthermore, the cost model can be used to optimize the parallel query execution plan and to map the algebraic operations to computer nodes.

The cost model was validated by measurements during the parallel query processing. The measurement was done on a network of different powerful computer nodes (SPARCStation 2, SPARCStation 4, SPARCStation 10), which are connected by an Ethernet-LAN (10 MBit/s). The following measurement results are considered in the load specification which is the basis of following investigations. We subdivide the load situations of the processors into three ranges: *small, middle and heavy* (Table 1). The mapping between work load situation depends on the CPU run queue length, in which the utilization is considered as a relation of the computing time and total time.

| Range | Work load | CPU run queue length |
|--------|-----------|------------------------|
| small | 0-40 % | 0-49 |
| middle | 40-80 % | 50-120 |
| heavy | 80-100 % | > 120 |

**Tab. 1**: Work load specification

On the base of a concrete query plan (Query 1) we put an artifically created load on computer nodes $s_j$, which were involved in the query processing. The measurement tests show that the neglect of the load profile produces large differences between the cost estimation results in dependence on true work load (Figure 6). If some load parameters are neglected, the response time is constant in spite of the changed load of single computer-specific resources.

To analyze the relationship between the computer node allocation and the behavior of response time, we compared the optimal load balancing results with non load balancing for Query 1 (Table 2).

| | Work load | | | |
|---|---------|---------|---------|---------|
| | 10 % | 30 % | 60 % | 90 % |
| + | 1230 ms | 1568 ms | 3727 ms | 6004 ms |
| * | 944 ms | 1295 ms | 2671 ms | 4305 ms |

**Tab. 2**: Response Time: Query 1

+ - without load balancing
* - with optimal load balancing

For this purpose, we only consider the general case with allocation of computer nodes depending on the respective load profile. Although the number of the allocated computer nodes is limited to three computers relative to the example query (Query 1), the reached results of the investigation are transferable to more complex queries.

Figure 7 shows an optimal load balancing due to a significant minimization of response time beginning from a work load of 40 %.

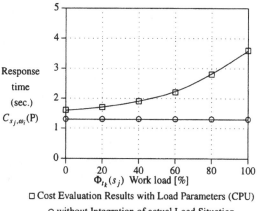

□ Cost Evaluation Results with Load Parameters (CPU)

o without Integration of actual Load Situation

**Fig. 6**: Comparison between the Cost Evaluation Results

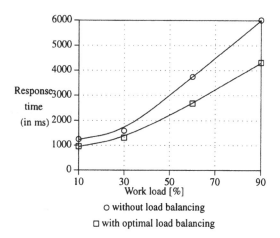

o without load balancing

□ with optimal load balancing

**Fig. 7**: Response Time: Query 1

We point out that the cost estimation result corresponds to the real response time with reaching accuracy *primarily by integration of the load parameters (basic load* $\Phi_{t_k}(s_j)$, *operator load* $\Phi_{t_k}{}'(s_j))$ in the current functions.

Based on the examination, we can assume the cost model offers an adequate approximation to the load behavior of a distributed system. Performance investigations of database queries can be executed by means of the cost model.

## 5 Conclusion and Future Work

By means of the introduced concept, a cost evaluation technique is available, allowing the integration of the current load situation on a computer node in the cost estimation of parallel query processing. This is a prerequisite to the determination of a qualified mapping between algebraic operations and computer nodes to find the optimal query execution plan for complex queries in a distributed DBMS.

Moreover, we considered especially the restrictions which follow from the pipelining mechanism, e.g. the storage requirements and the dynamic operator load variation. Due to the complexity of a distributed system, the exact specification and valuation of the effect of local load changes to the response time of a concrete query plan is hard to predict.

Until now, we could not present a complete experimental validation of the cost evaluation technique, because the prototype implementation is just in progress. Up to now we implemented the cost model, the load measurement component, the rewriting and the search module.

In future works we will study which estimation mechanism related to the error-propagation can be used to process a complex query.

Furthermore, case studies will be performed in order to compare the complexity, the accuracy and the costs of our static cost evaluation strategy with dynamic strategies.

Therefore, it is necessary to expand the cost model step by step until a flexible valuation is possible for all significant cost components of a database query. Later, a further validation of the cost model parameters will be done.

**Acknowledgements:**

We wish to thank our colleagues and students in the database research group of the University of Rostock: Andreas Heuer, Uwe Langer, Joachim Kröger and Anke Neumann for discussions and proposals and Ansgar Linke and Hans-Henning Kruse for implementing the prototype.

## References

[ApHY79] P. M. G. Apers, A. R. Hevner, and S. B. Yao, "Optimization Algorithm for Distributed Queries," *IEEE Trans. on Software Eng.*, 5, 3, pp. 57-68 (May 1979).

[BaWa89] K. M. Baumgartner and B. W. Wah, "GAMMON: A Load Balancing Strategy for Local Computer Systems with Multiaccess Networks," *IEEE Transactions on Computers*, 38, 8, pp. 1098-1109 (Aug. 1989).

[BeCh81] P. A. Bernstein and D. W. Chiu, "Using Semi-Joins to Solve Relational Queries," *Journal of the Association for Computing Machinery*, 28, 1, pp. 25-40 (January 1981).

[Bült89] G. v. Bültzingsloewen, "Optimizing SQL Queries for Parallel Execution," *SIGMOD Record,* 18, 4, pp. 17-22 (Dec. 1989).

[CaKu87] T. L. Casavant and J. G. Kuhl, "Analysis of three dynamic distributed load-balancing strategies with varying global information requirements" in *Proceeding of the 7th IEEE Int. Conf. on Distributed Computing Systems,* pp. 185-192 (Sept. 1987).

[CePe85] S. Ceri and G. Pelagatti, "Distributed Databases: Principles and Systems," *Mc Graw-Hill,* New York (1985).

[Cybe89] G. Cybenko, "Dynamic Load Balancing for Distributed Memory Multiprocessors," *Journal of Parallel and Distributed Computing,* 7, 2, pp. 279-301 (1989).

[DeGo93] M. Devarakonda and K. K. Goswami, "Prediction-Based Dynamic Load-Sharing Heuristics," *IEEE Transactions on Parallel and Distributed Systems,* 4, 6 (June 1993).

[DuKS92] W. Du, R. Krishnamurthy, and M-C. Shan, *Query Optimization in Heterogeneous DBMS* (1992).

[EnGH95] S. Englert, R. Glasstone, and W. Hasan, "Parallelism and its Price: A Case Study of NonStop SQL/MP," *SIGMOD Record,* 24, 4 (December 1995).

[FlLM94] G. Flach, U. J. Langer, and H. Meyer, "Cost-based Query Optimization in HEAD," *CS Technical Report,* 15, University of Rostock (1994).

[Flac95] G. Flach, "The Cost Evaluation of Database Queries in HEAD," *CS Technical Report,* 17, University of Rostock (1995).

[Fong86] Z. Fong, "The Design and Implementation of the Postgres Query Optimizer," *Technical Report,* CS Division, DEECS, University of California, Berkeley, California (Aug 1986).

[GoDa81] M. Gouda and U. Dayal, "Optimal Semijoin Schedules for Query Processing in Local Database Systems," *ACM SIGMOD,* pp. 164-175 (1981).

[HFLP89] L. M. Haas, J. C. Freytag, G. M. Lohman, and H. Pirahesh, "Extensible Query Processing in Starburst," *ACM TODS,* pp. 377-388 (Apr. 1989).

[Link94] A. Linke, "Load Measurement and Load Sharing in Heterogeneous Distributed Database Systems," *Master's thesis,* University of Rostock, Dept. of CS (May 1994).

[LuTa94] H. Lu and K.-L. Tan, "Load-Balanced Join Processing in Shared-Nothing Systems," *Journal of Parallel and Distributed Computing,* 23 (1994).

[MaLo86] L. F. Mackert and G. M. Lohman, "R* Optimizer Validation and Performance Evaluation for Distributed Queries," *Research Journal,* 5050, IBM Almaden Research Center, San Jose, California (Apr. 1986).

[Mare95] R. Marek, "A Cost Model of Parallel Query Processing in Shared-Nothing Database Systems," *In Proc. GI-Fachtagung "Datenbanksysteme in Büro, Technik und Wissenschaft" (BTW),* Dresden, Germany (March 1995).

[MaLR90] T. P. Martin, K. H. Lam, and I. Russel, "An Evaluation of Site Selection Algorithms for Distributed Query Processing," *Computer Journal,* 33, 1 (1990).

[MiCS88] K. P. Mikkilineni, J. C. Chow, and S. Y. W. Su, "Petri-Net-Based Modeling and Evaluation of Pipelined Processing of Concurrent Database Queries," *IEEE Trans. on Software Eng.,* 14, 11, pp. 1656-1667 (Nov. 1988).

[RaMa95] E. Rahm and R. Marek, "Dynamic Multi-Resource Load Balancing in Parallel Database Systems," *Proc. of the 21th VLDB Conf.,* Zurich, Switzerland (1995).

[SAC+79] P. G. Selinger, M. M. Astrahan, D. D. Chamberlin, R. A. Lorie, and T. G. Price, "Access Path Selection in a Relational Database Management System," *ACM* (1979).

[Zhou89] S. Zhou, "An Experimental Assessment of Resource Queue Lengths as Load Indices," UCB/CSD Rep. 86/298, CS Division, University of California Berkeley, USA (June 1986).

[Zhou88] S. Zhou, "A Trace-Driven Simulation Study of Dynamic Load Balancing," *IEEE Transactions on Software Engineering,* 14, 9, pp. 1327-1341 (Sept. 1988).

# High Performance OO Traversals in Monet*

Peter A. Boncz, Fred Kwakkel, Martin L. Kersten

University of Amsterdam, CWI
{boncz,kwakkel,mk}@cwi.nl

## Abstract

*In this paper we discuss how Monet, a novel multimodel database system, can be used to efficiently support OODB applications. We show how Monet's offbeat view on key issues in database architecture provided both challenges and opportunities in building a high-performance ODMG-93 compliant Runtime System on top of it.*

*We describe how an OO data-model can be mapped onto Monet's decomposed storage scheme while maintaining physical data independence, and how OO queries are translated into an algebraic language. A generic model for specifying OO class-attribute traversals is presented, that permits the OODB to algebraicly optimize and parallelize their execution.*

*To demonstrate the success of our approach, we give OO7 benchmark results of our Runtime System for both the standard pointer-based object navigation, and our declarative model based on a path-operator traversal library.*

*Keywords:* Object oriented databases, Performance, Benchmarking, Database programming languages Database architectures, Database Techniques, Parallel Systems.

## 1 Introduction

Engineering design and CASE are the prototypical database applications that require the database system to support complex and evolving data structures. Queries often involve -hierarchical- traversals and have to be executed with high performance to satisfy the requirements posed by an interactive application.

OODBs have been identified as the prime vehicle to fulfill these tough demands. It is in these application domains that traditional RDBMSs suffer most from the impedance mismatch, and fail to deliver flexibility and performance [7]. In recent years several – commercial – OODBs have entered the marketplace. Since "performance" in CAD/CAM or CASE applications has many faces, the OO7 benchmark was introduced as a yardstick for their success. It measures traversal-, update- and query evaluation performance for databases of differing sizes and object connectivity. The results published [5] indicate room for further improvement and a need for more effective implementation techniques.

---

* Parts of this work were supported by SION grant no. 612-23-431

This article describes how we tackled the OO7 functionality with our ODMG-93 compliant Runtime System called $MO_2$ [17] that was developed on top of Monet [4]. Monet is a novel database kernel that uses the Decomposed Storage Model (DSM [6]) because of its effectiveness in main-memory dominant environments. Through its use of virtual-memory techniques and operating system facilities for buffer management, Monet has been proven capable of handling both small and huge data-volumes efficiently [3].

Monet is a *multimodel* system; this means that its data can be viewed simultaneously in a relational, binary set-algebraic, or object-oriented manner. The $MO_2$ system is put at the task of translating between Monet's DSM- and the object-oriented data-model. This translation provides many opportunities for optimization, such as the *lazy attribute fetching* technique employed in $MO_2$ (see Section 3.1).

From the viewpoint of an OODBS, traversals specified in a persistent programming language like C++, result in a waterfall of individual object-fetches optimization cannot take place anymore. Helped by the physical data independence present in the $MO_2$ system, we managed to improve on this by offering a generic model for specifying complex traversals at a high level of abstraction. Traversals specified with this model can seamlessly be integrated with set-oriented query optimization and parallelization, for efficient execution on Monet.

## 2 Monet Overview

Monet is a novel database server under development at the CWI and University of Amsterdam since 1992. It is designed as a backend for different data models and programming paradigms without sacrificing performance. Its development is based on our experience gained in building PRISMA [1], a full-fledged parallel main-memory RDBMS running on a 100-node multi-processor, and current market trends.

Developments in personal workstation hardware are at a high and continuing pace. Main memories of 256 MB are now affordable and custom CPUs currently perform over 100 MIPS. They rely on efficient use of registers and cache to tackle the disparity between processor and main-memory cycle time, which increases every year with 40% [13]. These hardware trends pose new rules to computer software – and to database systems – as to what algorithms are efficient.

Another trend has been the evolution of operating system functionality towards micro-kernels, i.e. those that make part of the Operating System functionality accessible to customized applications. Prominent prototypes are Mach, Chorus and Amoeba, but also conventional systems like Silicon Graphics' Irix and Sun's Solaris increasingly provide hooks for better memory and process management.

### 2.1 Design Principles

Given the motivation and design philosophy outlined above, we applied the following ideas in the design of Monet:

- *perform all operations in main – virtual – memory*. Monet makes aggressive use of main-memory by assuming that the database hot-set fits into main-memory. All its primitive database operations work on this assumption, no hybrid algorithms are used. For large databases that exceed physical memory, Monet relies on virtual memory by *memory mapping* large files. In this way, Monet avoids introducing code to 'improve' or 'replace' the operating system facilities for memory/buffer management. Instead, it gives advice to the lower level OS-primitives on the intended behavior [2]. As Monet's tables take the same form on disk as in memory (no pointer swizzling), this memory mapping technique is completely transparent to its main-memory oriented algorithms.
- *binary relation model*. Monet stores all information in Binary Association Tables (BATs, see Figure 1). Search accelerators are automatically introduced as soon as an operator would benefit from their existence. They exists as long as the table is kept in memory; they are not stored on disk.

  This Decomposed Storage Model (DSM) [6] facilitates object evolution, and saves I/O on queries that do not use all the relation's attributes. These thin binary tables make for a kernel that needs to move relatively small data objects only, which is especially beneficial in main-memory environments (sinze data- movements are the main thing to optimize on), and easily outweighs the extra cost for re-assembling complex objects.
- employ *inter-operation parallelism*. Monet exploits shared-store and all-cache architectures. Unlike mainstream parallel database servers, like PRISMA [1] and Volcano [10], Monet does not use tuple- or segment-pipelining. Instead, the algebraic operators are the units for parallel execution. Their result is completely materialized before being used in the next phase of the query plan. This approach benefits throughput at a slight expense of response time and memory resources.

  A version of Monet designed to exploit efficiently distributed shared-nothing architectures is described in [15, 16]. A prototype runs on IBM/SP1.
- allow users to *customize* the database server. Monet provides extensibility much like in Gral [11], where a command can be added to its algebra, and its implementation linked into the kernel at any time. The Monet grammar structure is fixed, but parsing is purely table-driven on a per-user basis. Users can change the parsing tables at runtime by loading and unloading modules.

## 2.2 Algebraic Interface

Monet has a textual interface that accepts a set-oriented programming language called MIL (Monet Interface Language). MIL provides basic set operations, and a collection of orthogonal control structures that also serve to execute tasks in parallel. The – interpretive – MIL interface is especially apt as target language

---

[2] This functionality is achieved with the mmap(), madvise(), and mlock() Unix system calls.

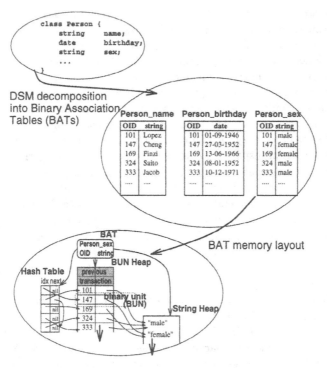

**Fig. 1.** Monet's decomposed storage scheme

for high-level language interpreters (SQL or OQL), allowing for modular algebra translation [11], in which parallel task generation is easy. Algorithms that translate relational calculus queries to BAT algebras can be found in [12, 15]

We show in an example what the BAT algebra looks like. Consider the following SQL query on relations company [comp#,name,telephone] and supply [supply#,comp, part, price]:

```
SELECT  company.name,
        company.telephone,
        supply.quantity
FROM    company, supply
WHERE   supply.comp = company.comp# AND
        supply.part = part_no AND
        supply.price < 0.50)
```

In Monet's SQL frontend, the relational database scheme will be vertically decomposed into five tables named comp_name, comp_telephone, supply_comp, supply_part and supply_price, where in each table the *head* contains an OID, and the *tail* contains the attribute value. The SQL query gets translated to the following MIL block:

```
{
    VAR m_supply, m_comp;
    VAR m_name, m_telephone, m_quantity;

    m_supply := SEMIJOIN(supply_part.SELECT(part_no),
                         supply_price.SELECT(0.0, 0.50));
    m_supply := MARK(m_supply);
    m_comp := JOIN(m_supply, supply_comp);
    {|
        m_name      := JOIN(m_comp, comp_name);
        m_telephone := JOIN(m_comp, comp_telephone);
        m_quantity  := JOIN(m_supply, supply_quantity);
    |}
    PRINT(m_name, m_telephone, m_quantity);
}
```

In all, the original double-select, single-join, three-wide projection SQL query is transformed in a sequence of 8 BAT algebra commands. The three last joins are placed in a parallel block {—..—}.

The dot notation "a.oper(b)" is equivalent to function call notation "oper(a,b)". Note that JOIN projects out the join columns. The MARK operation introduces a column of unique new OIDs for a certain BAT. It is used in the example query to create the new – temporary – result relation. The below table describes in short the semantics of the BAT commands used:

| BAT command | result |
|---|---|
| <AB>.mark | $\{o_i a \mid ab \in AB \wedge unique\_oid(o_i)\}$ |
| <AB>.semijoin(CB) | $\{ab \mid ab \in AB, \exists cd \in CD \wedge a = c\}$ |
| <AB>.join(CD) | $\{ad \mid ab \in AB \wedge cd \in CD \wedge b = c\}$ |
| <AB>.select(Tl,Th) | $\{ab \mid ab \in AB \wedge b \geq Tl \wedge b \leq Th\}$ |
| <AB>.select(T) | $\{ab \mid ab \in AB \wedge b = Tl\}$ |
| <AB>.find(T) | $\{a \mid aT \in AB\}$ |

# 3 MO$_2$: ODMG programming on Monet

When one would integrate a C++ application with a MIL (or even SQL) speaking Monet server, there is an impedance mismatch. To remedy this, in the MAGNUM project (underway since 1994) at the University of Amsterdam and CWI we have developed a ODMG-93 compliant database system nicknamed MO$_2$, that will (amongst others) be used as a tool to build a high-end GIS application.

The ODMG system consists of two parts: an ODL parser and an ODMG runtime library to be bound with the C++ application [8].

## 3.1 ODL Parser

An ODL definition defines both persistent and transient classes managed by the database system. ODL offers the usual OO features like inheritance, methods, objects and values, constructors (Set, Array,List, Struct etc) and binary relationships between objects. Note that ODL only defines the signature of object methods, the implementation must be done in the application language for which an ODL language binding exists. In our case we support both a C++ - and Java language binding.

The ODL parser accepts the data definitions, inserts those in the OODB data dictionary, and generates C++ header files with the corresponding class definitions.

In the C++ language binding, object references are implemented in a template class Ref<T> following a "smart pointer" approach.

The mapping of the ODMG object model to the Monet data-model is influenced by three considerations:

- The mapping must allow translation of OQL to an efficient MIL program. In particular, this means that object reconstruction from the decomposed tables – which is costly – must be avoided, set operations are performed on object identifiers only, and indexes can be used for the execution of selections and join operations on arbitrary attributes.
- The mapping must offer a large degree of data independence. Both C++ and Java applications must be able to share the data stored in the database. Furthermore, the addition of attributes to existing classes must have a low impact on the stored objects.
- In object hierarchy traversals such as OO7 a large number of objects are visited but only a small fraction of the attributes of the intermediate objects is used. "Lazy attribute fetching" is therefore a good technique to reduce disk I/O.

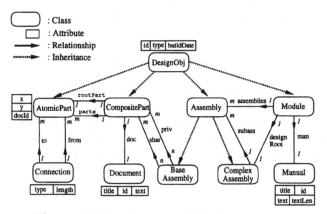

**Fig. 2.** OODB schema: the OO7 database

Objects are therefore fully decomposed in our design. Each attribute is stored as binary relation between the object identifier and the attribute value in class_attribute BATs. Each relationship is represented by a binary relation between the object identifiers of the two related objects.

In the case of the OO7 data-model (see Figure 2) the complete mapping of the 10 classes, 33 attributes, and 11 relationships of the OO7 database leads to 54 BATs in the Monet database.

## 3.2 ODMG Runtime

The ODMG runtime library deals with runtime object management. ODMG unites two paradigms, namely C++ persistent programming, where pointer traversals seamlessly permits browsing through the database tables, and the OQL part – a high level query language for bulk data retrieval.

Moving from a non-standardized OODB – as there exist many – to an ODMG compliant one, calls for a tight integration of the high-level OQL into the existing persistent programming system. Since OQL favors function-shipping solutions, preferably using complex query optimization and parallelization of tasks, there is a conflict of data allocation strategies, because the pointer traversal part of ODMG requires a data-shipping strategy to achieve efficiency.

The architecture of the Monet ODMG runtime system therefore incorporates a dual design. The client and server are peer-to-peer systems with different roles. The server system(s) are masters of their data: they are responsible for transaction management. The client, however, contains a functional complete copy of the server code to manage *transient* databases. This way, it can choose at runtime to cache tables and to execute operations locally or remotely.

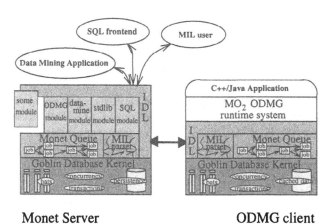

Fig. 3. The Monet Server and its Clients

Hiding the object implementation through the use of accessor functions get_attr() and put_attr() eliminates the need for object reconstruction at the client for navigational access. In other words, the data representation is the same at the client and server, so that query processing can be performed at either side. For this purpose the accessor functions and method code for new classes can be dynamically linked to the database server program.

At the moment of this writing, navigational access is supported and work is well underway to support full OQL. Section 5 presents the performance results for the traversal queries of the OO7 benchmark. In the future we will further optimize the Runtime System and reduce the granularity of locking it applies.

## 4 Efficient Object Traversals

Though OODBs provide for a seamless integration of application and database, they have also been criticized on the grounds that what effectively happens in OO class-attribute traversals is CODASYL-like "pointer chasing" [9]. Apart from the data independence issue, a piece of C++ code – say a complex loop – with object-referencing operations inside cannot be easily analyzed by the OODB to optimize complex traversals, let alone parallelize them. Such tasks are left to the programmer.

We think that this aspect of OODBs is a step backwards. For this reason, we felt there is a need for a way to specify OODB class-attribute traversals at a higher-level level of abstraction, such that they become amendable for optimization and efficient processing using a parallel platform.

Such high level constructs – generic as they may be – will never posses the expressive power as an arbitrary piece of C++ program. However, the model presented here captures a wide spectrum of traversals encountered in practice (most certainly those specified in the OO7 traversal queries).

### 4.1 Some Definitions

Our class traversal primitives require a few introductory definitions. We assume a class-attribute graph $\mathcal{G}$, which is a directed graph, where the nodes are classes, and the vertices the `relation` attributes in them.[3] These *attribute-vertices* start at the class of which the attribute is a member, and point to the class of the attribute. The class-attribute graph $\mathcal{G}$ also captures a second set of vertices representing inheritance relations, forming a forest of DAGs. Unless stated otherwise, when we use the term "reachable" we mean "reachable by attribute-vertices".

We define the following functions:

$$classes(\mathcal{G}) = \{C \mid C \text{ is a node in } \mathcal{G}\}$$
$$subclasses(P, \mathcal{G}) = \{C \mid P, C \in classes(\mathcal{G}),$$
$$C \text{ reachable from } P \text{ via inheritance-vertices}\}$$

The class-attribute graph can have objects as *instantiations* associated with it, which are captured by the extent $\mathcal{E}$:

$$\mathcal{E} = \{obj \mid obj \text{ instantiation of } C \in classes(\mathcal{G})\}$$
$$\mathcal{E}(P) = \{obj \mid obj \text{ instantiation of } C \in subclasses(P, \mathcal{G})\}$$

---

[3] We only describe relation attributes here, since value-attributes are not important in path definitions.

The complex paths we want to use are broader than the definition given in [2], in the sense that we want to be able to specify paths containing cycles and multiple subpaths from one class to the other.

Below we inductively define all possible paths $C_1 \overline{P} C_2$ as specified by a *path expression* $\overline{P}$:

$$C_1 \in classes(\mathcal{G}) \land$$
$$C_2 \in subclasses(C_1.\alpha) \Leftrightarrow C_1 \overline{C_1.\alpha} C_2 \tag{1}$$
$$C_1 \overline{P_1} C_2 \land C_2 \overline{P_2} C_3 \Leftrightarrow C_1 \overline{P_1 - P_2} C_2 \tag{2}$$
$$C_1 \overline{P_1} C_2 \land ... \land C_1 \overline{P_n} C_2 \Leftrightarrow C_1 \overline{[P_1,...,P_n]} C_2 \tag{3}$$

The notion of *reachability* of two objects $o_1 \in \mathcal{E}(C_1)$, $o_n \in \mathcal{E}(C_n)$, by a path $C_1 \overline{P} C_n$ can similarly defined over path expressions $\overline{P}$ as:

$$o_1 \overline{C_1.\alpha} o_n \Leftrightarrow o_1.\alpha = o_n \tag{4}$$
$$o_1 \overline{P_1 - ... - P_{n-1}} o_n \Leftrightarrow \forall i, 1 \le i < n : o_i \overline{P_i} o_{i+1} \tag{5}$$
$$o_1 \overline{[P_1,...,P_{n-1}]} o_n \Leftrightarrow \exists i, 1 \le i < n : o_1 \overline{P_i} o_n \tag{6}$$

A concrete instantiation $o_1.\alpha_1 - o_2.\alpha_2 - .. - o_n$ of a path $C_1 \overline{P} C_n$ between objects $o_1 \in \mathcal{E}(C_1)$ and $o_n \in \mathcal{E}(C_n)$ is called a *link*. The fact that two objects are reachable by a path implies that there is a (set of distinct) link(s) between them, following that path, and vice versa.

With this in mind, we can finally define the function $\mathbf{reachable}(\frac{o_1}{\overline{P}})$ as the *bag* of objects $o_n$, corresponding 1-1 to all distinct links $o_1.\alpha_1 - .. - o_n$ that are instantiations of path $C_1 \overline{P} C_n$, where $o_1 \in \mathcal{E}(C_1) \land \forall o_n : o_n \in \mathcal{E}(C_n)$. We refer to the order in which the objects are placed into the bag (which is arbitrary), as the *traversal order*.

## 4.2 Path Operators

Path expressions provide a handle to define the concept of *path operators*, which specify complex traversal patterns. Because the order in which a traversal algorithm visits the objects in a class-attribute hierarchy is important, we will define our path operators using pseudocode. Also, a traversal algorithm can visit a node more than once. It is for these reasons, that the path operators defined here work on ordered sets and ordered bags.

The $\mathbf{traverse}()$ traverses a path $\overline{P}$, starting from one object $o_1$, producing the $\mathbf{reachable}(\frac{o_1}{\overline{P}})$ bag of objects as a result:

```
FUNCTION traverse(src: OBJECT; p: PATHEXP;
                  f: FUNCTION) : BAG;
  VAR obj: OBJECT, dst : BAG;
  FORALL obj IN reachable(src, p) DO
    IF (f) THEN f(src,obj) FI;
    append(dst, obj);
  OD;
  RETURN dst;
END;
```

This trivial piece of pseudocode implies that some ordering criterion exist in visiting the destination objects reachable from the source object. The definition also allows some function to be executed on all nodes when they are visited.[4]

The second operator computes the closure set over a *cyclic* path starting at an input bag:

```
FUNCTION closure(src: OBJECT; dst: INOUT SET;
                 p: PATHEXP; f1, f2: FUNCTION);
  VAR obj: OBJECT, dst SET;
  FORALL obj IN reachable(src, p) DO
    IF (f1) THEN f1(src,obj) FI;
    IF (NOT obj IN dst) THEN
      append(dst, obj);
      closure(obj, dst, path, f1, f2);
      IF (f2) THEN f2(src,obj) FI;
    FI;
  OD;
  RETURN dst;
END;
```

This version of the closure operation uses a depth-first algorithm. Likewise, a breadth-first closure and other variants can be defined. Again, user-defined functions can be executed on the nodes when they are visited, or just when they are included in the closure.

## 4.3 Executing Path Operators

Path operators can be nested to specify complex traversal patterns. For example, the expression $traverse(closure(input, A.b-B.a), [A.c-C.e, A.d-D.e])$ starts traversal at the bag *input* and computes the closure over the loop $A_{\overline{A.b-B.a}}A$ (see Figure 5) and uses this set as input to traverse the two-branched path $A_{\overline{[A.c-C.e, A.d-D.e]}}E$ between $A$ and $E$ (see Figure 4).

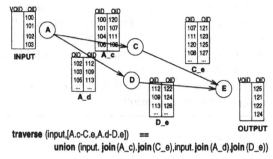

traverse (input,[A.c-C.e,A.d-D.e]) ==
union (input. join (A_c).join (C_e),input.join (A_d).join (D_e))

**Fig. 4.** Executing a traverse() operator

---

[4] further on, we will use a traverse() on an ordered source bag rather than a single source object, which executes a traverse on all its elements in order, returning the concatenation of all resulting bags.

Efficient execution of our path operators by Monet is relatively easy. As illustrated by the pseudo-code, the `traverse()` operator is equivalent to the join operator in Monet (see Section 2.2). Since the Monet's decomposition model vertically fragments all classes in binary relations named "class_attribute", traversing a path $P = A.a_1 - ... - A.a_n$ means joining the input bag with relation $A.a_1$, then joining its result with $A.a_2$, and again, until the last join with $A.a_n$, which forms the result of the operator. If the path has multiple branches $P = [P_1, ..., P_n]$, all branches are traversed first, and the results united (see Figure 4).

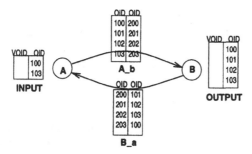

**closure** (input,A.b-B.a)  ==  input.**subgraph** (A_b.**join**(B_a))

**Fig. 5.** Executing a `closure()` operator

The `closure()` is implemented in Monet using the MIL operation `subgraph()`, which expects a single `[oid,oid]` BAT as the path relation. In contrast to `traverse()`, the `closure()` does not start joining the input bag with the "class_attribute" tables. Instead, it starts reducing the relations along the path *internally* using joins and unions until only a singular `[OID,OID]` path relation remains. Only then, it is fed as parameter with the input bag into Monet's `subgraph()` command.

## 4.4 Traversal Optimization

As opposed to a C++ pointer-based traversal, our nested path traversal operators give the OODB the whole view, such that it can work set-at-a-time and can optimize and parallelize traversal execution.

The relation attributes that connect the classes are essentially *join indices* [14], or OODB *nested indices* [2]. The closure operator first transforms a complex path to a singular one. In fact, it constructs a join index between the starting class and the ending class (which for `closure()` are one and the same).

For the traversal operators, the join index technique may also be applied. A complete path or (multiple) subpaths in the path can be collapsed into a join index. Although the construction cost for a join index maybe high, the investment of creating it can be turned into profit by re-using the index in later traversals.

It is clear, that the OODB optimizer has many options, of which some will, and others will not, be beneficial. The OODB should therefore use cost models incorporating parameters like mean fanout from objects along the classes-attribute path, the number of tuples in the input bag, the likelihood that a certain traversal will be executed again and others [14].

Path operators provide possibilities for parallel execution of traversals. Since both the `traverse()` as the `closure()` execute independent algorithms for the elements on their input bag, this bag can be fragmented, and given to different processing nodes for execution. The only communication required between nodes is at the end, when the results are united.

This article does not seek to investigate join index or traversal optimization cost-models; we just want to point out that high-level traversals provide opportunities for optimization and parallelization. The benchmark numbers in Section 5 have been obtained without attempting any optimization or parallelization.

### 4.5 ODMG Traversal Library

The high-level traversals discussed in this section are incorporated in Monet's ODMG system by means of a C++ template library. The library allows the programmer to construct nested path operators on his own classes.

```
// Path Class
template <class A, class B>
   class Path {
      Path(char *attr);              // outgoing attribute
      ~Path();
   }

// Path construction: && and || operators
template<class A, class B, class C>
   Path<A,C> Path::operator&&
      (const Path<A,B>& left,const Path<B,C>& right);

template<class A, class B>
   Path<A,B> Path::operator||
      (const Path<A,B>& left,const Path<A,B>& right);

// Path Operators: Traverse, Closure and Nest
template <class A, class B>
   class PathOperator {
      Bag<B> collect(Collection<A> root);
      int visit(Collection<A> root);
   }
template <class A, class B>
   class Traverse : public PathOperator<A,B> {
      Traverse(Path<A,B> path, void (fcn*)(Ref<A>,Ref<B>);
      ~Traverse();
   }
template <class A>
   class Closure : public PathOperator<A,A> {
      Closure(Path<A> path, void (pre*)(Ref<A>,Ref<A>),
                            void (post*)(Ref<A>,Ref<A>));
      ~Closure();
   }
template <class A, class C>
   class Nested : public PathOperator<A,C> {
```

```
    template <class B>
      Nested(Operator<A,B> op1; Operator<B,C> op2);
      ~Nested();
  }
```

The template classes are a direct translation of the model previously defined. They allow for some type checking to be done at runtime.[5]

The library user should first build a path expression, using instances of the Path class. Using the && (*and*) and || (*or*) operators, complex paths of resp. equation (2) and (3) can be assembled. The path operators Closure and Traverse can be constructed using such assembled paths. Path operators can be nested with the Nested operator. Materialization of a path operator is done by either the collect() method (which returns all visited objects), or the visit() method, which just returns a visit count.

## 4.6 Example

We now give an example of the use of these classes in a ODMG C++ binding, by showing how the OO7 Traversal 1 can be expressed:

```
 1 void oo7_t1(char *dbname) {
 2   Set<BaseAssembly> baseassbly, assbly;
 3   Ref<Assembly>    root;
 4   Database         database;
 5
 6   database->open(dbname);
 7   database->lookup(&root, "root");
 8   database->lookup(&baseassbly, "BaseAssembly.extent");
 9
10   Path <ComplexAssembly, Assembly> *p1 = Path("subAss");
11   Closure <Assembly> *o1 = Closure(p1);
12   assbly = p0->collect(root)->intersection(baseassbly);
13
14   Path <CompositePart,AtomicPart> *p2 = Path("rootPart");
15   Path <BaseAssembly,CompositePart> *p3 = Path("priv");
17   Traverse <BaseAssembly,AtomicPart> *o2 = Traverse(p2 && p3)
18
19   Path <Connection,AtomicPart> *p4 = Path("to");
20   Path <AtomicPart,Connection> *p5 = Path("to");
21   Closure <AtomicPart> *o3 = Closure(p4 && p5);
22
23   Nested<BaseAssembly, AtomicPart> *o4 = Nested(o2, o3);
24   printf("T1 #visited objects: %d.\n", o4->visit(assbly));
25   database->close();
26 }
```

We will now – step by step – show how the ODMG Runtime translates the above code to MIL: after some initialization, we fetch the *root* of the assembly hierarchy, and the extent of all *BaseAssemblies* (lines 7-8). This translates in the following MIL operations:

---

[5] except for attribute names: to do that, the C++ syntax would have to be extended in some way.

```
root := oo7_namedobjects.find("root");
baseassbly := oo7_namedobjects.find("baseassembly");
```

Lines 10-12 specify the path expression:
*closure(root,ComplexAssembly.subass)* of which the result is intersected with the previously fetched *baseassbly*. Monet constructs a BAT named *closure_root* with the previously fetched *root* as only element. Since the closure is to be computed on the single cyclic path *ComplexAssembly.subAss*, already represented in Monet by the binary association ComplexAssembly_subass, it doesn't have to be reduced to one with joins and unions. We just call the subgraph() with it, and the *closure_root* as source BAT, and semijoin the result with the *baseassbly*.

```
closure_root := new(oid,oid);
closure_root.insert(root,root);
leaves := subgraph(closure_root,
            ComplexAssembly_subAss).semijoin(baseassbly)
```

To retrieve all private root parts that are reachable from the selected base assemblies, we have to do a
*traverse(leaves,BaseAssembly.priv−CompositePart.rootPart)*. This traversal is executed in MIL with two joins:

```
rootparts := leaves.join(BaseAssembly_priv)
                    .join(CompositePart_rootPart);
```

The *traverse()* operator above can in fact be nested in the
*closure(leaves,AtomicPart.to−Connection.to)*, by substituting it in for "*leaves*" to obtain the nested path operator, as specified in lines 14-23. To execute the closure, two steps have to be taken. First, the closure path has to be reduced to a single relation, as follows:

```
connections := join(AtomicPart_to.reverse,
                    Connection_to);
```

(Note that joining two class-attribute relations might be an expensive operation, so an optimizing OODB might decide to save the *connections* BAT as a join-index for later re-use).

As a second step, the closure has to be executed on all elements in the *leaves* BAT, which contains all starting positions. Since we materialized the operator with visit(), we only have to return a visit count:

```
visited := 0; tmp := new(oid,oid);
rootparts@batloop() {
    tmp.clear;
    tmp.insert($2,$2);
    visited := visited + tmp.subgraph(connections).count;
}
```

The above piece of script, in which `visited` contains the final result, is the most expensive part of the T1 traversal. The *"@batloop()"* is a cursor-like Monet iterator, that iterates through all elements of a BAT, executing a MIL statement-block on all of them. Iterators in MIL can also be invoked in parallel: putting *"@[N]batloop()"* would have executed the block on at most $N$ elements from the BAT in parallel, providing an easy way to parallelize traversals.

# 5    OO7 Experiments

Our client platform was a Sun SPARCstation 20/50Mhz running Solaris, with 96 MB main-memory, 16KB data-, 20KB instruction and 1MB secondary cache, 1 Gb local disk (raw throughput: 10 MB/s) and 0.5 Gb swap space. It was connected with a similar Monet server via non-exclusive NFS over 10Mbit non-isolated ethernet. In this section we present results for three systems:

- $MO_2$ with C++ pointer-based navigational access. The implementation is a 95% match with the standard implementation available with the OO7 benchmark (see `ftp.cs.wisc.edu/oo7`).
- $MO_2$ with the Path Operator primitives. This implementation has only been done on the real traversal queries: T1 and T6 (full and sparse traversal), T2a,b,c (sparse,full and 3-fold attribute swap), and T3a,b,c (sparse,full and 3-fold indexed attribute update).
- A competitor from [5] as a reference. Since E/Exodus was the overall winner, we used these numbers. They have been corrected with a factor 5 to account for hardware differences with the original platform.

All numbers mentioned with the experiments are in seconds of elapsed time.

## 5.1    Traversal Queries

In the below table, we observe that for navigational $MO_2$ the numbers for the small database are slightly worse than the competition. Here Monet's approach with hash-lookups instead of pointer swizzling proves to bear slightly more overhead. For the medium database, the performance is very similar. We expect to improve the performance on sparse traversals (T6) by optimizations in the ODMG Runtime. The T1 is clearly faster, because of Monet's use of DSM: only the starting and ending points of the traversal must be materialized completely. This means that all attributes of intermediate classes, that are not relational attributes or not involved in the traversal, need not be accessed.

Note that for $MO_2$ T2 (swap-update) is in general more expensive than update T3 (toggle on single – indexed – attribute), whereas all competitors have T2 cheaper than T3. This is because the decomposed storage model implies that T2 accesses two tables, whereas T3 only one. This outweighs the extra cost of adapting the index in T3.

| fanout | Competitor (E/Exodus) | | | MO$_2$ (navigational access) | | | MO$_2$ (path operators) | | |
|---|---|---|---|---|---|---|---|---|---|
| | 3 | 6 | 9 | 3 | 6 | 9 | 3 | 6 | 9 |
| Small Database, Cold | | | | | | | | | |
| T1 | 7.0 | 8.5 | 10.1 | 10.6 | 17.0 | 23.4 | 3.6 | 15.1 | 8.6 |
| T6 | 3.8 | 3.8 | 3.8 | 3.2 | 4.8 | 6.4 | 1.5 | 1.5 | 1.3 |
| T2a | 7.3 | 8.8 | 10.3 | 11.4 | 17.6 | 23.8 | 2.8 | 2.9 | 2.9 |
| T2b | 7.9 | 9.3 | 12.0 | 12.2 | 18.6 | 25.0 | 12.3 | 13.7 | 18.0 |
| T2c | 8.1 | 9.5 | 12.2 | 13.4 | 20.0 | 26.8 | 18.5 | 26.3 | 30.9 |
| T3a | 8.0 | 9.8 | 12.3 | 11.0 | 17.2 | 23.6 | 1.3 | 1.5 | 3.2 |
| T3b | 17.5 | 20.2 | 28.0 | 11.6 | 18.2 | 24.8 | 14.4 | 10.1 | 17.8 |
| T3c | 43.8 | 48.9 | 70.5 | 12.4 | 19.0 | 25.6 | 16.5 | 18.6 | 32.0 |
| Small Database, Hot | | | | | | | | | |
| T1 | 2.1 | 2.6 | 3.0 | 6.6 | 12.0 | 17.8 | 3.3 | 8.8 | 7.8 |
| T6 | 0.2 | 0.2 | 0.2 | 0.3 | 0.3 | 0.3 | 1.0 | 1.6 | 1.0 |
| Medium Database, Cold | | | | | | | | | |
| T1 | 146.9 | 193.1 | 238.7 | 104.5 | 176.3 | 240.0 | 23.9 | 66.2 | 84.4 |
| T6 | 5.9 | 5.9 | 5.9 | 12.6 | 14.0 | 17.0 | 1.5 | 4.1 | 1.6 |
| T2a | 151.9 | 200.2 | 246.8 | 116.2 | 201.9 | 314.9 | 7.2 | 8.2 | 9.3 |
| T2b | 193.7 | 245.6 | 290.0 | 138.3 | 205.1 | 320.3 | 52.1 | 103.5 | 135.7 |
| T2c | 192.7 | 242.4 | 291.8 | 152.1 | 244.0 | 352.0 | 94.1 | 151.8 | 192.5 |
| T3a | 166.5 | 216.8 | 266.0 | 113.2 | 200.0 | 313.3 | 1.4 | 1.6 | 1.8 |
| T3b | | | | 119.9 | 212.9 | 318.8 | 47.4 | 103.6 | 152.1 |
| T3c | | | | 134.4 | 229.8 | 330.8 | 92.4 | 143.1 | 237.3 |
| Medium Database, Hot | | | | | | | | | |
| T1 | | | | 90.7 | 159.5 | 220.3 | 25.5 | 62.7 | 94.3 |
| T6 | | | | 0.3 | 0.4 | 0.5 | 1.1 | 2.2 | 2.1 |

As for the MO$_2$ numbers obtained with the path-operator class-library: with a factor 1-4 of difference this approach is the clear all-out winner. [6] Algebraic MIL operations work set-at-a-time and are more efficient than doing many single object-traversals. These results show crisp and clear that in order to achieve greater efficiency in complex OO traversals, one should use higher-level operations – whether it be path operators like we use, or some traversal-extension to a OQL-like language – such that the OODB can execute them efficiently, and in addition can employ standard query processing techniques like optimization and parallelization.

## 5.2 Queries T8-T9

Traversal T8 and T9 are operations on a large text block: *Manual_text* (1 MB). T8 counts all occurrences of the character 'i'. T9 compares the first and last character. The following performance figures are obtained for a medium database size (1MB of *Manual_text*).

---

[6] The reason that T3a and T2a seem even two orders of magnitude faster, is that the path-operator implementation only visits the to-be-updated objects. If all objects would have been visited, times would have been more similar to T1

| Query | Memory map | | Non Memory map | |
|---|---|---|---|---|
| | cold | hot | cold | hot |
| T8 (count) | 0.654 | 0.602 | 0.999 | 0.558 |
| T9 (compare) | 1.343 | 0.955 | 1.898 | 1.123 |

Monet allows you to specify for all BATs one of two different memory management strategies: loaded in memory, or mapped into virtual memory. For all measurements we used the latter strategy. This ensures BAT pages are swapped in memory only when required, and are therefore more efficient on low cache hit ratios. The performance data shows a faster response in the mapped version of T9 because here the first and last page are retrieved only.

## 5.3 Queries Q1-Q7

The performance results of the queries for the medium/9 database are shown below. We first discuss the results of Q1, in two different versions: in Q1 Monet only returns a set of OIDs, thereby taking advantage of its vertical decomposition strategy. The Q1a reconstructs tuples, by performing joins on the attributes. The difference in cold situations is due to BAT loading and building of index structures. The hot times clearly show the tuple reconstruction cost stays small (0.4 s).

| Query | Cold time | Hot time | Memory Size |
|---|---|---|---|
| Q1 | 0.77s | 0.56s | 2.0-2.8 Mb |
| Q1a | 1.82 | 0.94s | 6.0-6.9 Mb |

The other query results are as follows:

| Query | Cold time | Hot time | Competitor |
|---|---|---|---|
| Q2 (1%) | 0.62s | 0.61s | > 4s |
| Q3 (10%) | 0.67s | 0.64s | > 7s |
| Q4 | 0.85s | 0.64s | > 0.4s |
| Q5 | 0.84s | 0.82s | > 3s |
| Q7A (100%) | 1.94s | 1.78s | > 7s |
| Q7B (100%) | 2.5s | 2.2s | > 7s |

## 6 Conclusion

It was discussed how OO applications can be supported with Monet, a novel DBS with an unusual architecture. Firstly, our ODMG compliant $MO_2$ system maps an OO persistent programming interface onto decomposed tables in Monet. This mapping provides physical data independence, often hard sought for in OODBs. It also optimizes object-navigation by "lazy attribute fetching". Secondly, we introduced a derivate of the well-known concept of path-expressions to define path-operators. These provide an alternative – higher level – interface for specifying class-attribute traversals. We implemented the OO7 benchmark using $MO_2$ with and without this path-operator library. The comparison of results between the two and other OODBs shows that though bare $MO_2$ performs well, results superior to any competitor were achieved by the path operators, proving the importance of high-level query processing to performance in OODBs.

# References

1. P. M. G. Apers, C. A. van den Berg, J. Flokstra, P. W. P. J. Grefen, M. L. Kersten, and A. N. Wilschut. PRISMA/DB: A parallel main memory relational DBMS. *IEEE Trans. on Knowledge and Data Eng.*, 4(6):541, December 1992.

2. E. Bertino and W. Kim. Indexing techniques for queries on nested objects. *IEEE Transactions on Knowledge and Data Engineering*, 1(2), June 1989. Also published in/as: Mathematisch Centrum (Amsterdam), now CMCSC, TR-ACT-OODS,132-89, Mar.1989.

3. P. A. Boncz, , W. C. Quak, and M. L. Kersten. Monet and its Geographical Extensions: A novel approach to high performance GIS processing. In *Proc. EDBT'96 Conference, Avignon (France)*, March 1996.

4. P. A. Boncz and M. L. Kersten. Monet: An impressionist sketch of an advanced database system. In *Proc. IEEE BIWIT workshop, San Sebastian (Spain)*, July 1995.

5. M. Carey, D. J. DeWitt, and J. F. Naughton. The DEC OO7 benchmark. In *Proc. ACM SIGMOD Conf.*, page 12, Washington, DC, May 1993.

6. G. Copeland and S. Khoshafian. A decomposed storage model. In *Proc. ACM SIGMOD Conf.*, page 268, Austin, TX, May 1985.

7. J. Duhl and C. Damon. A performance comparison of object and relational databases using the Sun benchmark. In *Proc. ACM Conf. on Object-Oriented Programming Systems, Languages and Applications, ACM SIGPLAN Notices*, page 153, November 1988.

8. R.G.G. Catell et al. *The Object Database Standard*. Morgan Kaufman, 1993.

9. et al. Neuhold,E. and Stonebraker,M. Future directions in DBMS research. *ACM SIGMOD RECORD*, 18(1), March 1989. Also published in/as: ICCS, Berkeley, TR-88-1, Sep.1988.

10. G. Graefe. Encapsulation of parallelism in the volcano query processing system. In *19 ACM SIGMOD Conf. on the Management of Data, Atlantic City*, May 1990.

11. R. H. Gueting. Gral: An extensible relational database system for geometric applications". In *Proceedings of the 15th Conference on Very Large Databases, Morgan Kaufman pubs. (Los Altos CA), Amsterdam*, August 1989.

12. S. Khoshafian, G. Copeland, T. Jagodits, H. Boral, and P. Valduriez. A query processing strategy for the decomposed storage model. In *Proc. IEEE CS Intl. Conf. No. 3 on Data Engineering, Los Angeles*, February 1987.

13. A.R. Lebeck and D.A. Wood. Cache profiling and the spec benchmarks: A case study. *IEEE Computer*, 27(10):15–26, October 1994.

14. P. Valduriez. Join indices. *ACM Trans. on Database Sys.*, 12(2):218, June 1987.

15. C. A. van den Berg. *Dynamic Query Optimization*. PhD thesis, CWI (Center for Mathematics and Computer Science), February 1994.

16. C. A. van den Berg and M. L. Kersten. An analysis of a dynamic query optimisation scheme for different data distributions. In J. Freytag, D. Maier, and G.Vossen, editors, *Advances in Query Processing*, pages 449–470. Morgan-Kaufmann, San Mateo, CA, 1994.

17. C. A. van den Berg and A. van den Hoeven. Monet meets OO7. In *OO Database Systems Symposium of the Engineering Systems Design and Analysis Conference, Montpellier (France)*, July 1996.

# A Modular Compiler Architecture for a Data Manipulation Language

Suzanne M. Embury and Peter M.D. Gray

Department of Computing Science, King's College, University of Aberdeen,
Aberdeen, Scotland, AB9 2UE
E-Mail: {sme|pgray}@csd.abdn.ac.uk, URL: http://www.csd.abdn.ac.uk/~pfdm

**Abstract.** We describe a modular compiler architecture that has been developed for a functional data model DBMS. The architecture allows compilers for new sub-languages to be constructed rapidly, by reusing the components of the existing compiler, and allows new semantics and code generation strategies to be defined for existing language constructs. This point is demonstrated by the construction of a new compiler for an integrity constraint language, which required only two new modules to be added to the system. The most significant advantage of our architecture, however, is that it allows the DBMS itself to use the individual compiler modules, opening up a host of possibilities for run-time manipulation of application code.

Keywords: data manipulation languages, run-time compiling, semantic data models.

## 1  Introduction

The idea of a callable compiler was originally introduced into persistent languages, such as PS-Algol [33], as a way of overcoming the difficulties of building systems which must handle dynamically-introduced types in statically-typed languages. Programming environments, which support incremental development of code, are examples of such systems [13], as are database management systems (DBMSs). A callable compiler allows the implementation of embedded query languages, browsers and schema evolution capabilities, without sacrificing the security of static type checking [6]. However, as DBMS technology has advanced, the increasing need to manipulate not only the structure of data at run-time, but also its semantics, has meant that the ability to invoke compiler functions "on the fly" has become important for DBMSs themselves, and not just for the languages which implement them. The aim of a DBMS is to take over responsibility for routine management tasks from the user, many of which involve manipulation of code as well as data; deciding which code needs to be recompiled after a schema change, for example, or re-optimised as the cost of evaluating alternative access paths changes. Furthermore, as DBMSs are increasingly being seen as components in larger (possibly distributed) systems, the ability to combine, analyse and transform code retrieved from different sources is increasing in importance. Since DBMSs are organised around *data models* [17], with well-defined semantics, rather than *type systems*, and since they can rely on the availability of a repository of information about both the structure and semantics of the data (the metadata), the potential for more far-reaching and "intelligent" manipulation of code is far greater than it is for a programming language, with its low-level, low-semantics type system and minimal runtime metadata storage.

To perform this kind of manipulation requires the invocation of a compiler by a running program, but a callable compiler in the usual sense is too coarse-grained. It implements only a single function, transforming source text into executable code, and thus forces the DBMS to represent and manipulate code in one of these two forms—neither of which are suitable for the task. Source text is too "flat". Before it can be manipulated, it must be parsed and converted into some internal data structure, and before the modified code can be executed, it must be translated back into source language form, and parsed all over again by the compiler. The target language representation, on the other hand, is much too low-level to be easily manipulated. It is designed for efficient execution, and thus concentrates too much on storage semantics details, with only a weak representation of the original semantics.

What we need, then, is not a monolithic callable compiler, but one in which the front end and the back end can be invoked independently—the former to parse the source text and turn it into some format convenient for automatic manipulation, and the latter to take programs expressed in the internal format and convert them into executable code. This scheme allows us to represent code internally in the format which is best for the analysis and transformations we want to carry out, without the overheads of continual reparsing, or the need to implement the extra translation routines.

The extra flexibility gained by this division suggests the idea of splitting the compiler up into a series of independently callable modules, each implemented as a transformer from input to output, and each performing some particular step in the compilation process: parsing, optimisation, code generation, etc. This would provide the DBMS with an assortment of tools for manipulating code in various ways, which could either be used individually (for example, when recompiling some method code from its internal representation), or in different combinations, opening up a host of possibilities for automated run-time maintenance of code.

This paper describes the implementation of a compiler along these modular lines for the data manipulation language Daplex [29], in the context of P/FDM [18, 9], a Prolog implementation of Shipman's Functional Data Model. We begin (Sect. 2) with a brief overview of the Daplex language itself, and discuss some of the compilation issues it presents. Section 3 then describes the architecture of our compiler, and how it has been divided into independent modules. Section 4 gives a description of the intermediate code format used to represent program code within P/FDM, and Section 5 gives some examples of the novel ways in which the compiler modules can be used to extend system functionality. Finally, we discuss some of the issues raised by the idea of modular architectures for database language compilers, including the slightly unusual role played by Prolog in our system (Sect. 6), and conclude (Sect. 7).

```
create private module unidb

declare person ->> entity
declare name(person) -> string
key_of person is name

declare lecturer ->> person

declare student ->> person

declare year(student) -> integer
declare course ->> entity
declare code(course) -> string
declare year(course) -> integer
key_of course is code

declare takes(student) ->> course
declare teaches(lecturer) ->> course;
```

**Fig. 1.** A simple university database schema

## 2 Overview of the Daplex Language

Daplex is a high-level, functional style language that was designed as a "conceptually natural" interface to the Functional Data Model [29]. It consists of two sub-languages—one for data definition (the DDL) and one for data manipulation (the DML). The DDL allows the specification of FDM schemas, and the classes and functions which they contain. The schema given in Fig. 1, for example, describes a simple university database with classes storing information about people (person) and courses (course). The person class is divided into two subclasses, student and lecturer. The attributes of each class are modelled as functions mapping instances of the argument class onto either single values of the result type (indicated by a single-headed arrow) or sets of such values (indicated by a double-headed arrow).

Programs in the DML consist of a specification of one or more sets of database values, followed by a sequence of operations (called "actions") which must be performed on the elements of the sets. For example, the following program updates the database to ensure that all third year students are registered for all third year courses, and displays details of the updates made:

```
for each s in student such that year(s) = 3
   for each c in course such that year(c) = 3
include c into takes(s)
print(name(s), 'now registered for course', code(c));
```

The examples given above illustrate the distinction between the DDL and DML sub-languages of Daplex. The two sub-languages are not completely disjoint, however, as fragments of DML may be embedded within schemas to define methods:

```
define num_courses(s in student) -> integer in unidb
    count(takes(s));
```

This DDL method definition uses a DML set specification (`count(takes(s))`) to describe the result of the num_courses function intensionally (rather than as a set of stored mappings). Another important distinction is that programs expressed in the DML are compiled (into Prolog) while DDL schemas are interpreted directly into calls to the data definition primitives of P/FDM. This difference can be seen clearly in the architectures of the two sub-language compilers, which share a common front-end but which have quite different back-ends.

Before we move on to the description of the modular compiler architecture, it is worthwhile to consider the ways in which Daplex differs from a conventional programming language, and what effect this has on the requirements for compiling such a language. Firstly, the separation of data definition and data manipulation in Daplex means that new data structures cannot be declared within a data manipulation program. This greatly simplifies the process of statically type checking programs, and eases the optimisation and analysis of DML code. In fact, our implementation of Daplex goes further than this in that data update (or state change of any kind) is restricted to the actions part of each DML program. So, for example, in the program given above, which registers third year students on third year courses, it would be illegal for either the update or the `print` statement to appear in front of or between the two `for each` loops. Set specifications, then, are kept completely free of side effects, in order that they may be treated as referentially transparent for optimisation and analysis purposes. This is true even when methods are called within set expressions, as the syntactic structure of Daplex forces users to declare whether methods are side-effect free or not when they are defined.

The implication of this separation of data definition and manipulation for the language compiler is that complex symbol tables need not be maintained during compilation. All data structure information is stored in an easily available form in the metadata, and may be accessed by the compiler at any time. Otherwise, we need only keep track of which variables are currently in scope, and what their type is, using a simple list structure.

The second point to note about the compilation of Daplex is that the target language (Prolog) is itself relatively high level. This means that many of the usual difficulties of code generation (such as register allocation, and run-time memory management) are not applicable to our compiler, with the result that issues for the design of our much higher-level intermediate code format are rather different than for a conventional compiler. This is discussed further in Sect. 4, where we look at the use of ZF-expressions for representing code.

Finally, we note that although our target language is dynamically typed, Daplex programs themselves are statically type-checked against the available metadata. This gives us the flexibility of Prolog's weak type system for system code, while giving the user the extra security of a strongly-typed language. Runtime type checks are built into the data manipulation primitives provided by P/FDM and therefore come free of compilation effort. There is admittedly some performance cost with this, as the run-time checks cannot be optimised and may be performed more times than is necessary, but this is a small overhead compared to the cost of executing each primitive.

## 3   The Modular Compiler Architecture

### 3.1   The Data Manipulation Language Compiler

The major building blocks which make up the Daplex compiler are essentially those which would be found in any standard programming language compiler [1]. The DML compiler, for example, consists of a pipeline of the following units:

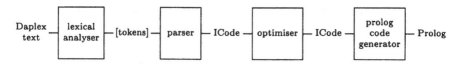

Each of these units is constructed as an independent module which may be called in isolation from any of the others. The **lexical analyser** accepts Daplex text as input and produces from this a list of lexical tokens. This list is passed on to the **parser** module, which uses Prolog's concise and flexible DCG rule facility to convert the input into an intermediate code format. In fact, the parser consists of two sub-modules:

The **syntactic & semantic analyser** parses the token list, and performs some basic semantic analysis and type checking. Its output is a parse tree, constructed of nested Prolog terms, which describes the entire input program. This is then passed to the **ICode generator**, which transforms the full parse tree into the simpler intermediate code format. This format, which we call ICode, is based upon ZF-notation [26, 18]. It retains the semantic content of the parse tree representation, while discarding much of the accounting and type information required only for parsing. It describes only the essential semantics of the input program, while the parse tree also contains information about exactly which syntactic constructs were used to express these semantics. A more detailed description of the intermediate code format is given in Sect. 4.

Once an ICode version of the program being compiled has been constructed, it is passed to the Daplex query optimiser [20, 21]. Like the parser, this module is split into sub-modules:

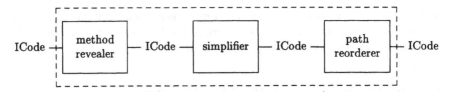

However, unlike the parser's sub-modules, each of these operates as a transformer from ICode to ICode, and is therefore a candidate for independent use. The first optimising sub-module, the **method revealer**, walks the given ICode structure looking for calls to intensionally defined functions (i.e. method functions), and, where possible, replaces each such function call with its intensional definition. This allows "global" optimisation of the query with, for example, removal of common sub-expressions from within method definitions [14, 21]. For example, the method revealer would replace the expression num_courses(s1) with:

    count(takes(s1))

This may require renaming of some duplicated variables, but is an otherwise straightforward process, since method bodies are stored in ICode format, ready for revelation.

Having revealed the definitions of all suitable method functions, the expanded ICode program is passed on to the **simplifier** sub-module. This module performs conventional optimisations, such as removal of common sub-expressions, and of invariants from within loops, producing a pared down version of the original program. This new version, still in ICode format, becomes the input of the last optimising sub-module, the **path reorderer**. This module performs the kinds of optimisations most commonly associated with database query languages, in that it uses accumulated statistics about the size of the various database classes, and a cost model of database access, to search for the cheapest way to navigate between the data items specified in the query. The result produced by this is a standard ICode representation of the program, except that the ordering of the individual components is now significant, in that it specifies the execution ordering chosen by the optimiser as being the best it could find.

The final module in the DML compiler is the **Prolog code generator**, which translates an ICode structure into a fragment of Prolog code that implements the required path semantics. The code generator module is order preserving, so that the relative ordering of the ICode constructs within the list is mirrored in the ordering of the goals in the resulting Prolog fragment. This is important as the ICode ordering is the only means of communicating the navigational path chosen by the path reorderer to the other modules.

This module completes the transformation of Daplex DML programs from text strings to Prolog goals. The resulting code fragments are either executed immediately and discarded, or are labelled and stored in the metadata for future use, according to the user's instructions.

## 3.2   The Data Definition Language Interpreter

The arrangement of compiler modules described above is specific to the DML. The interpreter for the Daplex DDL has the following alternative modular arrangement:

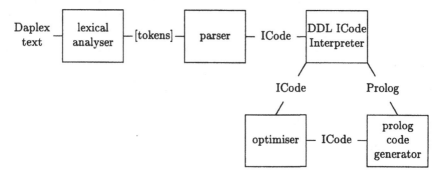

Here, the same lexical analyser and parser that were used in the DML compiler are reused to generate an ICode representation of the data to be defined. Once such a representation has been produced, it is passed to a new module, the **DDL ICode interpreter**. This module walks the input ICode, making appropriate calls to the data definition primitives of P/FDM as it goes. This otherwise straightforward process is complicated only by the need to handle method definitions and their embedded DML expressions. When an intensional definition is encountered by the DDL interpreter, it invokes the standard optimiser and code generator modules to generate a fragment of Prolog that will compute the result of the function, given its argument values. This code fragment is then passed to the relevant data definition primitive, along with the original ICode definition, for storage in the metadata.

From this we can see that the only real difference between the two language processors is the way in which the basic modules are connected together. Having implemented the Daplex DML compiler, we had only to add the new syntactic rules to the parser, and to build the interpretation module for the new ICode constructs, in order to build the DDL interpreter. The remaining modules were used unchanged. This was possible because we had standardised on an expressive but easily manipulable intermediate code format that could serve as a basis for the interchange of program semantics between modules, and as a "storable" but declarative representation for making behavioural information (i.e. methods) persist.

# 4 The Intermediate Code Format

The intermediate code format used in the current Daplex compiler is an extension of that designed for the original compiler [26], which was based on ZF-notation[1]. In this notation, a set is described by a pattern, giving the form of the elements of the set, and a declarative specification of what values are set members. For example, the set of third year students is described by the ZF-expression:

```
[ s | s ← student; year(s) = 3 ]
```

The pattern (here just the variable s) is given to the left of the '|' symbol, and the set specification to the right. Set specification consists of lists of *generators* for variables, having the form "var ← set", and predicates, called *restrictions*, which act as filters on the generated values. So our example set specification consists of a single generator, assigning student instances to the variable s, and a single restriction, filtering out those student instances whose **year** attributes evaluate to something other than the value 3.

The Daplex compiler uses a very similar form to this for representing sets. For example, the Daplex set:

```
s in student such that year(s) = 3
```

is represented internally by the ICode list:

```
[ generate(student, var(1)),
  restrict(year, [student], [var(1)], var(2)),
  expression(=, var(2), 3)
]
```

The **generate/2** term takes a class name and a variable, and corresponds to the ZF-expression generator construct. The restriction "**year(s) = 3**" is represented by the remaining two constructs. The set description would then be translated into the following fragment of Prolog:

```
( getentity(student, V1),
  getfnval(year, [V1], V2),
  V2 = 3
)
```

Here, **getentity/2** is the primitive provided for enumeration of class instances, with the result variable (V1) being bound to successive instance identifiers on backtracking. Similarly, **getfnval/3** takes a function name, a list of argument values and a result variable, and attempts to apply the function to produce the result. Thus, this fragment of Prolog, when executed, will bind the variable V1 to all **student** instances for which the **year** function evaluates to 3, one by one, on backtracking.

---

[1] This terminology is taken from [32]. Subsequently, the terms *list comprehension* and *set comprehension* have been applied to the same notation.

The intermediate code format contains constructs describing all the unique semantic concepts described by the Daplex DDL and DML, ranging from declarations of new schema elements:

```
declaration(SchemaName, NewSchemaElements, MethodFiles)
```

to DML imperatives, like the update example given on page 3:

```
imperative(InputVars, SetICode, ActionICode)
```

Our intention here is not to give a detailed description of our particular intermediate code format, but to give enough of a flavour to illustrate the features that are desirable in such a format, given the modular architecture described here. As it stands, our format lacks many of the control structures commonly found in more traditional languages (such as **while** and **repeat** loops) or any notion of destructive assignment to program variables, since Daplex itself lacks these features. There is no reason why structures to support these concepts could not be added to our intermediate format, although we would certainly lose some of the ease with which ICode can be analysed and transformed with the introduction of unrestricted state change. The important point is that, unlike other intermediate code formats (such as 3 place codes, or reverse polish notation), ICode retains most of the source code semantics explicitly. This makes regeneration of the original source program from the internal representation is relatively straightforward, but does not mean that we have had to sacrifice ease of code generation. It is admittedly not as compact as more conventional formats, but this is not a problem for us, as data manipulation programs are unlikely to grow to such a size that memory limitations become a significant factor—especially given the possibility of holding temporarily unused code on disk.

Because manipulation of ICode constructs is the principal task of most of the compiler modules, we have found it useful to construct a library of routines for analysing and manipulating ICode in common ways, and to provide these on the same basis as the callable compiler modules. This library consists of

- routines which test fragments of ICode for particular properties, e.g. whether a method function is called, or a particular variable is used.
- routines which compare arbitrary pieces of ICode, e.g. for equivalence up to code ordering, or for inclusion of one fragment of ICode within another.
- routines which transform arbitrary ICode fragments, e.g. creating a copy of the given ICode in which every variable is replaced by a new variable guaranteed to be unused in the current compilation cycle. Another example routine takes an ICode representation of a predicate, and returns the ICode representation of its negation.

Any of these library routines can be used either in the construction of new compiler modules, or to prepare ICode as input for existing modules. For example, `reorder_icode(+ICode, -ReorderedICode)` is a library routine which orders the constructs in a given piece of ICode so that all variable dependencies are respected. This procedure can be used to prepare unoptimised (and therefore unordered) ICode for input to the Prolog code generator module.

# 5 A New Use for the Compiler Modules

The redesign of our Daplex compiler as a collection of independently callable modules has already proved its value in the ease with which it has allowed us to make extensions to the functionality of the P/FDM system. In order to demonstrate this point, we will describe one of these new features in some detail, and outline a couple of other extensions which have made use of the compiler modules.

The extension we shall present in detail is the implementation of a new Daplex sub-language for the expression of semantic integrity constraints [10]. The Daplex DML already contains a rich set of constructs for describing predicates, including the standard universal and existential quantifiers (each, some and no), and three special numerical quantifiers (at most <n>, at least <n> and exactly <n>). For example, the following is the Daplex expression of the constraint that no student may take a course from a year higher than the student's year:

```
constrain each s in student
so that no c in takes(s) has year(c) > year(s);
```

We have reused the existing syntactic constructs in the constraint language, in order to keep it as close to the DML as possible. This not only has the advantage of allowing database designers to specify constraints in a language with which they are already familiar, but it also means that we can reuse the existing ICode constructs for quantified predicates as the internal representation for integrity constraints.

For each constraint, the compiler must generate a fragment of Prolog code that will check the entire database for validity relative to that constraint. This code is executed before the constraint is accepted by the DBMS, as we do not want to allow integrity constraints which are already violated when they are defined. It is also executed whenever a disabled constraint is re-enabled (to ensure that the constraint has not been violated while disabled), and is therefore stored in the metadata for future use. The constraint language compiler must also work out which update events may cause a violation of the constraint, and produce fragments of Prolog code to check the validity of the constraint for each such update [2]. For a certain class of constraints, the compiler is able to produce checking fragments which perform the minimum of retrieval required, while for the rest it uses a much simpler code generation strategy but produces more inefficient code.

Here, then, is the modular arrangement of the constraint sub-language compiler:

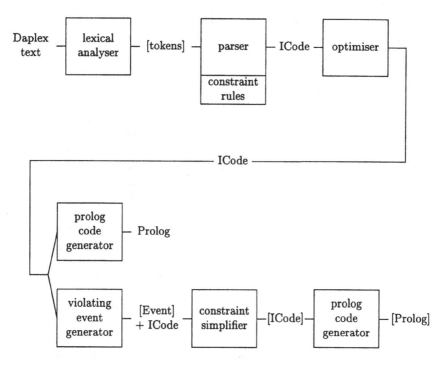

The lexical analyser, optimiser sub-modules and Prolog code generator modules have all been reused *unchanged* in the constraint language compiler. The parser module has been extended with three new syntax rules (and two of the existing rules have been modified) to allow the use of the new keyword `constrain`, to introduce quantified predicates as constraint declarations.

The Prolog code generator module appears in two places in the compiler's architecture because it is performing two different compilation tasks. Its first use is to translate the ICode representation of the constraint into the check for validity of the entire database—which it does by translating the optimised representation of the constraint into Prolog as if it were an ordinary DML predicate. In fact, if we were not concerned about efficiency of constraint checking, we could have implemented the entire constraint compiler with no new modules at all, since the standard compiler modules are all that is needed to generate legal (but inefficient) constraint checking code.

Not surprisingly, then, the two new modules are concerned with minimising the number of times constraints are checked (the **violating event generator**) and the amount of work required for each check (the **constraint simplifier**). The task of this module is to transform the constraint into pieces of ICode which describe, for each update event, the minimum check needed to test validity of the constraint relative to that update. Since the result of this module is a collection of legal ICode fragments, we can call the existing Prolog code generator once more, to generate the Prolog code that will actually perform the simplified check. This code can then be stored in the metadata for execution when data is updated. In addition, we record the ICode representation of the constraint, and the details of the events which may violate it. This information is required primarily for efficient location of constraint checks at run-time, but it is also useful for maintaining the consistency of the metadata during schema evolution (for example, deleting constraint checks when constraints are deleted, deleting constraints when schema elements they depend on are deleted).

The constraint compiler illustrates how our modular approach allows us to change the semantics of how Daplex code is translated, by inserting modules which transform the ICode before the code generation stage. We have also been able to produce compilers for new target languages, SQL [23, 17] and CHIP [11], by plugging in new code generation modules. These are not just simple isomorphic changes of format. In one case, we are changing to a very different, relational storage schema. In the other, we are introducing a radically different execution strategy involving non-deterministic search over constraints. Nonetheless, in both cases we were able to reuse a great deal of the existing compiler, and share the same metadata structures.

However, as we have said, the modular approach not only has the advantage of encouraging code reuse in compiler development; it also opens up new possibilities for the run-time manipulation of program code by DBMSs. For example, if there are many constraints to be checked after a particular update, it would be possible to extract the ICode versions of each constraint check from the metadata, join them all together in a conjunction, and then optimise the conjunction as a whole, before converting it into Prolog for execution. This would remove any duplicated expressions and avoid redundant checking. Along similar lines, another possibility for run-time manipulation of code by the DBMS might be the automatic re-optimisation of method code overnight. Methods (like all Daplex programs) are optimised to take the cheapest path relative to the database statistics known at compile-time. However, over time, these statistics will change as the database is updated, and the path chosen for evaluation of methods may become inefficient. Under our modular architecture, the DBMS could re-optimise methods likely to have been affected by database updates overnight, so that the user always runs code that is tuned for the current database statistics[2].

## 6   Discussion

The nearest neighbours to our modular compiler are the persistent languages we began with, which have been extended with the notion of linguistic reflection [30] in order to overcome the limitations of static type checking for certain applications. While the earliest extensions used strings to represent the code to be

---

[2] A similar idea to this has been proposed for persistent programming environments by Cutts [7].

manipulated at run-time (i.e. the source language text), later implementations have realised the limitations of this approach and have moved towards the two-way split of the compiler that allows the internal form of the code to be accessed by the calling program [7, 12]. As we have seen, this is certainly an improvement over a flat source text representation, although it still falls short of the flexibility of the full modular approach. Extra transformations may be inserted into the compilation process, but only at one point (where the front end and the back end are divided), and there is no possibility of dropping phases of the standard translation, or of reordering them.

Certainly there is nothing in principle to prevent the callable compilers provided by these persistent languages from being implemented as a collection of independent modules. It is doubtful, however, whether such systems could take full advantage of the modular approach, since the possibilities for analysis and transformation of such low-level, procedural code are much more limited than for a high-level, declarative data manipulation language, with all the semantic support offered by a well-defined data model. This is the pay-off for the loss of low-level performance improvements in a language such as Daplex. In a DBMS context, we also benefit in that all important metadata generated during the compilation process is retained in an easily accessible, persistent form, for use by later invocations of the compiler modules, or by other system components. This is a completely different philosophy from that underlying the construction of standard programming language compilers, in which symbol tables and other internal structures are designed for use by one process (the compiler) in the course of a single invocation.

A modular approach has also been suggested for extensible database systems (e.g. EXODUS [4] and GENESIS [3]), in order to allow the creation of DBMS's which are tailored to the needs of specific applications. However, extensibility of language components in such systems has focussed almost exclusively on query optimisers [15, 19, 25, 27, 28] rather than on compilers in general. Some of these optimisers (the Starburst optimiser [19], for example) have been implemented along similar lines to our compiler, with components of the optimiser operating as transformers on a common internal format, while others (such as the Volcano Optimiser Generator [15]) take a rule-based approach, and confine their modularity to rule-independence. The aim of these extensible systems, whether DBMS's or query optimisers, is either to allow the construction of customised components, or to facilitate the introduction of new facilities and implementation techniques into existing systems. While our own architecture shares these advantages to some degree, we are also interested in providing modular components for use by the DBMS itself, and it is for this reason that we believe that the modular approach is so attractive for data manipulation language compilers.

The success of the modular compiler architecture advocated in this paper depends critically on the availability of a suitable intermediate code format. Such a format must be:

- expressive, i.e. able to encode all the semantics expressible by the source language—at as high a level as is consistent with the other requirements.
- easy to generate from the source code, and (more importantly) easy to convert to executable code. The latter transformation is the more important of the two as it will potentially be made more often than the parsing transformation, which should ideally occur only one per code fragment. However, this requirement should not be achieved at the expense of the semantic content of the format.
- easy for the DBMS's internal code to construct and deconstruct.
- suitable for theoretically verifiable analysis and transformation (e.g. for optimisation).
- most importantly, well-defined and stable. If an intermediate code format is to be published as the accepted means of communication between modules, then programmers making independent use of these modules must be confident that they will be shielded from changes to that format, and that the interface between modules will remain static.

The intermediate code format described in this paper satisfies all these requirements. It is unusual in that it is relatively close to both the source language (Daplex) and the target language (Prolog), although this is probably due to the high-level of the target language. It is certainly easy to analyse and transform, and has been shown to be amenable to all the major optimising transformations proposed for relational query languages [31]. Moreover, it is computationally complete, and is therefore more expressive than relational algebra—the traditional intermediate format for database query languages. Finally, it has a formally-defined semantics, based on the $\lambda$-calculus [8].

We have also benefited greatly from the choice of Prolog as the implementation language for the compiler modules. The advantages of Prolog for traditional compiler writing have already been documented [34, 5] but we have found the language to be particularly congenial for the kinds of high-level code transformations required by the modular compiler architecture. The ease with which complex data structures can be constructed and manipulated means that it is as easy, if not easier, to program directly with ICode structures than with Daplex text strings. This is not true in a conventional language, in which code must be represented internally by some complex data structure, unless some specialised program editor was being used which could provide a view of the source text version of the data structure, for the programmer to manipulate [24]. Moreover, it is equally convenient to work with partially-instantiated ICode structures in Prolog, which means that the compiler (or whatever) does not have to commit itself to details of the generated code or to postpone operations until it has the required information.

But perhaps most significant has been the use of Prolog's searching and pattern-matching abilities. These allow us to build templates as partially instantiated ICode fragments, and then ask Prolog to search for matches within a given piece of ICode. Prolog will return a fully instantiated copy of the template for each match found. For example, the following code fragment indicates how we can retrieve a list of all constructs which generate values for a particular variable (V) occurring in a fragment of ICode (ICode):

```
findall(Generator, (
    member(Generator, [generate(_, V),
                       generate(_, _, _, _, V), ...]),
    icode_member(Generator, ICode)
), Generators).
```

Thus, we are using Prolog as a language for *unification programming* [21], rather than for logic programming *per se*. Certainly, it is these features (i.e. non-determinism and unification) which appear to give Prolog the edge over other declarative languages, in which working with partial data structures is not supported. Prolog's weak and dynamic typing system is also an advantage for the systems programmer dealing with highly complex data structures like our ICode format, particularly as it allows new constructs to be added to the format without affecting the validity of the code which uses the unexpanded version.

## 7  Conclusions

We have described the architecture of a compiler for the Daplex language, which is composed of independently callable modules, each implementing some transformation over well-defined inputs and outputs. The modules currently implemented are:

- lexical analyser: text → token list
- parser: token list → ICode
- optimiser: ICode → ICode
  - method revealer: ICode → ICode
  - simplifier: ICode → ICode
  - path reorderer: ICode → ICode
- prolog code generator: ICode → Prolog
- DDL ICode interpreter: ICode
- violating event generator: ICode → [Event]
- constraint simplifier: [Event] + ICode → [ICode]

Of course, a modular design for a compiler is really a natural consequence of the application of good software engineering principles, and certainly our re-designed compiler has proved to be easier both to maintain and extend than its earlier incarnation. But the real benefit of the modular architecture (and the main contribution of this paper) is that it provides a set of basic building blocks for manipulating units of the language, which can be combined in different ways in order to perform different functions. This opens up the possibility of much faster compiler development for new sub-languages (as we have found in practice with our constraint language compiler in Sect. 5) and also of novel ways of manipulating code fragments at run-time, giving the DBMS almost the same basic capabilities as the database maintenance programmer in terms of code manipulation.

The implementation of the modular compiler required a certain amount of discipline, both in designing the intermediate format, which acts as a communication protocol between modules, and in ensuring that each module is truly independent and does not rely on any side effects being made by other modules. But we were helped in this by our choice of implementation language, as Prolog lends itself readily to the idea of passing complex data structures as parameters to procedures, to be taken apart by the unification mechanism. In addition, the availability of the DBMS's metadata as a store of information about the available data types (i.e. schema elements) means that there is no need to clutter the module interfaces with more parameters by which to communicate this information—yet another reason why the modular architecture is so well suited to the database environment.

In standard compiler technology, the use of an intermediate language is recognised as being an important factor in improving the portability of the resulting system [35]. This is because changes in the compiler caused by target language differences will be localised in the routines which translate the intermediate code into the final executable code. Similarly, in DBMSs, the use of an intermediate representation for stored code insulates the system from changes in the external environment; when the version of the programming language used as the target for the database compiler changes, or even when the language itself changes, it will only be necessary to insert a new code generation module into the compiler. All code retrieved from disk after this will automatically be recompiled to the new target language. This is a view of code that will become increasingly common, as we move towards new uses of database technology in distributed system and distributed knowledge bases:

> "... we must take seriously the proposition that some data is so long-lived that it may well outlast the programming languages currently in fashion. Thus, we must beware of the legacy problems caused by having fragments of code, compiled by elderly compilers for aging languages, existing in large OODB or knowledge bases. There are already problems of legacy software, where people dare not replace procedures or change data formats, since they do not know what side effects this may have. By hanging on to knowledge as high-level constraints and code-generating it for new forms of storage organisation we keep it fresh and active." [16]

The modular compiler architecture described in this paper takes a first step towards providing the programmer support that will be required to implement database systems with these kinds of capability. The code manipulation facilities discussed here will also play in important role in regaining the performance lost in the move away from tightly-compiled low-level code to high-level declarative representations. This will be achieved by making more use of semantics to perform "global" optimisations not possible for systems restricted to dealing with low-level code fragments.

# Acknowledgements

The DML and DDL compilers described in this paper are based on an original compiler implemented by Norman Paton, who also designed the intermediate code format of which ours is an extension. This original compiler was rewritten by Graham Kemp and Zhuoan Jiao, and the authors would like to thank them for their patience and help in re-implementing the compiler yet again according to the architecture described here. This work has also benefited from discussions with Scott Leishman, and from the thoughtful comments of the anonymous referees. Suzanne Embury is supported by a grant from the EPSRC.

# References

1. A.H. Aho, R. Sethi, and JD. Ullman. *Compilers - Principles, Methods and Tools.* Addison Wesley, Reading, Massachusetts, USA, 1985.
2. N. Bassiliades and P.M.D Gray. CoLan: a Functional Constraint Language and Its Implementation. *Data and Knowledge Engineering*, 14:203–249, 1994.
3. D.S. Batory, T.Y. Leung, and T.E. Wise. Implementation Concepts for an Extensible Data Model and Data Language. *ACM Transactions on Database Systems*, 13(3):231–262, September 1988.
4. M.J. Carey, D.J. DeWitt, D. Frank, G. Graefe, M. Muralikrishna, J.E. Richardson, and E.J. Shekita. Tha Architecture of the EXODUS Extensible DBMS. In K. Dittrich and U. Dayal, editors, *International Workshop on Object-Oriented Database Systems*, pages 52–65, Pacific Grove, September 1986. IEEE Computer Society Press.
5. J. Cohen and T.J. Hickey. Parsing and Compiling Using Prolog. *ACM Transactions on Programming Languages and Systems*, 9(2):125–163, April 1987.
6. R.L. Cooper, M.P. Atkinson, A. Dearle, and D. Abderrahmane. Constructing Database Systems in a Persistent Environment. In P.M. Stocker, W. Kent, and P. Hammersley, editors, *Proceedings of the 13th VLDB Conference*, pages 117–125, Brighton, 1987. Morgan Kaufmann Publishers, Inc.
7. Q.I. Cutts, R.C.H. Connor, G.N.C. Kirby, and R. Morrison. An Execution-Driven Approach to Code Optimisation. Technical Report FIDE/94/99, FIDE Technical Report, 1994.
8. S.M. Embury. A Formal Semantics for the Daplex Language. Technical Report AUCS/TR9504, University of Aberdeen, Dept. of Computing Science, King's College, Aberdeen, U.K., October 1995. Accessible as http://www.csd.abdn.ac.uk/~pfdm/postscript/embury.1995b.ps.
9. S.M. Embury. User Manual for P/FDM V.9.1. Technical Report AUCS/TR9501, Dept. of Computing Sc., University of Aberdeen, U.K., AB9 2UE, January 1995. Accessible as http://www.csd.abdn.ac.uk/~pfdm/postscript/user.manual.ps.
10. S.M. Embury and P.M.D. Gray. Compiling a Declarative, High-Level Language for Semantic Integrity Constraints. In R. Meersman and L. Mark, editors, *Proceedings of 6th IFIP TC-2 Working Conference on Data Semantics*, Atlanta, USA, May 1995. Chapman and Hall.
11. S.M. Embury and P.M.D. Gray. Planning Complex Updates to Satisfy Constraint Rules Using a Constraint Logic Search Engine. In T. Sellis, editor, *Proceedings of 2nd International Workshop on Rules in Database Systems (RIDS'95)*, LNCS No. 985, pages 230–244, Glyfada, Athens, Greece, September 1995. Springer-Verlag.

12. A. Farkas and A. Dearle. Octopus: a Reflective Language Mechanism for Object Manipulation. In C. Beeri, A. Ohori, and D.E. Shasha, editors, *Proceedings of the Fourth International Workshop on Database Programming Languages – Object Models and Languages*, pages 50–64, Manhattan, New York City, August 1993. Springer-Verlag.

13. J.W. Goodwin. Why Programming Environments Need Dynamic Data Types. In D.R. Barstow, H.E. Shrobe, and E. Sandewall, editors, *Interactive Programming Environments*, Frontier Series, pages 414–425. McGraw-Hill Book Company, 1984.

14. G. Graefe and D. Maier. Query Optimisation in Object-Oriented Database Systems: a Prospectus. In *Advances in Object-Oriented Database Systems: Proc. OODBS-II*, 1988.

15. G. Graefe and W.J. McKenna. The Volcano Optimizer Generator: Extensibility and Efficient Search. In *Proceedings of the Ninth International Conference on Data Engineering (ICDE)*, pages 209–218, Vienna, Austria, April 1993. IEEE Computer Society.

16. P.M.D. Gray. Knowledge Reuse through Networks of Large KBS. In D. Bowers, editor, *Proceedings of 12th British National Conference on Databases*, LNCS 826, pages 13–22. Springer-Verlag, July 1994.

17. P.M.D. Gray and G.J.L. Kemp. Object-Oriented Systems and Data Independence. In D. Patel, Y. Sun, and S. Patel, editors, *Proc. 1994 International Conference on Object Oriented Information Systems*, pages 3–24, London, December 1994. Springer-Verlag.

18. P.M.D. Gray, K.G. Kulkarni, and N.W. Paton. *Object-Oriented Databases: a Semantic Data Model Approach*. Prentice Hall Series in Computer Science. Prentice Hall International Ltd., 1992.

19. L.M. Haas, J.C. Freytag, G.M. Lohman, and H. Pirahesh. Extensible Query Processing in Starburst. In J. Clifford, B. Lindsay, and D. Maier, editors, *SIGMOD 89 Conference*, pages 377–388, Portland, Oregon, 1989. ACM Press.

20. Z. Jiao. *Optimisation Studies in a Prolog Object-Oriented Database*. PhD thesis, University of Aberdeen, Aberdeen, Scotland, November 1992.

21. Z. Jiao and P.M.D. Gray. Optimisation of Methods in a Navigational Query Language. In C. Delobel, M. Kifer, and Y. Masunaga, editors, *Second International Conference on Deductive and Object-Oriented Databases*, pages 22–42, Munich, December 1991. Springer-Verlag.

22. P. Kanellakis and J.W. Schmidt, editors. *Proceedings of the Third International Workshop on Database Programming Languages – Bulk Types and Persistent Data*, Nafplion, Greece, August 1991. Morgan Kaufmann Publishers, Inc.

23. G.J.L. Kemp, J.J. Iriarte, and P.M.D. Gray. Efficient Access to FDM Objects Stored in a Relational Database. In D.S. Bowers, editor, *Directions in Databases: Proceedings of the Twelfth British National Conference on Databases (BNCOD 12)*, pages 170–186. Springer-Verlag, 1994.

24. G.N.C. Kirby, R.C.H. Connor, and R. Morrison. START: a Linguistic Reflection Tool Using Hyper-Program Technology. Technical Report FIDE/94/96, FIDE Technical Report, 1994.

25. G. Mitchell, U. Dayal, and S.B. Zdonik. Control of an Extensible Query Optimizer: A Planning-Based Approach. In R. Agrawal, S. Baker, and D. Bell, editors, *Proceedings of the 19th VLDB Conference*, pages 517–528, Dublin, 1993. Morgan Kaufmann Publishers, Inc.

26. N.W. Paton and P.M.D. Gray. Optimising and Executing Daplex Queries Using Prolog. *The Computer Journal*, 33:547–555, 1990.

27. A. Rosenthal and U.S. Chakravarthy. Anatomy of a Modular Multiple Query Optimiser. In F. Bancilhon and D.J. DeWitt, editors, *Proceedings of the 14th VLDB Conference*, pages 230–239, Los Angeles, 1988. Morgan Kaufmann Publishers, Inc.

28. E. Sciore and J. Sieg, Jr. A Modular Query Optimiser Generator. In *Proceedings of the Sixth International Conference on Data Engineering (ICDE)*, pages 146–153, Los Angeles, California, USA, February 1990. IEEE Computer Society.

29. D.W. Shipman. The Functional Data Model and the Data Language DAPLEX. *ACM Transactions on Database Systems*, 6(1):140–173, March 1981.

30. D. Stemple, R. Morrison, and M.P. Atkinson. Type-Safe Linguistic Reflection. In Kanellakis and Schmidt [22], pages 357–360.

31. P. Trinder. Comprehensions, a Query Notation for DBPLs. In Kanellakis and Schmidt [22], pages 55–68.

32. D.A. Turner. Miranda: a Non-Strict Functional Language with Polymorphic Types. In J.-P. Jouannaud, editor, *Proceedings of the IFIP Int. Conf. on Functional Programming Languages and Computer Architecture*, Lecture Notes in Computing Science, Vol. 201, pages 1–16, Nancy, France, September 1985. Springer-Verlag.

33. Universities of Glasgow and St. Andrews Technical Report PPRR-12-88. *PS-Algol Reference Manual*, 1988. 4th edition.

34. D.S. Warren. Logic Programming and Compiler Writing. *Software — Practice and Experience*, 10(2):97–125, 1980.

35. D.A. Watt. *Programming Language Processors*. Prentice Hall International, 1993.

# Querying Graph Databases Using a Functional Language Extended with Second Order Facilities

Robert Ayres[1] and Peter J H King[2]

[1] Brunel University, Department of Computer Science and Information Systems,
Uxbridge, Middlessex UB8 3PH, United Kingdom
email Robert.Ayres@brunel.ac.uk
[2] Birkbeck College, University of London, Department of Computer Science, Malet
Street, London WC1E 7HX, United Kingdom
email UBACW02@dcs.bbk.ac.uk

**Abstract.** This paper presents the functional database language Hydra which extends previous such languages with *associational* facilities enabling a user to pose queries about the ways in which values and entities in the database are related to each other. These associational facilities work by treating the database as a graph and following all the arcs from a node or finding paths between nodes. The nodes of the database graph correspond to entities or values in the application domain and the arcs to associations between those entities and values. From the perspective of Hydra this database graph is viewed in terms of functions between sets of entities and values. Associational facilities are provided by built-in second-order primitives which use schema-level information to determine what arcs may be associated with a node or as the basis for searching for an instance-level path. Results from associational primitives are returned in the form of lists of functions which may be displayed to the user or directly applied to other parameters. The associational facilities provided are fully integrated into a computationally complete language in the style of Miranda. This integration allows complex queries to be answered, which are beyond the power of conventional database query languages.

*Keywords* Graph-databases, functional databases, functional programming, semantic networks.

## 1 Introduction

In this paper we present Hydra, a functional database programming language which has been extended with second order facilities, and show how these facilities may be used to express and answer queries which are beyond the power of conventional database query languages. The motivation for the design and development of Hydra came from considering the needs of non-standard database applications, such as criminal intelligence systems, where the information held is non-homogeneous and where the connections between entities are likely to form the object of queries.

Conventional database systems are not well adapted to querying data which has an inherently graphical form. This is due to a combination of inappropriate data models and inadequate query languages. Currently most databases are based on record-oriented data models which have a number of semantic inadequacies [Ken79]. Such models do not provide support for object identity and the associations between entities and values are not explicitly modelled or recorded. For example the fact that someone has age 29 may be recorded by the appearance of 29 as an attribute in a particular record. However the relationship between the entity modelled by the record and the value 29 cannot be directly retrieved. This means that record-oriented data models provide no direct support for applications where there is a need to model a network of entities and connections between them. In object-oriented systems the problem of identity is addressed by the use of surrogates [HOT76] but there is still no explicit modelling of links between entities or values. Moreover most query languages implemented over such data models provide no support for path-related queries.

In order to properly model the semantics of many real world applications a graph-based data model is preferable. In such a model entities and values form the nodes in a graph and the associations between those values are represented by arcs between the nodes. Graph-based data models include the Binary-Relational Model [Abr74] and the Functional Data Model [Shi81]. In these models entities are represented by surrogates and relationships between entities and values by binary-relations or functions respectively. The distinction between the ways in which attributes (values associated with an entity) and relationships (associations between entities) are represented disappears — all associations are modelled uniformly through the use of binary-relations or functions. Note that the use of graph-based data models results in no loss of expressive power compared to record-based models — any $n$-ary relation can always be reexpressed in terms of $n + 1$ binary-relations or simple functions.

In the database query language FQL [BFN82] the functional view of data is used along with functional programming techniques to obtain a powerful database query language. The complete integration of a functional database with a functional language was first achieved in FDL [PK90]. In FDL the database schema and contents are expressed in terms of function declarations and definitions. Functions may be defined both extensionally and intensionally and may be incrementally updated thus achieving a complete integration of data and computation.

Functional database languages such as FDL are computationally complete in the sense that they provide equivalent computational power to the $\lambda$-calculus. However the $\lambda$-calculus is a theory of anonymous functions whereas in a functional database information is represented using named functions. Moreover the names of these functions carry semantics. Consequently the criterion of computational completeness is not, of itself, sufficiently strong to ensure that all queries a user might ask can be answered. For instance the question

What is the connection (if any) between John and 29?

corresponds, in a functional database, to a query to find a function which when applied to the surrogate representing *John* returns the result 29. For example, the function **age** would be an answer if, in the database, *John* were defined to have age 29. Queries such as this are second order since they are quantified over all functions in the database and are not supported in conventional query languages.

The database language Hydra, presented in this paper, contains a number of built-in, second order primitives which allow queries about the ways in which database values are connected to be answered. We term such facilities and queries which use them **associational**. These queries are answered by treating the database as a graph in which nodes represent entities or values and arcs correspond to associations between entities. The queries we seek to support entail following all the paths from a node or finding paths between nodes.

Support for finding schema-level links or paths between types is provided in EFDM [AK84] where such paths are displayed to the user when a new function is declared. This facility is intended to help users avoid adding redundant functions and is not integrated into the query language. Thus the EFDM facility cannot be used to inspect the presence of paths between entities in the instance-level data. Recently some systems, such as GraphLog [CM90] have been developed which emphasize the graphical nature of certain types of data. However such systems are essentially graphical front ends to logic programs and provide a visual metaphor for clausal logic rather than new functionality.

In the rest of this paper we first give an overview of the main features of Hydra, we then present an extended example of how the integration of the associational facilities of Hydra with general functional programming facilities allows us to program database queries which carry out searches for associations between entities. Finally we present our conclusions.

## 2 Overview of Hydra

Hydra is a computationally complete functional database language. In the overview below we concentrate on the features which are necessary to understand our example of the use of Hydra's associational facilities. A general presentation is given in [Ayr95].

### 2.1 The Organisation of Data

In Hydra data is organised according to the Binary-Relational Model — that is as sets of atomic values linked by binary relations [Abr74]. Since Hydra is a functional language this data is defined and accessed from a functional perspective. Thus the database is viewed at the language level in terms of atomic values associated by functions of a single parameter. Any binary relation $R$ over two sets $A$ and $B$ can be viewed in terms of a function from one set to the powerset of the other. This function, $f$ say, of type $A \rightarrow \mathcal{P}(B)$ may be defined for any parameter $x$ as $f(x) = \{y|(x,y) \in R\}$. The definition of the function $f$ corresponds to following the relation $R$ "forwards" — we can also envisage a function induced by following it in the other direction. We call such functions **inverses** and, in Hydra, they are denoted by prefixing a function name with a tilde sign. Thus the function $\sim f$ is defined as $\sim f(x) = \{z|(z,x) \in R\}$. When the underlying relation $R$ itself represents a partial function then the relation can be represented directly as a function of type $A \rightarrow B$. Thus a relation such as **children** (associating a parent with an arbitrary number of children) induces a set-valued function, whereas a relation such as **age** (associating each person in the database with at most one integer value) induces an ordinary function. We use the terms multi-valued function and single-valued function to distinguish between these two cases. Note that in Hydra all inverses are considered to be multi-valued. Thus although the data is modelled using a Binary-Relational model the view of the data presented at the language-level is closer to that of the Functional Data Model [Shi81].

## 2.2 Data Definition and Retrieval

The atomic values which may appear in the database graph are either surrogates representing application entities or are values drawn from one of the built-in types integer, string, and boolean. Surrogates are organised into classes according to the kind of application entities which they are being used to represent. One or more entity classes may be introduced using the keyword **entity**, thus the statement:

    entity person, location;

introduces classes of surrogates to represent persons and locations. Application entities are represented by visible surrogates which must begin with an uppercase letter. The statement:

    location ::+ KingGeorge, SmallBillsGarage, WhiteSwan;

adds three new surrogates to the class **location**. The extent of an entity class is dynamic — further entities may be added, or removed as with the statement:

    location ::- WhiteSwan;

which removes **WhiteSwan** from the class **location**. Surrogates may also be generated by the system or modified — these features are described in [AK95].

Application data is represented by a set of functions called **primary functions**. For example information about where people work may be captured by a primary function **works_at** from **person** to **location** declared as follows:

    primary works_at :: person -> location;

This function associates at most one location with a person. Note that, in contrast to DAPLEX, function names may not be overloaded.

Where more than one entity or value may be associated a multi-valued function is used. Thus a function recording the locations people frequent may be declared as follows:

```
primary frequents :: person -> [location];
```

Note that at the storage level such functions are held in a form which implies no ordering of the results which they return. However since the locations returned by the application of **frequents** to a person will appear in an arbitrary though consistent order, the function is viewed as being list-valued at the level of the Hydra language. Primary functions must be consistent with the binary relational model, that is they must associate a single atomic value with either one or an arbitrary number of atomic attributes.

The set of declarations of primary functions define a database schema. Thus the declarations above along with the following declarations:

```
primary associate :: person  -> [person];
primary relative  :: person  -> [person];
primary age       :: person  -> int;
primary address   :: location -> string;
```

form part of the schema of a criminal intelligence database as shown in Figure 1, where multi-valued functions are represented by arcs with double-headed arrows.

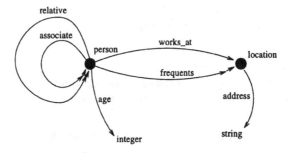

**Fig. 1.** Schema of a Criminal Intelligence Database

The definitions of primary functions correspond to the instance-level database. To record that a person Joyce works at the King George pub the defining equation:

```
works_at Joyce  = KingGeorge;
```

is entered. Primary functions may be defined by a mixture of extensional and intensional equations. Thus we can define general values for primary functions which will hold in the absence of a particular defining equation. For instance we can use a variable parameter (which must begin with a lowercase letter) as in:

```
age x = 21;
```

to define the default age for any person to be 21. Primary functions may be incrementally defined or modified thus entering the equation:

```
age Joyce = 39;
```

defines the age of Joyce as 39. An equation may be removed from a primary function definition by entering an equation with no right hand side. Thus:

```
age Joyce = ;
```

removes the age held for Joyce and:

```
age x = ;
```

removes the default age equation.

Since extensional equations for multi-valued functions (such as **associate** and **frequents** in our example) are stored in unordered format it is possible to modify *extensional* equations for those functions using set-oriented operations. For example the statement:

```
associate  Richard =+ Mary, Ronald, Sean;
```

adds **Mary**, **Ronald** and **Sean** to the set of **Richard**'s associates. Further associates may be added or removed. For instance:

```
associate  Richard =- Sean;
```

removes **Sean** from the set of **Richard**'s associates.

Information is retrieved by applying primary functions to parameters. The application of a primary function to a parameter is evaluated using best-fit pattern-matching. Hence to evaluate the query:

```
associate Richard;
```

the system first looks for defining equations with **Richard** on their left hand side. In this instance it will find that **Richard** has the two associates **Mary** and **Ronald** and the result will be returned as a list such as:

```
[Mary, Ronald]
```

Note that the order of elements in this list is arbitrary but consistent between changes to the database. Had the system found no precise match for the parameter **Richard** it would then have searched for a general defining equation of the form:

```
associate x = ... ;
```

If no matching pattern is found then an empty list would be returned. When pattern-matching fails for a single-valued function the evaluator returns the null-value — denoted by ?? in Hydra.

Application of a primary function to a value can be thought of as following the instance level arcs forwards. We may also follow these arcs backwards by using an inverse function. These are automatically maintained by the Hydra system and are obtained by prefixing the function name with a tilde. Hence the query `~works_at KingGeorge;` returns a list of people who work at the King George pub. Inverse functions such as `~works_at` are always list-valued.

## 2.3  General Computational Facilities

Primary functions along with entity classes are sufficiently expressive to model application data but not powerful enough to express general computation. To provide computational facilities Hydra provides a separate class of functions called **secondary** functions.

Since secondary functions are provided for computation and data-structure manipulation their declarations and definitions are not constrained by data model considerations. As with primary functions, a secondary function must be declared before its definition is given. Thus a general polymorphic function to append two lists may be declared as:

```
secondary append :: ['a] -> ['a] -> ['a];
```

where 'a is a polymorphic type variable. The definition of a secondary function must be given in one go and cannot be upated. Separate patterns in the definition are separated by a vertical bar, thus:

```
append (x:xs) ys = x : append xs ys |
append    [] ys = ys                 ;
```

where : is the infix list-constructor. Pattern matching for secondary functions is top to bottom, each pattern being tried in turn until a match is found or the function returns a null value.

Hydra also supports user-defined types which, although they do not form part of the data model, can be used along with the general computational facilities provided by secondary functions. User-defined types may be polymorphic or recursive. Thus a general tree type may be defined as:

```
tree 'a ::= Tree (tree 'a) (tree 'a)
          | Leaf 'a;
```

and `Tree (Tree (Leaf 1) (Leaf 2)) (Leaf 3)` is a value of type `tree int`. Secondary functions may be defined to manipulate such structures — for instance, the function `flatten` defined as:

```
secondary flatten :: (tree 'a) -> ['a];

flatten (Tree l r) = append (flatten l) (flatten r) |
flatten (Leaf x)   = [x]                            ;
```

uses pattern-matching on user-defined constructors and converts trees to lists.

In Hydra there is no difference between an expression which carries out computation and manipulation and one which is evaluated by accessing the database. Thus from a user perspective all functions behave in the same way when used in expressions or the defining bodies of functions and, provided no type constraints are violated, primary and secondary functions can be used interchangeably. Thus the default equation for a primary function lookfor_at of type person -> [string] which returns a list of addresses where someone might be found may be given as:

```
lookfor_at p = map address (works_at p : frequents p);
```

where map is a secondary function which applies a function to each element in a list.

Hydra supports list comprehension syntax. Thus the list of associates of Joyce who are over 21 is given by the comprehension:

```
[p | p <- associate Joyce | age p > 21];
```

which can be paraphrased as *Select all* p, *such that* p *is an associate of Joyce and the age of* p *is over 21.* List comprehensions are, like the select-from-where syntax of SQL, essentially syntactic variations on the notation used in Zermelo-Fraenkel set-theory. Since the notation was originally conceived for specifying sets it is well adapted for specifying queries on bulk data. Note however that list comprehensions differ from sets in that they specify a list, the order of whose elements is defined in terms of the results of the comprehension's sub-expressions.

## 2.4 Associational Facilities

Among the associational facilities of Hydra are two built-in functions from, and to. These primitives find all the primary functions which are applicable to a particular value. For instance, given the state of the schema shown in Figure 1, the expression:

```
from Richard;
```

returns the list:

```
[associate, relative, ml.age, ml.works_at, frequents]
```

of functions[3] which can be applied to the parameter Richard — that is primary functions with person domain. The single-valued functions age and works_at are coerced to be list-valued by composing them with the function ml, defined in the Hydra standard environment as follows:

---

[3] Note that when Hydra expressions are evaluated a reference to a named function is not replaced with its internal definition until it is applied to sufficient parameters to be reduced. This allows function names to be preserved after compilation and returned as results where appropriate.

```
secondary ml :: 'a -> ['a];

ml x = if (isnull x) [] [x];
```

where `isnull` returns `True` if applied to a null value. This coercion ensures that all the functions in the result list are themselves list-valued — this facilitates subsequent manipulation of the result. Similarly the built-in function `to` returns a list of all the inverse functions which can be applied to a value. Thus the expression:

```
to Richard;
```

returns the list:

```
[~associate, ~relative, ~works_at, ~frequents]
```

Both these primitives work by retrieving the type of their parameter and then inspecting the set of primary function declarations to find those functions which can be applied to the parameter. Were a user to declare a new function, such as:

```
primary leaseholder ::  location -> person;
```

then `to Richard;` would now return:

```
[~associate, ~relative, ~works_at, ~frequents, ~leaseholder]
```

reflecting the modified schema. Further associational primitives which are provided include `like` which retrieves database entities or values of the same type as its parameter, and `link` and `trail` which retrieve instance-level paths connecting database entities. These primitives are described in [Ayr95].

Some of the results returned by associational primitives are not well-typed according to the standard polymorphic type system used in most functional languages. This problem is resolved by the provision in Hydra of a new type called **universal**, denoted by a question-mark, which represents the union of all types. Thus a list such as:

```
[1, True, []]
```

has type `[?]` and the result returned by

```
from Richard;
```

is considered to have type `[person -> [?]]`. Support for such heteromorphic lists allows the database to be queried in ways which would not be possible within the framework of a conventional functional-programming style type system.

The universal type can be supported because type information is retained at run-time allowing the system to determine how each value in a heteromorphic result should be displayed. Several features of Hydra make use of this type information, including the equality test which can be used to compare values of any type. Thus:

```
1 == Richard
```

evaluates to **False** rather than giving rise to a type error. This interpretation of the equality test is required in order to allow the user to reason with and manipulate heteromorphic results. The use of the universal type means that type checking must be carried out on the basis of type-containment. This is similar to the approach needed in the presence of class-hierarchies [CP95, Mit91]. The type system and associated type checking algorithm are explained in [Ayr95].

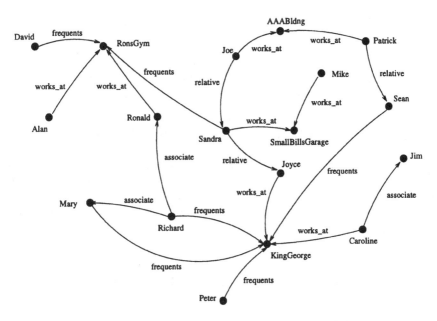

**Fig. 2.** Portion of Instance-Level of Criminal Intelligence Database

Associational facilities, along with type-heteromorphism, give a considerable increase of query power. Given a specific value or entity (node) we can retrieve all adjacent values or entities (nodes one arc away). Thus, given the database shown in Figure 2 the result of the list-comprehension

```
[(f, x) | f <- append (from Richard) (to Richard)
        | x <- f Richard];
```

is [(associate,Mary),(associate,Ronald),(frequents,KingGeorge)]. This query cannot be posed in other functional database languages since it is second-order, the primitives from and to are quantified over all primary functions, and its result is not well-typed according to the strict typing they employ. Second-order facilities permit queries to be formulated without a knowledge of function names – this facility is important in applications where the schema may be subject to frequent modification.

Associational queries, such as the one above, can be abstracted into functions. For example we can define a secondary function to find the nodes adjacent to a given database node as:

```
secondary adjacent :: ? -> [?];
```

```
adjacent x = [n | f <- append (from x) (to x) | n <- f x];
```

The query (adjacent Joe) would return:

```
[Sandra, AAABldng]
```

Note that the heteromorphic type of this function does not result in any type-insecurity since the type-checker ensures that heteromorphic results are never passed to functions unable to process them.

## 3   An Example of the Use of Associational Facilities

In this section we give an extended example to show how associational facilities can be used in conjunction with general functional programming techniques to answer queries which are beyond the power of conventional database query languages. In particular, the ability to treat the database as a network and follow any arcs from a node allows us to search for direct or indirect associations. Hence given a statement such as

*I saw Alan and Mike drinking in the King George pub with two other people. They left in a van with* AAA Building Contractors *written on the side.*

we can explore a database of criminal intelligence information to determine who the unknown people *might* be. To do this we reexpress the problem as follows:

- we have 4 known entities — **Alan, Mike, KingGeorge,** and **AAABldng,**
- we wish to search the database to find "candidates" for the 2 unknown entities. These candidate entities are those which are closest on aggregate to each of the known entities. We do this by assigning relative weights to nodes in the database graph according to their distance (in terms of number of arcs) from each of the known entities.

Below we show how associational primitives can be used to produce a list of weighted candidate entities. Our approach has three main parts:

200

- we first weight the nodes in the vicinity of a particular start node,
- we then combine the weighted nodes obtained from different start nodes,
- finally we sort by weight the list of nodes obtained so that the most likely
  "candidates" appear first.

**Weighting Nodes in the Vicinity of a Value** The component weights due
to a particular start node are assigned by first allocating a user-specified weight
to the start node and then propagating this value to other nodes in the vicinity
— decrementing it by 1 for each arc traversed, stopping when the weight reaches
0. Hence, given the instance-level database shown in Figure 2, if we assign the
node **David** the weight 3 then we would give **RonsGym** the weight 2 and **Alan,
Ronald**, and **Sandra** the weight 1. The weight assigned to a node reachable by
more than one route from a given start node is obtained by following the shortest
path.

We define a function **weightnodes** to allocate component weights with respect
to a given start node and user-assigned initial weight. We use integer weights,
representing the node Joe with weight 9 by the pair (Joe,9). Thus **weightnodes**
takes a weighted node as its start point and returns a list of weighted nodes. It
is declared and defined as follows:

```
secondary weightnodes :: (?, int) -> [(?,int)];

weightnodes (node,weight) = wnsx ([], [(node,weight)]);
```
This definition uses the auxiliary function **wnsx** to carry out the weighting, de-
fined as follows:

```
secondary  wnsx :: ([(?,int)],[(?,int)]) -> [(?,int)];

wnsx (ns,[]) = ns                                                      |
wnsx (ns,ls) = wnsx (newvicin (append ns ls,[]) (frontier ls));
```
This function takes a pair of lists of weighted nodes representing the weighted
vicinity of the start node. The first list represents the internal nodes of this
vicinity and the second its frontier. Each time **wnsx** recursively invokes itself
it expands this vicinity by 1 arc until the weight has reduced to 0. Thus the
initial user-supplied weight determines how large an area of the database will
be inspected. Hence the expression **weightnodes (Mary,2)** will evaluate to the
list of weighted nodes:

```
[(Mary,2), (Richard,1), (KingGeorge,1)]
```
given the database shown in Figure 2. The definition of **wnsx** makes use of the
function **frontier**, defined as follows:

```
secondary  frontier :: [(?,int)] -> [(?,int)];

frontier ls = [(n,w - 1) | (l,w) <- ls | n <- adjacent l
                                       | w > 1];
```

which takes a list of weighted nodes and returns a list of adjacent nodes weighted with a reduced weight — provided that weight exceeds 0. The function **adjacent** is defined in the previous Section in terms of associational primitives and could not be defined in the absence of such primitives.

The definition of **wnsx** also uses the function **newvicin** which updates a pair of lists representing a weighted vicinity with a list of weighted nodes corresponding to the new "frontier" of the vicinity. In this process duplicate nodes are eliminated and remaining nodes retain their highest weighting. **newvicin** is defined as:

```
secondary newvicin :: ([(?,int)],[(?,int)]) -> [(?,int)]
                                    -> ([(?,int)],[(?,int)]);


newvicin (ns,ls)    [] = (ns, ls)                               |
newvicin (ns,ls) (x:xs) = if ((isnew x ns) and (isnew x ls))
                             (newvicin (ns,x:ls) xs)
                             (newvicin (ns,  ls) xs)           ;
```

The auxiliary routine **isnew**, which tests if a new weighted node is already present in a list of weighted nodes, is defined as:

```
secondary isnew :: (?,int) -> [(?,int)] -> bool;

isnew (x,i)         [] = True                        |
isnew (x,i) ((y,j):ys) = if (x == y)
                            False
                            (isnew (x,i) ys);
```

**Combining the Weights Obtained** We now need to combine the lists of weighted nodes obtained from distinct start nodes. Each node in the result list of weighted nodes receives the sum of weights assigned from each of the start nodes. Any node which is not reached from each start node is eliminated. The function to combine two lists of weighted nodes is defined as:

```
secondary  combine :: [(?,int)] -> [(?,int)] -> [(?,int)];

combine xs ys = [(x, i+j)| (x,i) <- xs | (y,j) <- ys| x == y];
```

Hence the expression:

```
combine [(David,2), (RonsGym,1)] [(RonsGym,1), (Alan,2)]
```

evaluates to `[(RonsGym, 2)]`.

To determine the overall weightings of nodes in the database, given an initial weight and a list of start nodes, we use **centre** defined as:

```
secondary  centre  :: int -> [?] -> [(?,int)];

centre d   [x] = weightnodes (x,d)                              |
centre d (x:xs) = combine (weightnodes (x,d)) (centre d xs);
```

Hence, the expression **centre 2 [Alan, David]** evaluates to **[(RonsGym,2)]** given the database state shown in Figure 2.

**Sorting Weighted Nodes** When several nodes are returned the most central node can be found by sorting the list by weight. This can be done using the function **sortp** defined as follows:

```
secondary sortp  :: [('a,int)] -> [('a,int)];

sortp         [] = []                                          |
sortp ((x,i):xs)
      = append (sortp [(y,j)|(y,j)<-xs|      j > i ])
               ((x,i):(sortp [(y,j)|(y,j)<-xs| not (j > i)])));
```

which is based on the quicksort algorithm.

We can now express our original motivating query as

```
sortp (centre 4 [Alan, Mike, KingGeorge, AAABldng]);
```

which searches the database for a region 3 arcs distant from each of these start nodes. This query evaluates to:

```
[(Sandra,8),(RonsGym,6),(Joe,6),(Joyce,6),(SmallBillsGarage,6)]
```

We have thus identified *Sandra, Joe*, and *Joyce* as possible drinking companions. We have also found that *Ron's Gym* and *Small Bill's Garage* may have served as a contact points for the group.

# 4  Conclusion

Conventional database systems limit retrieval to entity-oriented queries — queries corresponding to questions such as *What is the relationship between Sandra and Mike?* are not supported. Hydra provides the facilities to answer such queries by means of associational primitives. Moreover, we have shown that integrating associational facilities into a computationally complete functional language obtains a significant increase in semantic power allowing us to evaluate queries which cannot be expressed in conventional query languages.

The current UNIX/C implementation of Hydra is being used for application experimentation on criminal intelligence databases of the kind used in our example. Typical response times for queries of the form `centre 4 ...` on a database of several hundred entities are of the order of a few seconds. The authors believe such response times to be acceptable in the context of the facilities being provided (which are not available in standard systems). Nevertheless the performance can undoubtedly be improved and different implementation techniques are being investigated.

# References

[Abr74]   J. R. Abrial. Data semantics. In J. W. Klimbie and K. L. Koffeman, editors, *Data Base Management*, pages 1–59. North Holland, 1974.

[AK84]   M. P. Atkinson and K. G. Kulkarni. Experimenting with the functional data model. In P. Stocker, editor, *Databases — Role and Structure*, pages 311–338. Cambridge Univeristy Press, 1984.

[AK95]   R. Ayres and P. J. H. King. Entities, functions, and surrogates in functional database languages. In Bob Werner, editor, *Proceedings of Basque International Conference on Information Technology, BIWIT 95*, San Sebastian, Spain, July 1995. IEEE Computer Society Press.

[Ayr95]   R. Ayres. *Enhancing the Semantic Power of Functional Database Languages*. PhD thesis, Birkbeck College, University of London, August 1995.

[BFN82]   P. Buneman, R. E. Frankel, and R. Nikhil. An implementation technique for database query languages. *ACM Transactions on Database Systems*, 7(2):164–186, June 1982.

[CM90]   Mariano P Consens and Alberto O Mendelzon. GraphLog: A visual formalism for real life recursion. In *Proceedings of the Ninth ACM SIGACT-SIGMOD-SIGART Symposium on Principles of Database Systems*, pages 404–416, 1990.

[CP95]   S. Courtenage and A. Poulovassilis. Combining inheritance and parametric polymorphism in a functional database language. In Carole Goble and John Keane, editors, *Advances in Databases, Proceedings 13th British National Conference on Databases, BNCOD 13*, pages 24–46, Manchester, United Kingdom, July 1995. Springer-Verlag, LNCS 940.

[HOT76]   P Hall, J Owlett, and S J P Todd. Relations and entities. In G M Nijssen, editor, *Modelling in Data Base Management Systems*. North Holland, 1976.

[Ken79]   William Kent. Limitations of record-based information models. *ACM Transactions on Database Systems*, 4(1):107–131, 1979.

[Mit91]   J. C. Mitchell. Type inference with simple subtypes. *Journal of Functional Programming*, 1(3):245–285, July 1991.

[PK90]   A. Poulovassilis and P. J. H. King. Extending the functional data model to computational completeness. In *Proceedings of EDBT'90*, pages 75–91, Venice, Italy, 1990. Springer-Verlag, LNCS 416.

[Shi81]   D. Shipman. The functional model and the data language DAPLEX. *ACM Transactions on Database Systems*, 6(1):140–173, March 1981.

# SQL+i:
# Adding Temporal Indeterminacy to the Database Language SQL

Antony Griffiths and Babis Theodoulidis
Department of Computation, UMIST, Manchester, M60 1QD, UK.
{tagriff | babis}@sna.co.umist.ac.uk
http://www.co.umist.ac.uk/~timelab

**Abstract.** This paper introduces SQL+i, a temporal relational database management system[1] (TRDBMS) whose aim is to incorporate both determinate, indeterminate, and relative temporal facts which may be declared at multiple and even mixed levels of granularity in a uniform, natural, and unambiguous manner. We use the SQL query language as the basis for the SQL+i query language, utilising a temporal algebra whose aim is to reduce any periods of indeterminacy to a minimum level whilst still maintaining the consistency of the database. By means of a motivating example, we present our underlying model of time and the SQL+i temporal data types, along with the data definition and manipulation language extensions necessary to manipulate SQL+i relations and data.

## Section 1. Introduction

The need to represent indeterminate temporal information in TRDBMSs has been presented in [14], and a system to accommodate such information has been proposed using probabilistic methods [4]. Other researchers have proposed general constraint satisfaction methods to limit the occurrence time of events [9], methods utilising fuzzy set theory [12], and systems which use temporal rules in order to deduce further information [11]. We utilise some of the general constraint satisfaction methods proposed by [9] together with a temporal algebra which reduces the period of indeterminacy of temporal attributes stored in relations in the TRDBMS. We recognise that whilst in many UoDs (universes of discourse) a probabilistic approach to temporal indeterminacy may be sufficient, in some application domains such as legal and medical databases a period of indeterminacy should not be reduced by external factors, as any bias towards certain data may have unpredictable or undesirable consequences.

We recognise also that temporal indeterminacy may originate from our natural inclination to perceive the timing of facts only in relation to the timing of other previously known facts. If we subsequently update our original knowledge then the timing of the related facts must therefore be reviewed. SQL+i recognises this need by introducing relative temporal constants which may be related to previously stored

---

[1] According to the classification schema of [16] SQL+i is actually an historical RDBMS.

database facts which may possess either determinate or indeterminate semantics through constraint propagation techniques. This work follows naturally from the large amount of research into planning applications [1][8]. We also introduce a non-monotonic update operation '*append*' which allows relative temporal facts to be maintained when further knowledge about the original relationship between facts is made available.

One factor which has been noted to generate indeterminate temporal data is the concept of scale [14]. By this notion a known temporal fact at a declared level of granularity is indeterminate with respect to all finer levels of granularity. To overcome this problem we place added emphasis on the temporal analysis of the intended UoD by allowing the database designer to specify the minimum level of granularity for both the SQL+i schema and each relation contained within the schema, and default transformations which can be performed on the SQL+i temporal data types which define how facts declared at finer levels of granularity than the minimum are semantically interpreted.

The following sections present a motivating example which will be used throughout the paper, we then present the underlying model of time on which SQL+i bases its fundamental notions of time. Section 4 introduces the SQL+i temporal data types and their determinate and indeterminate variants, whilst in section 5 we present the extensions used to declare, manipulate, and compute relative temporal facts. Section 6 briefly presents an overview of the extended temporal algebra, and we conclude with the proposed extensions to the SQL query language.

## Section 2.  A Motivating Example

In this section we present an example SQL+i database whose purpose is to record the information collected from witness statements regarding a hypothetical bank robbery. This database will provide the examples used in the later sections, the notation and methods used in deriving the example data will be discussed when appropriate. A summary of the robbery information is as follows.

The robbery occurred in Liverpool over the New Years bank holiday in 1990. The robbery was not discovered until the following day when the manager opened the branch for business. From eye-witness reports it can be ascertained that the robbery started at some time between midnight and 6am and ended between 6pm and midnight on New Years Day. The prime suspect for the robbery is a convicted 'safe cracker' called Mike. He was in Manchester before the robbery started and arrived in Paris at least 3 hours after the robbery finished. He has no corroboratory evidence regarding his exact whereabouts between the time he left Manchester and the time he arrived in Paris. He is unsure of the time he left Manchester, except that it was before the time of the robbery, but has a witness that saw him at his home in Southport between 9am and 9:15am on the day before the robbery. To simplify this case study we have made the naive assumption that there is no notion of a journey time between Manchester and Liverpool.

We can create the Suspects and Offence relations shown in tables 1 and 2 to store the above data. The primary keys for the relations are composed of the underlined attributes.

| Offence | | | |
|---|---|---|---|
| $ | Crime | Location | when |
| 1 | Robbery | Liverpool | [| 1990/1/1 0am ~ 1990/1/1 7am | - | 1990/1/1 7pm ~ 1990/1/2 1am |) |

Table 1: Offence Relation.

| Suspects | | | |
|---|---|---|---|
| $ | Name | Location | when |
| 2 | Mike | Southport | [ | 1989/12/31 9am | - | 1989/12/31 10am | ) |
| 3 | Mike | Manchester | [ | mindate ~ 1990/1/1 7pm | - | mindate+1 ~ 1990/1/1 7pm | ) |
| 4 | Mike | Paris | [| 1990/1/1 10pm ~ 1990/1/2 4am | - | 1990/1/1 11pm ~ 1990/1/2 4am |) |
| 5 | Mike | Travelling | [ | mindate ~ 1990/1/1 7pm | - | mindate ~ mindate+1 | ) |

Table 2: Suspects Relation.

A relation in SQL+i is created through an extended SQL create table operation. The Offence relation can be created as follows:

create table Offence (Crime char(32), Location char(32), when interval
valid-time when non-decomposable below hour)

This statement creates the Offence relation with the specified list of attributes, and stores in the extended system catalogs the fact that the *when* attribute represents the valid-time of each fact stored in the relation. Furthermore the granularity for the relation is set to hour, and for interval valid-time attributes the non-decomposable clause specifies that the valid-time represents the interval only when considered as a whole at the declared granularity of the relation. If this clause specified 'decomposable', then the stored data is applicable to each chronon in the interval. In an SQL+i schema each tuple has a unique system generated identifier - termed its surrogate ($) - and is timestamped with either an instant or an interval valid-time attribute. The surrogates aid the storage of relative temporal facts and are explained further in section 5. In contrast with the proposed TSQL2 extension to support temporal indeterminacy [14], the valid-time attributes of an SQL+i relation can store both determinate, indeterminate, or relative temporal facts. The database designer therefore does not need to create relations whose temporal semantics are fixed at the time of their creation.

## Section 3. The Underlying Model of Time

This Section defines the primitive notions and assumptions that are necessary for the definition of our model of time. This model will serve as the basis for the underlying time line and its calendar system. The model that we adopt places special emphasis on three concepts that we feel are of fundamental importance. Namely the formalism should; adopt semantics that are as close to our natural and intuitive perception of time; be computationally viable; be flexible.

SQL+i assumes that time is linear, dense, and infinite. Whilst these decisions allow us to create a time line whose basic elements are potentially infinitesimally small and infinite in range - and thus capable of modelling the temporal domain of any UoD - we still need to achieve computational viability. We therefore allow each SQL+i schema to specify the earliest and latest dates that are relevant to the UoD being modelled, and a minimum level of granularity below which no temporal assertions can be made. By these methods we create an time line which is specific to the individual schema, thus maintaining a flexible system. Any temporal assertions made at the minimum level of granularity may therefore be considered to be instantaneous in terms of the schema in which they are defined.

To develop a useful model of the temporal domain of the UoD we must construct a human representation of our time line, therefore a calendar is constructed which uses the schema-specific minimum granularity as its most fundamental level of abstraction. Instants can therefore be said to exist at the minimum level of granularity permitted by the system, these instants are termed chronons. The calendar then uses these primitives to construct temporal constants at progressively coarser level of granularity. The earliest and latest chronons that the schema permits (namely $d_{min}$ and $d_{max}$) are included in the time line, thus the set of chronons which constitute the schema-specific time line is denoted by Chronons:

$$\text{Chronons} = \left\{ t \mid d_{min} \leq t \leq d_{max} \wedge (d_{min}, d_{max} \in \text{Chronons}) \right\}$$

We also extend the notions of schema-wide earliest and latest chronons and minimum granularity by recognising that individual relations within an SQL+i schema may have need for temporal constraints which are specific to them. We therefore allow each relation to have its own earliest and latest chronons with the added stipulations that these must be members of the schema's declared time line, and that the minimum granularity of an individual relation must be coarser than or equal to the schema minimum granularity. If no relation-specific constraints exist then the schema-wide constraints are used as defaults. In all examples we will assume that the appropriate constraints are retrieved by SQL+i from the system catalogs.

SQL+i has adopted the dating conventions of the Gregorian calendar so that users may express temporal constants at all the commonly used granularity levels. These levels form a hierarchical structure with the coarsest level of granularity being the year level and the finest level of granularity being the nanosecond level, with the exclusion of week.

Many DBMS have gaps in the levels of granularity supported. For example, it is perfectly legitimate to declare the temporal constant "1990/06/23" which is at the day level of granularity, but not "1990/04" which is at the month level of granularity. SQL+i however allows temporal constants to be quoted at any level of granularity, the only restriction imposed is that the fields in a temporal constant must be declared in the order shown below. This allows the implicit granularity of the temporal constant can be calculated.

```
<Determinate_instant_value>  ::=  <date_literal> [ ERA [ <time_literal> [ MERIDIAN ] ] ]
<date_literal>         ::=  <years_value> [ <separator> [ <months_value>
                                 [ <separator> <days_value> ] ] ]
<time_literal>         ::=  <hours_value> [ : <minutes_value>
                                 [ : <seconds_value> [ . <milliseconds_value>
                                 [ <micro_seconds_value> [ <nano_seconds_value> ] ] ] ] ]
```

# Section 4. Temporal Constants in SQL+i

SQL+i introduces three data types which can be used to model temporal data, they are namely instants, intervals, and spans. Each of these data types can have either determinate or indeterminate semantics, the instant and interval data types may also be declared relative to another stored database fact or temporal constant. The following sub-sections discuss these options and their possible semantic meanings.

## 4.1 The Instant Temporal Data Type

An instant has been defined as an isolated instant in time, it is said to occur at time $t$ if it occurs at any time during the chronon represented by $t$ [5]. We qualify this definition by stating that if it is known during which chronon an instant occurred, then the instant is determinate. It can be seen from this definition that a determinate instant can still occur at a time that is not completely known. For example, if we define the size of our schema chronon to be 1 day, then any instant defined at a finer level of granularity (e.g. second) can only be said to occur at some time during the chronon in question. To remove this ambiguity we can place a fixed semantic meaning to any instant defined at a granularity less than the schema chronon size. SQL+i allows the database creator to choose from the following semantic options:

- Option A: Assume *start of* semantics. Using this option each instant is considered to occur at the start of the chronon in question. For example, if the user inputs the determinate instant | 1994/06/16 11:30am | with the schema chronon set to 1 day, this will be stored as | 1994/06/16 |.

- Option B: Assume *end of* semantics. Using this option each instant is considered to occur during the next chronon in the calendar. Using the previous example this will be stored as | 1994/06/17 |. For example, 'end of' semantics can be used to model a product's use-by date.

- Option C: Assume *nearest to* semantics. Using this option the instant is either rounded down to the start of the chronon that it occurs in, or rounded up to the next chronon. Using the previous example this will be stored as | 1994/06/16 |, if however the input instant constant were | 1994/06/16 12:30pm |, this would be stored as | 1994/06/17 |. 'Nearest-to' semantics can be used to record periodic events, therefore ensuring regularly spaced readings.

- Option D: Disallow instant temporal constants with a granularity finer than that of the schema chronon level.

Any instant constants that exist at a coarser granularity than the schema chronon have their unused fields padded out with their minimum valid value, thus if the schema chronon size has been set to second, then the instant temporal constant | 1994/06 | will be stored internally as | 1994/06/01 ad 00:00:00am |, the initial granularity of the temporal constant is however maintained as part of the instant's timestamp. All instant constants are delimited by vertical bars. This also conforms to the proposed TSQL2 language specification [14].

An indeterminate instant is an isolated instant in time that is known to have happened, but the exact chronon during which it occurs is either uncertain or is unknown. This does not model the situation where it is uncertain if an instant occurred at all. An indeterminate instant is described by stating the two chronons which delimit its possible existence period. This period of indeterminacy is always assumed to be a half-open time interval. Therefore an indeterminate instant $| t_L \sim t_U |$ is defined as:

$$| t_L \sim t_U | \; = \; \big\{ \, t \in \text{Chronons} \mid t \leq t_L \wedge t < t_U \wedge$$
$$\neg \exists \, t' \in \text{Chronons} \mid t' \geq t_L \wedge t' < t_U \wedge t' \notin | t_L \sim t_U |$$
$$\wedge \; t_U - t_L \geq 1 \text{ chronon} \big\}$$

Indeterminate instant constants can be created by either specifying the two determinate instants which delimit the possible existence period of the indeterminate instant, or an interval can be quoted which spans the period of possible existence of the indeterminate instant. For example, the fact "Mike travelled at some time in January 1994" can be specified using the two input methods as either (assuming a schema chronon of 1 day) | 1994/01/01 ~ 1994/02/01 | or | ?1994/1? |, where the tilde symbol '~' is used to denote a period of indeterminacy and any temporal constant enclosed by question marks is deemed to be an interval over which the indeterminacy holds. The starting and ending chronons of an indeterminate instant may be quoted at different levels of granularity.

SQL+i also supports the notion of relative time. Declaring instant temporal constants relative to other database facts is fully discussed in section 5.

## 4.2 The Interval Temporal Data Type

An interval is defined as the time between two instants [5]. To fully describe a determinate interval we must therefore either define the determinate instants that start and end the interval, or its starting or ending instant qualified with the duration of the instant. In SQL+i interval temporal constants use the bracketing conventions given in table 3, this allows users to create interval temporal constants with the end point semantics which are most natural to them.

| Symbol | Meaning |
|---|---|
| [ | interval is closed at the lower end |
| ( | interval is open at the lower end |
| ] | interval is closed at the upper end |
| ) | interval is open at the upper end |

Table 3: The Interval Delimiting Tokens

SQL+i always stores and internally manipulates interval temporal constants as half-open intervals. Their internal representation is therefore:

$$[ \, | \, t_L \, | \, - \, | \, t_U \, | \, ) \; = \; \{ \, t \in \text{Chronons} \, | \, t_L \leq t < t_U \; \wedge$$
$$\neg \exists \, t' \in \text{Chronons} \, | \, t' \geq t_L \wedge t' < t_U \wedge t' \notin [ \, | \, t_L \, | \, - \, | \, t_U \, | \, )$$
$$\wedge \, t_U - t_L \geq 1 \text{ chronon} \}$$

Interval constants require the definition of default semantics for the interpretation of an interval whose duration is less than 1 chronon. For example, if the interval in question is [ | 1994/06/01 10:30:26 | - | 1994/06/01 10 | ) with the schema chronon set to 1 day, then SQL+i recognises two options which determine how this can be interpreted.

- Option A: Disallow interval temporal constants with a duration of less than 1 system chronon.

- Option B: Transform the input interval temporal constant to the shortest determinate interval available. Using this method the interval in the example above will be transformed to have duration of 1 day and will be stored as [ | 1994/06/01 | - | 1994/06/02 | ).

An indeterminate interval is bounded by *at least* one indeterminate instant. This means that the exact existence period of the interval is therefore uncertain. An indeterminate interval is described by stating the 2 instants that delimit its possible existence period, these are called the *lower bound* and *upper bound* respectively. An indeterminate instant $[ | \, t_L^- \sim t_L^+ \, | \, - \, | \, t_U^- \sim t_U^+ \, | \, )$ is therefore defined as:

$$[\,|\,t_L^-\sim t_L^+\,|\,-\,|\,t_U^-\sim t_U^+\,|\,) \;\equiv\; \big\{\, t \in \text{Chronons} \;\big|\; t \in |\,t_L^-\sim t_L^+| \;\wedge\; t \in |\,t_U^-\sim t_U^+|$$

$$\wedge \;\neg\,\exists\, t' \in \text{Chronons} \;|\; t' \geq t_L^- \;\wedge\; t' < t_U^+ \;\wedge\; t' \notin [\,|\,t_L^-\sim t_L^+\,|\,-\,|\,t_U^-\sim t_U^+\,|\,)$$

$$\wedge \; t_U^- - t_L^- \;\wedge\; t_U^+ - t_L^+ \geq 1\text{ chronon }\wedge$$

$$\exists\, p \in |\,t_L^-\sim t_L^+\,| \;\wedge\; \exists\, q \in |\,t_U^-\sim t_U^+\,|\;|\;|\,q - p\,| \leq 1\text{ chronon}\big\}$$

Although this definition allows $t_L^+$ to be after $t_U^-$, when an instanciation of the constant is required the interval that is returned must satisfy the implicit constraint $t_U^- > t_L^+$. By this method the stored indeterminate interval models a set of possible determinate intervals subject to any schema or relation constraints as discussed below.

SQL+i allows a great deal of flexibility in the way in which indeterminate interval temporal constants are declared. For example, if we wish to store the timing of the Eastminster Bank robbery, we can declare this as
[ | 1990/1/1 0am ~ 1990/1/1 7am | - | 1990/1/1 7pm ~ 1990/1/2 1am | ). An indeterminate interval therefore represents the set of possible real world values that the database fact may take. If we subsequently discover that the robbery started at exactly (at the hour level of granularity) 6am and ended at 8pm then the above example can be updated to [ | 1990/1/1 6am | - | 1990/1/1 9pm | ).

SQL+i allows users to place schema-wide or relation-specific constraints on the minimum and maximum duration of an interval. This facility allows users to accurately model the temporal requirements of the UoD. These constraints are expressed by placing a quantitative binary constraint of the form $(\delta_{max} - \delta_{min} \in D)$, where D is the minimum or maximum duration of intervals in the schema or relation expressed as a span (discussed in section 4.3). The constraints placed on the schema or individual relations are expressed through SQL+i's extended data definition language (DDL), the general form of which is:

<modify_statement>  ::=  MODIFY (<schema> | <relation>) TO  <new_default>

where <new_default> is the new constraint or default setting for the named schema or relation. A full description of the extended modify statement is given in the appendix.

If we placed a constraint on the Offence relation which stated that the maximum duration of any offence is 6 hours then the updated determinate interval then becomes [ | 1990/1/1 6am | - | 1990/1/1 1pm | ).

Declaring interval temporal constants relative to other database facts is discussed in section 5.

## 4.3 The Span Temporal Data Type

A span has been defined as a directed duration of time [5]. A span therefore has a length but has no specific starting or ending chronons, in this sense it is an unanchored set of chronons which can either refer to a positive or negative duration of time. As with instants and intervals, spans require the definition of default semantics for the interpretation of span constants whose duration is less than 1 schema chronon. Spans use the same options as intervals for this purpose.

Spans are enclosed by percentage marks in order to distinguish them from the other SQL+i data types, they are quoted as signed multiples of a valid granularity. For example, the duration "6 weeks" would be created as %6 weeks%. We distinguish between determinate spans, which have known durations, and indeterminate spans which have a duration that is either imprecise or unknown. Indeterminate spans are specified by declaring an upper and lower limit on the duration of the span. For example, the duration "between 6 and 7 weeks" would be created as %6 ~ 7 weeks%. The maximum and minimum duration of a span is once again specified by the minimum and maximum duration constraints on the schema or relation. There is no need to consider relative semantics for either determinate or indeterminate spans as by definition an unanchored set of chronons cannot exist at a specific location on the schema time line.

# Section 5.   Relative Temporal Constants

In an SQL+i database all facts may be declared with either determinate or indeterminate temporal semantics, however only instants and intervals may also be declared relative to another (previously recorded) database fact. Relative time has been defined as meaning that "the valid-time of a fact is related to either the valid-time of another fact or the current time, now" [5]. This definition however merely links the valid-time of a particular database fact to a calendar defined instant or interval. If we look at a dictionary definition of the term relative we find the following "having meaning or significance only in relation to something else; not absolute" [2]. This definition captures somewhat more of the semantics of relative temporal facts as supported by SQL+i. Moreover for TRDBMSs, a relative temporal fact can be defined as a database fact whose valid-time is not only linked to the valid-time of another database fact, but whose existence in the database is wholly dependant on the existence of the said database fact and any changes that are made to it. In other words it constantly and permanently mirrors the valid-time of the fact that it is related to.

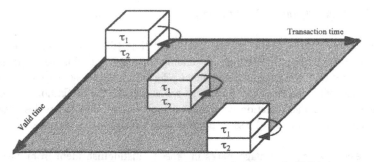

Figure 1: Child Relative Facts Mirroring their Parent's Valid-time

Figure 1 illustrates this linkage between the valid-time of a child tuple $\tau_1$ and its parent tuple's ($\tau_2$) valid-time in an TRDBMS. As the transaction time[2] in the database changes, any modification to the valid-time of $\tau_2$ will be reflected in the corresponding valid-time of $\tau_1$. Before a child fact $\tau_1$ can be stored relative to the parent fact $\tau_2$ the following preconditions must be satisfied; $\tau_2$ must already exist and be uniquely identifiable in some relation in the database; the data type of $\tau_1$ and $\tau_2$ must be either instant or interval; $\tau_1$ cannot be related to itself.

We assume that each tuple has a system generated identifier, and that each tuple is timestamped with either an instant or an interval valid-time attribute. For ease of recognition we shall term the previously stored database fact the parent fact, and the new fact that is defined as being relative to the parent fact the child fact. This does not mean that a parent fact cannot itself be a child fact in another relationship.

## 5.1 Declaring Relative Temporal Constants

To declare the valid-time of a tuple with relative temporal semantics, we must first find the surrogate value of the tuple which is to be the parent of the new database fact. This value can then be used to link the valid-times of the child and parent tuples in the database. The child tuple can be related to the parent tuple with any of the thirteen temporal relationships identified by James Allen [1]. The temporal relationship between the parent and child tuples can also be qualified through the use of an optional temporal distance between the tuples, this is defined as a span. For example, if we wished to record in the database that "Project P3 will start between 6 and 7 days after project P2 has finished", the temporal relationship between the two tuples will be 'before', and this is offset by the indeterminate span %6 ~ 7% days.

Not every tuple stored with relative temporal semantics will make sense. For example, it is not semantically correct to state that a child tuple with an instant valid-time can be related to a parent tuple whose valid-time is an interval with the

---

[2] The transaction time of a database fact is the time when the fact was stored in the database, as contrasted to its valid-time which is the time when the fact is true in the modelled reality.

relationship 'contains'. To achieve semantically correct relative temporal statements the data type of the child tuple is identified through the syntax of the child's timestamp, and the data type of the parent tuple through its surrogate value. The relationship between them is tested for semantic correctness for the combination of temporal data types. Furthermore, only the 'before' and 'after' temporal relationships are semantically correct when a temporal offset is used in the statement. For example, the statement "Project P3 Occurred 6 weeks during project P2" is nonsensical, and would therefore raise an error.

After semantic analysis, the temporal constant is processed and using the time-duration and time-boundedness rules for the target relation, and the date which represents the most constrained valid-time of the child tuple is inserted in to the target relation. In order to identify the Surrogate value of the parent tuple, relative temporal constants require an additional select clause in their declaration. The general form of a relative temporal constant is therefore:

<token> [<offset>] <modifier> ( <sub-select statement> ) <token>

For example if we insert the fact "Mike arrived in Paris at least 3 hours after the robbery ended" we can use the following declaration:

```
insert into Suspects ( Name, Location, Valid_time )
values ('Mike', 'Paris', [ %3 hours% after
( select valid-time from Offence
where Crime = 'Robbery' and Location = 'Liverpool') ))
```

## 5.2   Storage of Relative Temporal Data

SQL+i uses a temporal constraint network (TCN) to represent and reason about the relative temporal facts that it stores. The TCN consists of a set nodes $\{ N_1, ..., N_n \}$, each of which represents an instant or interval relative temporal fact, each node being related to every other node by a vector consisting of a set of qualitative constraints. Each new relative temporal fact added to the database forms a node in the TCN, the vector relating it to its parent fact consisting of the singleton constraint supplied as part of the child fact. We term this user supplied vector the *primary vector*.

In a TCN of n nodes and $n(n - 1)/2$ vectors each node will be connected by $(n - 1)$ vectors as each vector $V_{ij}$ connecting nodes $N_i$ and $N_j$ implies an equivalent vector $V_{ji}$ which is omitted from the network. In an SQL+i database we only store the most constrained representation of the child fact's valid-time. This is computed by using the qualitative relationship stored in the primary vector and the valid-time of the parent fact. The remaining vectors are used to help maintain the consistency of the TCN and to aid the retrieval of tuples during select operations. We use the three-consistency algorithm developed by Allen [1] to maintain the temporal integrity of the TCN and to propagate the results of all new temporal assertions that are added to the network. For an extensive worked example of this algorithm the reader is directed to [8]. The timestamp of the child tuple always maintains the most up-to-date representation of the tuples valid-time. Every update to the parent tuple's valid-time is reflected in the child tuple's valid time.

It has been noted by [10] that although this algorithm detects all inconsistencies between neighbouring nodes (termed arc-consistency), it does not guarantee the consistency of the TCN as a whole. Thus any path between nodes $N_i$ and $N_j$ is not guaranteed to be consistent (termed path-consistent). In an SQL+i database we are only interested in explicitly storing and maintaining the valid-time of the child fact as computed through its relationship to the parent fact and their primary vector. It is therefore sufficient to only enforce arc-consistency within the TCN.

It is quite likely that at some time during the propagation process the primary vector will contain a set of constraints which has more that one member. Disjunctive information of this type cannot place special emphasis on any particular member of the set of constraints, we cannot therefore maintain the valid-time of the child tuple using a calendar representation. Any such tuple which is returned as the result of a successful retrieval operation must therefore have its valid-time computed at retrieval time.

If we examine the initial facts in our case study we can ascertain that our prime suspect claims he in Manchester before the time of the robbery, and that he was in Paris at least 3 hours after the robbery ended. These claims can be translated into the two relative assertions; Time(Mike in Manchester) before Time(Robbery), and Time(Mike in Paris) at least 3 hours after Time(Robbery). These assertions can be used to create the initial TCN shown in figure 3. The relationship between the nodes 'Mike in Manchester' and 'Mike in Paris' is a derived vector formed as a result of the three-consistency algorithm.

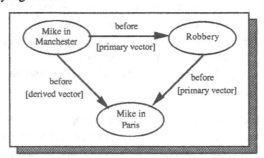

Figure 2: Initial Temporal Constraint Network

The quantitative temporal information contained in the second of the above temporal facts is termed an offset, and is maintained as a discrete field in the timestamp of the child fact. The valid-time of the child fact must therefore be computed at retrieval time. Other researchers have proposed separate parallel storage structures for maintaining quantitative temporal information [7] [3], our proposal removes this need but in the process we loose some of the temporal reasoning capabilities of their systems.

It should be noted that in our motivating example we are only considering interval valid-time attributes, there is however no reason why we cannot consider the relationships between interval and instant nodes in our network. To achieve this end we follow the proposal forwarded by [13] for general temporal constraint networks. By this method we use 6 transitivity tables to compute the composition of the basic relations between facts of differing temporal types.

When the consistency algorithm has run to completion, and no inconsistent relationships are found, any nodes that have had their primary vector updated are added to a list. Any node in this list have the valid-time of the corresponding tuple in the database updated using the algorithms described in section 5.6. Any inconsistent relationship in the temporal constraint network represents an inconsistent state of the UoD. If this occurs we must rollback the network (and hence the state of the database) to its state before the relative temporal assertion that caused the inconsistency was introduced.

We can deduce two further relative temporal facts from our example to the TCN. Firstly that the time Mike was in Manchester meets the time he was travelling, and secondly that the time he was travelling meets the time he was in Paris. The implications of these new facts can be propagated through the TCN to produce the final TCN shown in figure 4.

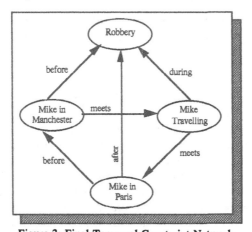

Figure 3: Final Temporal Constraint Network

It will be noticed that if the primary key constraint for the Suspects relation were {Name, Location}. When we add the two tuples ('Mike', 'Travelling', [met_by 0x3)) and ('Mike', 'Travelling', [meets 0x4)) the primary key constraint is violated. The Suspects relation is however a valid-time relation, therefore this conflict can be used to our advantage by utilising the underlying temporal algebra to merge together the valid-time attributes of the conflicting tuples to form a single unique tuple. This operation is briefly described in section 6.

## 5.3 A Non-monotonic UPDATE Operation

The SQL+i *append* clause transforms the SQL update operation [15] into a non-monotonic update for relative temporal facts. If we were to use a standard SQL update operation on a relative temporal fact, then all previous knowledge that has been stored and derived about the fact will be replaced by the new knowledge, this is in effect a monotonic operation. If we wish to add to the knowledge about the temporal relationship between two relatively stored database facts we can use the append operation to maintain our original knowledge, add the new knowledge, and propagate its effects throughout the network of stored relative facts. The general form of the altered update operation is therefore:

```
update <tablename>
[ from <tablename> {, <tablename> } ]
[ set <columnname> = <expression> {, <columnname> = <expression> } ]
[ append <relationship> {, <relationship> } ]
[ where <search_condition> ]
```

For an existing vector $R_{ij}$ and new qualitative relation(s) $\{r_1, ..., r_n\}$ that are appended to the tuple that satisfies the search condition, the new constraint is defined as:

$$R_{ij} \Leftarrow R_{ij} \cup (r_1 \cup \ldots \cup r_n)$$

Using this variant on the update operation we can directly manipulate the connecting vectors in the TCN without the need for deleting and re-inserting existing nodes and vectors.

## 5.4 Algorithms for Computing Relative Temporal Constants

In this section we briefly describe the algorithms used to compute the most constrained quantitative representation of a child fact from the input qualitative information. The algorithms perform reasoning on the basis of the relationships between the possible starting and ending chronons of the parent and child tuple valid-times. These algorithms can be viewed as extensions of the research carried out by [6] [7] [13] to transform qualitative temporal data into its quantitative counterpart, our extensions incorporate indeterminate semantics into this work.

The algorithms determine the temporal data type of the valid-time attribute of the parent tuple R and whether this contains determinate or indeterminate data. This information is then transformed, using the temporal modifier P and any offset $\omega$, into the target return data type. Any temporal constraints on the child tuple's relation or on the schema as a whole are also considered by the algorithms.

| Parent Type | Parent Representation | Child Representation |
|---|---|---|
| Det_instant | $\|R\|$ | $\|(R - \omega_U) \sim (R - \omega_L + 1\text{chronon})\|$ |
| Indet_instant | $\|R_L \sim R_U\|$ | $\|(R_L - \omega_U) \sim (R_U - \omega_L)\|$ |
| Det_interval | $[\|R_L\| - \|R_U\|)$ | $\|(R_L - \omega_U) \sim (R_L - \omega_L)\|$ |
| Indet_interval | $[\|R_L^- \sim R_L^+\| - \|R_U^- \sim R_U^+\|)$ | $\|(R_L^- - \omega_U) \sim (R_L^+ - \omega_L)\|$ |

Table 4: Relationships between Child and Parent Fact End-points.

For reasons of brevity the we only present the method for returning the child representation from a generic indeterminate offset $\omega_L \sim \omega_U$ and the temporal modifier *before*, these are presented in table 4.

Figure 4 shows the possible starting and ending periods of a parent indeterminate interval R. The graphical representation of the child fact is shown below for the indeterminately qualified modifier *before*. It should be noted that when an indeterminate parent fact is qualified by an indeterminate offset then this introduces a second level of indeterminacy for the possible end points of the period of indeterminacy of the resultant child fact. The indeterminate instant temporal constants introduced into the SQL+i language cannot fully express this 'double indeterminacy', we therefore return the largest possible period of indeterminacy for the child fact, as shown in figure 4.

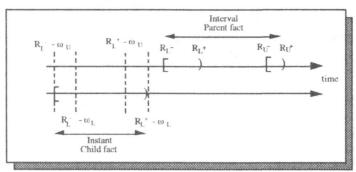

Figure 4: Graphical Representation of Child Fact using the Indeterminately Qualified Modifier 'before'

It should be noted that if the inclusion of an offset results in the earliest or latest possible chronon of the child fact occurring before or after $d_{min}$ or $d_{max}$ then the modifier is recalculated to enforce the consistency of the constraints.

## Section 6. Extending the Temporal Algebra to Support Indeterminacy

SQL+i uses a temporal relational algebra which ensures that any two tuples in a relation are maximal. More specifically; for any valid-time relation R, if $R(a_1, ..., a_{i-1}, u_i, a_{i+1}, ..., a_n)$ and $R(a_1, ..., a_{i-1}, v_i, a_{i+1}, ..., a_n)$ are two distinct tuples of R, where the non-temporal attributes $a_1$, ..., $a_n$ are identical, and the valid-times of the two tuples ($u_i$ and $v_i$) have common points (i.e. they either overlap, touch, or are equal), then these tuples must be coalesced into one tuple with a valid-time equal to the union of the initial valid-times. If either of the tuple's valid-times is indeterminate then these are coalesced in a manner analogous to that described in section 5.6. For example, when we add the simplified relative facts

('Mike', 'Travelling', [ met_by 0x3 )) and ('Mike', 'Travelling', [meets 0x4)) to the Suspects relation we obtain the following tuple valid-times:

[ | mindate ~ 1990/1/1 7pm | - | mindate+1 ~ maxdate+1 | ) and
[ | mindate ~ 1990/1/2 4am | - | 1990/1/1 11pm ~ 1990/1/2 4am | ).

If we coalesce these intervals we obtain the result:

[ | mindate ~ 1990/1/1 7pm | - | mindate ~ mindate+1 | ).

## Section 7.   Concluding Remarks and Future Work

Indeterminate temporal data can occur in many, if not most, application domains. Whilst is it generally agreed that it would be beneficial to be able to store such data, is uncertain what degree of credibility should be attributed to it. In some UoDs we can use the experience of domain experts and past experience to help us to formulate reasoning strategies based on the credibility that has been assigned to the stored data. There are however many domains in which vital decisions must be made on often uncertain temporal information where any form of bias can have undesirable results. We have therefore proposed a TRDBMS which can utilise expert domain knowledge in the production of the temporal model of a UoD, yet which does not predispose the formulation of a decision based on factors external to the available facts.

We are presently implementing our work using the INGRES RDBMS platform. This system allows designers to create user-defined data types and operations on these types. Future work on the SQL+i project will consider methods for the inclusion of relative temporal constraints on relations. The development of a graphical interface and methods for both the DDL and DML to SQL+i which will facilitate the use of both relative temporal constants and temporal constraints are also under investigation.

This paper does not consider a delete or monotonic update operation. At the present time these operations are being investigated in terms of their implications to relative temporal data, especially for their effect on implementation efficiency.

## Appendix.   SQL+i Language Extensions

### 1.   <data type>

| | | |
|---|---|---|
| <instant type> | ::= | INSTANT [<open paren> <default parameters> <close paren>] |
| <interval type> | ::= | INTERVAL [<open paren> <default parameters> <close paren>] |
| <span type> | ::= | SPAN [<open paren> <default parameters> <close paren>] |

```
<default parameters>   ::= DECOMPOSABLE
                        |  NON-DECOMPOSABLE BELOW <granularity level>
```

## 2.  `<modify statement>`

```
<modify statement>    ::= MODIFY (<schema> | <relation>) TO <new default>

<new default>         ::= <chronon default>
                       |  <earliest chronon default>
                       |  <latest chronon default>
                       |  <max duration default>
                       |  <min duration default>
                       |  <instant default>
                       |  <interval default>
                       |  <span default>

<chronon default>        ::= CHRONON <granularity level>
<early instant default>  ::= EARLIEST INSTANT <instant constant>
<late instant default>   ::= LATEST INSTANT <instant constant>
<max duration default>   ::= MAXIMUM DURATION <span value>
<min duration default>   ::= MINIMUM DURATION <span value>
<instant default>        ::= INSTANT DEFAULT <instant default>
<interval default>       ::= INTERVAL DEFAULT <interval default>
<span default>           ::= SPAN DEFAULT <span default>

<instant default>     ::= START OF
                       |  END OF
                       |  NEAREST TO
                       |  DISALLOW

<interval default>    ::= TRANSFORM
                       |  DISALLOW

<span default>        ::= TRANSFORM
                       |  DISALLOW
```

# References

[1] Allen, J. F.: Maintaining Knowledge About Temporal Intervals. Commun. of ACM, 26(11), pp. 832 - 843, 1983.

[2] Collins English Dictionary - 3rd Ed.. HarperCollins Publishers 1991.

[3] Dechter, R., Meiri, I., Pearl, J.: Temporal Constraint Networks. Artificial Intelligence, 49(1-3), pp. 61 - 95, 1991.

[4] Dyreson, C. and Snodgrass, R.: Valid-time Indeterminacy. Proc. of the 9th Int. Conf. on Data Engineering, pp. 335 - 343, 1993.

[5] Jensen, C.S., Clifford, J., Gadia, S.K., Segev, A., Snodgrass, R.T.: A Glossary of Temporal Database Concepts. SIGMOD Record, 21(3), Sept. 1992.

[6] Kautz, H. and Ladkin, P.B.: Integrating Metric and Qualitative Temporal Reasoning. In Proc. of AAAI-91, Anaheim, CA, 1991.

[7] Keretho, S. and Loganantharaj, R.: Qualitative and Quantitative Time Interval Constraint Networks. In Proc. 1991 ACM Computer Science Conf. pp. 239 - 246. Pub. ACM 1991.

[8] Keretho, S. and Loganantharaj, R.: Reasoning about Networks of Temporal Relations and Its Applications to Problem Solving. Journal of Applied Intelligence, 3, pp. 47 - 70. 1993.

[9] Koubarakis, M.: Representation and Querying in temporal databases: The power of temporal constraints. Proc. of the Int. Conf. on Data Engineering. pp. 327 - 334. Vienna, Austria, April 1993.

[10] Loganantharaj, R., Mitra, D., Gudivada, V.N.: Consistent Singleton Models of a Temporal Constraint Network. In Proc. 1992 IEEE Int. Conf. on Robotics and Automation vol. 2. pp. 1192 - 1196. Niece, France, May 1992. IEEE Comput. Soc. Press 1992.

[11] Maiocchi, R., Pernici, B., Barbic, F.: Automatic Deduction of Temporal Information. ACM Trans. on Database Systems, 17(4), pp. 647 - 688. Dec. 1992.

[12] Martin, R., Barro, S., Bosch, A., Mira, J.: Modelling the representation of time from a fuzzy perspective. Cybernetics and systems, 25(2), pp. 217 - 231. 1994.

[13] Meiri, I.: Combining Qualitative and Quantitative Constraints in Temporal Reasoning. In Proc of AAAI-91, pp. 260 - 267, 1991.

[14] The TSQL2 Temporal Query Language. Snodgrass, R.T. (Ed.). Kluwer Academic Publishers. 1995.

[15] van der Lans, R.F.: The SQL Standard. A Complete Reference. Prentice-Hall, 1992.

[16] McKenzie, L.E. & Snodgrass, R.T.: Evaluation of Relational Algebras Incorporating the Time Dimension in Databases. ACM Computing Surveys, Vol. 23(4), December 1991.

# Pearls, Swine and Sow's Ears: Interface Research Inside a Multinational Bank

Matthew Chalmers

Ubilab
Union Bank of Switzerland, Bahnhofstrasse 45, 8021 Zürich, Switzerland
Matthew.Chalmers@ubs.com
http://www.ubs.com/research/ubilab/Staff/chalmers.html

**Abstract.** Inside the Union Bank of Switzerland (UBS), as with many other corporations, timely access to the right information determines the success or failure of work goals. Ubilab is the UBS information technology research lab, and it develops new information tools and advises on technology trends for the bank. New technology, however, bears a risk of unbalancing established practices. Bank employees such as traders and analysts see the potential of new technologies but their reactions to the pressure to be up to date with the latest technology may not be what a researcher expects. They cannot afford to take excessive risks, are used to relatively basic technology, and are fully occupied handling their everyday work. They may consider researchers' 'pearls of wisdom' to be unsuitable, irrelevant or unhelpful. Their work practices are advancing, as of course is database system and interaction research, but these directions are not the same and this divergence weakens both sides. By pointing out some of the contrasts and similarities between everyday information use and mainstream database interaction, I hope to spark off discussion about this separation and what can be done to reduce it.

## 1   Introduction

At first glance, one might consider that modern corporations' reliance on vast amounts of data would validate database research in its many forms. The well–known difficulties of 'information overload' and usability might suggest that all corners of such a corporation would actively encourage and quickly employ advances in database systems and their interfaces.

Such a Utopian view is far from the truth. In fact, the relationship of a research laboratory within a large corporation is a difficult balance between pragmatism and risk: short–term development needs and financial pressures within the corporation have to be balanced with the fundament of such laboratories' existence: longer–term goals of research and discovery. Arising from this is a problem which the author feels may ultimately diminish support for database research. This is that the everyday use of information is at odds with the way that most database systems work, and that if anything the gap between practice and research in database interaction is widening.

By looking at mainstream database interaction and at some front desk work in my own corporation, I hope to offer examples of this gap. Also, by using examples fromsome of Ubilab's research in information visualisation, I will offer some suggestions as to how it might be reduced.

## 2 Information Access

The stereotypical image of foreign exchange and bond traders has become familiar to many, with the frantic activity of the 'pit' having been often shown in films and novels. Huge amounts of data stream through such workplaces. Along with news feeds of textual information, the traders concentrate on real–time data showing the rises and falls of prices and other economic values. These rising and falling values are recorded over time, building up databases of *time series* which are in turn the basic material for prediction and analysis. Electronic trading systems are starting to spread around the world's exchanges, distributing over networks and accumulating databases of the ongoing trades. Much work is now being done from trading rooms out in the individual banks (and similar institutions). Electronic exchange systems have accelerated the rate at which decisions must be made; the pace of work is intense.

Although a few more modern workstations are appearing, the majority of traders' and analysts' (the 'quants') desks have PCs with very basic tools for data management. Each person usually handles a small area of financial instruments and does not roam expansively over the large set of data available. If they do query some larger database it will be in a relatively cursory way, as query languages are too complex: boolean expressions tend to be either very short or used with little confidence in the result.

Usually, spreadsheets are used for analysis and display of a small number of time series, allowing relatively simple graphing and analysis e.g. calculating correlation matrices and looking for periodicity. Larger numbers of series make for cluttered graph plots and unwieldy matrices, making analysis and exploration difficult. They also may mean delay and confusion: the former may mean that market opportunities are missed, while the latter may mean financial over–exposure or loss. Since speed and low risk are two of the most essential features of traders' work, they need to be able to construct their own analyses quickly and understandably, wait seconds (and not minutes or hours) for answers, and thus obtain clear timely results that they trust. It can also be noticed that databases for newsfeeds and similar textual data, and their correlation to time series data, are not usually used.

All in all, the number of items that can be handled effectively is constrained. In both spreadsheets and database front–ends, users can only compare data in simple ways. Simple graphs and matrices, linear lists of database query matches: such structures are weak in conveying the richness of the stored data. The context of an item matching some query, the inter–relationships of the retrieved set, the relationship of that set to previous work, the patterns that would be apparent from an overview of the full data set — all these things are discarded in traditional database interfaces. Queries are too often a fumbling grasp into the black box of the database. Instead of an ongoing interactive process, each query essentially conforms to a batch mode of operation: the query is composed, sent off for processing, and executed in sterile isolation from the user.

Some of these issues are at the core of the author's project at Ubilab. This relatively new project is centred on the visualisation of complexly structured data such as collections of time series and corpora of textual data. We are exploring techniques for efficiently laying out high–dimensional data in the form of maps or landscapes, which can be browsed and explored graphically [Chalmers93, Chalmers95]. We are trying to design easily perceivable representations of this data so that people can better maintain

Figure 1. A layout constructed from 331 time series, each of dimensionality 60. Selected items in the bottom right have their titles shown, revealing a group of brewery companies and a set of German DAX indices. Areas of roughness show less reliable subregions.

cognizance of — a 'feel' for — the entire data set. A map generated by one of our research prototypes and visualised using the DIVE virtual environment system [Fahlén] is shown in Figure 1.

Efficiency of layout production is one of the main threads in this work. Layout should ideally be fast enough to either keep up with the dynamics of the data (real–time feeds are at the core of many traders' work) or to be used interactively the desktop.

Complex analyses of large amounts of data, which cannot run on the desk of the fast–moving trader but instead require overnight processing on some large shared machine, will not get used very much. (Analysts may have more time for such tools, however.) To some extent this stems from the need for tailorability of analyses to the data sets of particular interest to the trader. Large global analyses may become useful shared references or resources, but what traders often push for is the analysis that no–one else has. With this they may then gain a (usually brief) competitive advantage in their area of concern.

With such concerns in mind, we have been developing efficient incremental algorithms for layout. Based on spring–based models for numerical optimisation, these have evolved from the $O(N.logN)$ iteration time algorithm presented in [Chalmers92], and are focused on textual and time series data sets whose dimensionality is roughly in the range $10^2$ to $10^5$ — perhaps significantly exceeding the number of items modelled ($10^2$ to $10^4$). Although details of our current work are left as the subject of another paper, we are now using linear iteration time algorithms which drastically out–perform the author's earlier techniques and the standard $O(N^2)$ force based techniques. We plan to run a pilot implementation of our programs inside the main part of the bank this summer or autumn, so as to obtain feedback from those working there.

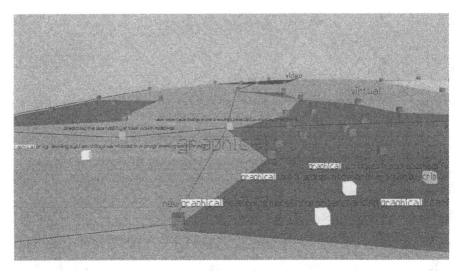

Figure 2. Imageability features build upon basic layout positions of 252 articles on HCI, with an overall dimensionality of 3871. Static features such as clusters or districts help with orientation and navigation. A few documents are dynamically but randomly chosen to be highlighted with a medium colour and have their titles shown, with a bias based on nearness to the eye. Topic words are also dynamically placed in the scene according to density of occurrence in the field of view and word usage history. Clicked–on words start searches which colour documents white.

Positions in space plotted in 2– or 3D are not enough to make such graphical representations useful, legible, and imageable. One has to reveal structure and detail while avoiding occlusion and clutter [Tufte]. Another main thread of the Ubilab work is visualisation design, with the aims of imageability and ease of interaction being paramount. We wish to open up the database so that as people move through it and work within it, they maintain awareness of patterns within the data, can navigate their way through it, and can quickly find what they are looking for.

The layout algorithms are but one side of this. Although we do have numerical metrics of layout quality, based on the mechanical stress of spring systems, they are indifferent to more subtle qualities of the layout. We have found that two layouts may have identical stresses but, subjectively, one makes better sense and is easier to use. Therefore we vary layout parameters and models so as to improve this 'feel', which is evidenced in such features as the perceived consistency of spatially proximate objects, and the degree of separation and 'clumpiness' of clusters. This aspect of our work is design rather than hard science. We do not have objective measures for everything that makes a good layout. It is emphasised, however, that treating this work as craft — a mixture of design and science — is unavoidable, or even desirable, given the influence of human perception on the quality of system interfaces.

Another side of this 'opening up' of the database is therefore the information design: the tailoring of the positions of objects as mentioned above and also the addition of static and dynamic features for imageability. Figure 2 shows an example. Static imageability features include the shoreline, local areas of surface roughness and also the clusters of objects based on geometric proximity (sometimes combined with higher–dimensional proximity) and found using the method of [Ingram].

Dynamic features are further subdivided into two types: view–specific and view–independent. Specific to the current field of view are successively sampled words and documents. A few appear as the user moves through the space, and more are shown when motion stops. The orientation of text is kept orthogonal to the view of the user as he or she moves. This aids legibility for that user and also helps support awareness of the activities of others (a topic discussed further in the following section). Independent of the viewpoint are indicators of usage frequency which are shown only on demand. This usage information reflects past activity by all users as measured by mouse selection, keyword search hits, &c., and is updated within the virtual environment as such activities progress.

To close this section on basic information and its access, note that with time series there are few simple key fields to search on. Instead, other organising principles are often used, such as hierarchies of groups of time series, dividing the database by country, by industrial sector, investment type and so forth. Such hierarchies may not be uniform in structure e.g. one branch representing a country may well have different criteria for the subdivision of each of its children. One child may be divided by industrial sector while another may use company names. This lack of uniformity may make more standard database models less attractive. Relational databases also are weak in helping with the detection of patterns or with queries relying on the sequential nature of time series, because the relations — sets — do not have such time dependencies built into them. These issues have given rise to another project within Ubilab, Calanda [Dreyer].

## 3  Information Use and Collaboration

The traditional *á la crier* system of the traditional exchange is full of human interaction as well as interaction with information on display boards and individual desks. Traders are visible to each other when they make bids and offers. When planning their work they use their experience of their fellow traders as much as the raw data on prices and rates. In this way they build and use their feel for the market.

As pointed out in [Parikh] when describing the Chicago Mercantile Exchange, traders may easily be executing a trade roughly once a minute. Some controversy has arisen over the electronic system being introduced there, in particular with it being regarded as restrictive and slow. Parikh and Lohse suggest that a major factor against the electronic system was the way in which traders lost the ability to see the whole market and its participants. They find the context of their work diminished, both in terms of other parts of the market and other people. Larger banks may be less prone to this in sectors where they have a large proportion of the market, but in other areas and for smaller banks, this problem becomes more severe.

It is also interesting to see how interaction and collaboration between traders is still a vital part of the work in the more modern trading rooms, even though far fewer people are now physically co–located. As has been described in [Heath], traders in the same room weave together their individual work with collaborative activities. As well using the data on the many screens stacked on their desks, traders maintain a peripheral awareness which allows them to refine their own work as well as their colleagues'. While they focus on their localised tasks related to a particular area of the market, they are still aware of the work going on around them. They will pass on useful information that they come across and will also monitor enough of their colleagues' activity so that they can offer help if the situation demands it. Much as discussed in [Rodden], they do this part of their everyday work without the help of the information system. In fact one might say in spite of it.

Supporting the richer variety of ways in which people interact is a difficult task, but it is important that we break away from the idea that only one person uses one retrieved item of data for one instant of time. Where information comes from, who else is interested in it, what has been done with it previously, what could we potentially do with it: we work with these issues as well as the raw data values. These issues can change how we perceive and use information, making us adjust our perception of what is useful, significant or interesting. Usage and collaborative issues therefore should affect how we design interfaces to databases, even though at the lower data management levels we still enforce more traditional rules of control and consistency.

'Collaborative tools' in the commercial world usually refers to workflow systems, which tend to enforce a strict notion of work roles which has been considered outmoded and naive by sociologists for many years, and which has even led to the epithet 'naziware'. Only in very proceduralised work environments do such systems work as expected. An interesting example of how in a more normal environment such systems are subverted by users so that they can get their 'real' work done is given in [Bowers].

In the visualisation group at Ubilab we have been using information on past usage and other users in less tightly structured (and structuring) ways. We wish to take advantage of past activity so as to enrich information presentation, and we also offer mutual awareness of users' ongoing activity within the data. To some extent we are motivated by work on using the information of others such as [Goldberg], where raw data is supplemented by user–derived information on quality or interest.

The usage indicators mentioned in the previous section are a simple manifestation of this. We plan to push much further in this aspect, hoping to feed back more of the expressed interests and activities of users into both the added imageability features and the layout process itself. We also hope to obtain and display usage information on financial trades — who traded what when — data currently used only for auditing purposes. This example of usage information should stir in the reader a new set of concerns: privacy and security. Although the virtual environment offers synchronously working people the opportunity to see each others' ongoing activities, making these transient activities retrospectively accessible to others may lead to problems of invasiveness. At this stage we have not implemented schemes to handle this, but we do acknowledge both the problem and the existence of previous work in this area such as [Bellotti]. By combining usage information with the raw data, in a way that is appropriate to the sensitivities (both perceptual and social) of the people using it, we may then regain and even enhance the rich and varied information that forms their work environment and which current mainstream systems ignore.

## 4   Conclusion

People such as traders are at the leading edge of the use of information. In their everyday work, they are faced with a scale and dynamism of information which few others routinely encounter. There are many ways in which the systems used to manage and present this information do not fit their needs and habits. Research should be aware of this incongruence and adapt itself accordingly. Some of Ubilab's first steps toward doing so have been mentioned in this paper.

Traders have new products for data analysis continually cast before them. Developers present pearls of wisdom wrapped in grand claims of performance and accuracy, bigger profits and lower risk. Although traders know that new technology has the potential to help and smooth their work, their scepticism is kept strong by a stream of over–complex and ill–fitting technology. If we, as researchers, work without full regard to users then we will be trying to make silk purses out of sow's ears. Instead, systems to handle complex information should exhibit a broader view of interaction. In the future our systems will be better used and our clients and customers better served when we take the complexities of use seriously.

# 5  Acknowledgments

The author wishes to thank Rob Ingram for his postdoc work at Ubilab on clustering, and also Roberto Brega, Christoph Pfranger and Raimond Reichert, who implemented many of the features described here. Thanks also to Düri Schmidt, whose comments helped firm up the paper.

# 6  References

[Bowers]      J. Bowers, G. Button & W. Sharrock, Workflow from Within and Without: Technology and Cooperative Work on the Print Industry Shopfloor, *Proc. 4th European Conf. on Computer Supported Cooperative Work, (ECSCW'95)*, pp. 51–66, Kluwer, 1995.

[Bellotti]    V. Bellotti & A. Sellen, Design for Privacy in Ubiquitous Computing Environments. In G. de Michelis, C. Simone and K. Schmidt (Eds.), *Proc. 3rd European Conf. on Computer Supported Cooperative Work, (ECSCW'93)*, pp. 77–92. Kluwer, 1993.

[Chalmers92]  M. Chalmers & P. Chitson, Bead: Explorations in Information Visualisation, *Proc. ACM SIGIR'92 (*Copenhagen, June 1992), published as a special issue of SIGIR Forum, ACM Press, pp. 330–337, 1992.

[Chalmers93]  M. Chalmers, Using a Landscape Metaphor to Represent a Corpus of Documents, *Proc. European Conference on Spatial Information Theory*, Elba, September 1993. Published as *Spatial Information Theory*, Springer Verlag LNCS 716, A. Frank & I. Campari (eds.), pp. 377–90, 1993.

[Chalmers95]  M. Chalmers, Design Perspectives in Visualising Complex Information, *Proc. IFIP 3rd Visual Databases Conference*, Lausanne, Switzerland. Published as *Visual Database Systems 3: Visual Information Management*, S. Spaccapietra & R. Jain (eds.), Chapman & Hall, pp. 103–111, 1995.

[Dreyer]      W. Dreyer, A. Kotz Dittrich & D. Schmidt, Research Perspectives for Time Series Management Systems. *ACM SIGMOD*, Vol. 23, No. 1, March 1994

[Fahlén]      L. Fahlén et al., A Space Based Model for User Interaction in Shared Synthetic Environments, *Proc. ACM InterCHI'93*, pp. 43–48, 1993.

[Goldberg]    D. Goldberg et al., Using Collaborative Filtering to Weave an Information Tapestry, *Comm. ACM* 35(12), pp. 61–70, 1992.

[Heath]       C. Heath, M. Jirotka, P. Luff & J. Hindmarsh, Unpacking Collaboration:

Interactional Organisation in a City Trading Room, *J. CSCW* 3(1), pp. 147–165, 1995.

[Ingram]    R. Ingram, & S. Benford, Legibility Enhancement for Information Visualisation, *Proc. IEEE Visualization 95*, (Atlanta, Oct 1995), pp. 209–216, 1995.

[Parikh]    S. Parikh & G. Lohse, Electronic Futures Markets versus Floor Trading: Implications for Interface Design. *Proc. CHI'95* (Denver, May 1995), ACM Press, pp. 296–303, 1995.

[Rodden]    T. Rodden, J. Mariani & G. Blair, Supporting Collaborative Applications. *J. CSCW,* 1(1), 1992.

[Tufte]     E. Tufte, *Envisioning Information*, Graphics Press, 1990.

# Dissemination-Based Information Systems: Your Data May Be Where You Least Expect It

Stanley B. Zdonik

Brown University, Dept. of Computer Science

**Abstract.** This talk examines a new architecture for distributed information systems that is based on the idea that asymmetry in communication channels will require a new approach to data delivery. Most current information systems require processes to pull (i.e., request) data from external information sources. We advocate the use of broadcast or push as a way to deliver data in asymmetric situations. A dissemination-based information system is one that can balance the use of pull and push to suit the current parameters of the network and the requirements of the applications.

This talk will discuss a particular form of dissemination that uses the communication channels as a storage medium. We will describe a new proposal called broadcast disks which pushes data from storage servers to clients in a cyclic fashion in advance of any request. By appropriately choosing the frequency of broadcast for each data item, we can simulate an arbitrarily fine-grained memory hierarchy in the wires of such a network. We will discuss how servers should organize their broadcast and how clients can use their local cache to adjust to a particular broadcast. Preliminary results will be presented.

# Microsoft Database Technologies - An Inside View

Nigel Stanley

ICS

**Abstract.** Microsoft is a multi-faceted organisation with a diverse set of products ranging from the end-user consumer title "The Yellow School Bus" through to enterprise wide mission critical systems such as Windows NT and Micrsoft SQL Server. This apparent product mismatch may wrongly position Microsoft within the minds of IT professionals — often to the detriment of the Microsoft database and enterprise computing groups.

Interesting fact number 1 — If the Microsoft database and developer tools group was incorporated as a separate company, it would be second only to Oracle in terms of licence sales.

The Microsoft database architecture is maturing along the road to a component-based architecture. The presentation will cover this architecture in some detail, including the workings of the Microsoft jet database as used by Microsoft Access and Visual basic. Jet is fairly advanced in its database workings, including the ability to undertake heterogeneous joins, expose object interfaces to both SQL Server and Oracle and optimise a range of diverse queries.

Micrsoft SQL Server has developed into a full fledged RDBMS able to compete well technically with the likes of Oracle and Informix. The talk will focus on some of the innovative technical features of the product including replication and SQL DMO — the high level object oriented interface now exposed in version 6.0.

ODBC has matured into the *de facto* connectivity standard with Windows clients. It has an interesting history, and this will be examined along side the multi-tiered approach to heterogeneous connectivity.

# Predicate-Maintained Queries: An Active OODBMS for Financial Applications

Mark Butterfield, Nicholas Caine, Stephen Ross-Talbot

Nomura Research Institute

**Abstract.** Hoodini (Highly Object-Oriented Development in Nomura International) is one of the largest object-oriented developments being undertaken in the City of London's financial community. The whole ethos behind Hoodini is to build a true three-tier client-server architecture to allow the distribution of processing in an effective manner. The three tiers, presentation, business logic and resource are bound together using various "new" technologies including Teknekron's Transaction Express, Rendezvous and Iona's Orbix for communication, Sybase and Object Design's ObjectStore for storage resources and a dynamic Model View Controller (MVC) based toolkit for presentation.

One of the many problems that Hoodini seeks to address is active distribution of semi-static data to a trader's workstation. ObjectStore is the base technology that addresses this requirement. ObjectStore is used as a persistent front-end cache with Sybase offering secure longer-term storage. This presentation explores the ways in which ObjectStore has been used to address this requirement. In particular the concept design and implementation of "Predicate Maintained Queries" (PMQ).

A PMQ is a query which is always kept up-to-date. Objects that are created, updated or deleted may results in potential changes to one or more PMQs. A PMQ in this context is a predicated notification based on set membership.

# Universal Data Mangagement

Andy Bailey

Oracle

**Abstract.** Universal data management is managing all types of data for all types of applications. The presentation will start by highlighting some of the key industry trends and basic computing models and move onto information management within those models. It will highlight the requirements and techniques for managing different types of data such as relational, multimedia, spatial, text etc.

# Index of Authors

# Lecture Notes in Computer Science

For information about Vols. 1–1026

please contact your bookseller or Springer-Verlag

Vol. 1061: P. Ciancarini, C. Hankin (Eds.), Coordination Languages and Models. Proceedings, 1996. XI, 443 pages. 1996.

Vol. 1062: E. Sanchez, M. Tomassini (Eds.), Towards Evolvable Hardware. IX, 265 pages. 1996.

Vol. 1063: J.-M. Alliot, E. Lutton, E. Ronald, M. Schoenauer, D. Snyers (Eds.), Artificial Evolution. Proceedings, 1995. XIII, 396 pages. 1996.

Vol. 1064: B. Buxton, R. Cipolla (Eds.), Computer Vision – ECCV '96. Volume I. Proceedings, 1996. XXI, 725 pages. 1996.

Vol. 1065: B. Buxton, R. Cipolla (Eds.), Computer Vision – ECCV '96. Volume II. Proceedings, 1996. XXI, 723 pages. 1996.

Vol. 1066: R. Alur, T.A. Henzinger, E.D. Sontag (Eds.), Hybrid Systems III. IX, 618 pages. 1996.

Vol. 1067: H. Liddell, A. Colbrook, B. Hertzberger, P. Sloot (Eds.), High-Performance Computing and Networking. Proceedings, 1996. XXV, 1040 pages. 1996.

Vol. 1068: T. Ito, R.H. Halstead, Jr., C. Queinnec (Eds.), Parallel Symbolic Languages and Systems. Proceedings, 1995. X, 363 pages. 1996.

Vol. 1069: J.W. Perram, J.-P. Müller (Eds.), Distributed Software Agents and Applications. Proceedings, 1994. VIII, 219 pages. 1996. (Subseries LNAI).

Vol. 1070: U. Maurer (Ed.), Advances in Cryptology – EUROCRYPT '96. Proceedings, 1996. XII, 417 pages. 1996.

Vol. 1071: P. Miglioli, U. Moscato, D. Mundici, M. Ornaghi (Eds.), Theorem Proving with Analytic Tableaux and Related Methods. Proceedings, 1996. X, 330 pages. 1996. (Subseries LNAI).

Vol. 1072: R. Kasturi, K. Tombre (Eds.), Graphics Recognition. Proceedings, 1995. X, 308 pages. 1996.

Vol. 1073: J. Cuny, H. Ehrig, G. Engels, G. Rozenberg (Eds.), Graph Grammars and Their Application to Computer Science. Proceedings, 1994. X, 565 pages. 1996.

Vol. 1074: G. Dowek, J. Heering, K. Meinke, B. Möller (Eds.), Higher-Order Algebra, Logic, and Term Rewriting. Proceedings, 1995. VII, 287 pages. 1996.

Vol. 1075: D. Hirschberg, G. Myers (Eds.), Combinatorial Pattern Matching. Proceedings, 1996. VIII, 392 pages. 1996.

Vol. 1076: N. Shadbolt, K. O'Hara, G. Schreiber (Eds.), Advances in Knowledge Acquisition. Proceedings, 1996. XII, 371 pages. 1996. (Subseries LNAI).

Vol. 1077: P. Brusilovsky, P. Kommers, N. Streitz (Eds.), Mulimedia, Hypermedia, and Virtual Reality. Proceedings, 1994. IX, 311 pages. 1996.

Vol. 1078: D.A. Lamb (Ed.), Studies of Software Design. Proceedings, 1993. VI, 188 pages. 1996.

Vol. 1079: Z.W. Raś, M. Michalewicz (Eds.), Foundations of Intelligent Systems. Proceedings, 1996. XI, 664 pages. 1996. (Subseries LNAI).

Vol. 1080: P. Constantopoulos, J. Mylopoulos, Y. Vassiliou (Eds.), Advanced Information Systems Engineering. Proceedings, 1996. XI, 582 pages. 1996.

Vol. 1081: G. McCalla (Ed.), Advances in Artificial Intelligence. Proceedings, 1996. XII, 459 pages. 1996. (Subseries LNAI).

Vol. 1082: N.R. Adam, B.K. Bhargava, M. Halem, Y. Yesha (Eds.), Digital Libraries. Proceedings, 1995. Approx. 310 pages. 1996.

Vol. 1083: K. Sparck Jones, J.R. Galliers, Evaluating Natural Language Processing Systems. XV, 228 pages. 1996. (Subseries LNAI).

Vol. 1084: W.H. Cunningham, S.T. McCormick, M. Queyranne (Eds.), Integer Programming and Combinatorial Optimization. Proceedings, 1996. X, 505 pages. 1996.

Vol. 1085: D.M. Gabbay, H.J. Ohlbach (Eds.), Practical Reasoning. Proceedings, 1996. XV, 721 pages. 1996. (Subseries LNAI).

Vol. 1086: C. Frasson, G. Gauthier, A. Lesgold (Eds.), Intelligent Tutoring Systems. Proceedings, 1996. XVII, 688 pages. 1996.

Vol. 1087: C. Zhang, D. Lukose (Eds.), Distributed Artificial Intelliegence. Proceedings, 1995. VIII, 232 pages. 1996. (Subseries LNAI).

Vol. 1088: A. Strohmeier (Ed.), Reliable Software Technologies – Ada-Europe '96. Proceedings, 1996. XI, 513 pages. 1996.

Vol. 1089: G. Ramalingam, Bounded Incremental Computation. XI, 190 pages. 1996.

Vol. 1090: J.-Y. Cai, C.K. Wong (Eds.), Computing and Combinatorics. Proceedings, 1996. X, 421 pages. 1996.

Vol. 1091: J. Billington, W. Reisig (Eds.), Application and Theory of Petri Nets 1996. Proceedings, 1996. VIII, 549 pages. 1996.

Vol. 1092: H. Kleine Büning (Ed.), Computer Science Logic. Proceedings, 1995. VIII, 487 pages. 1996.

Vol. 1093: L. Dorst, M. van Lambalgen, F. Voorbraak (Eds.), Reasoning with Uncertainty in Robotics. Proceedings, 1995. VIII, 387 pages. 1996. (Subseries LNAI).

Vol. 1094: R. Morrison, J. Kennedy (Eds.), Advances in Databases. Proceedings, 1996. XI, 234 pages. 1996.

Vol. 1095: W. McCune, R. Padmanabhan, Automated Deduction in Equational Logic and Cubic Curves. X, 231 pages. 1996. (Subseries LNAI).

Vol. 1096: T. Schäl, Workflow Management Systems for Process Organisations. XII, 200 pages. 1996.

Vol. 1097: R. Karlsson, A. Lingas (Eds.), Algorithm Theory – SWAT '96. Proceedings, 1996. IX, 453 pages. 1996.

Vol. 1098: P. Cointe (Ed.), ECOOP '96 – Object-Oriented Programming. Proceedings, 1996. XI, 502 pages. 1996.

Vol. 1099: F. Meyer auf der Heide, B. Monien (Eds.), Automata, Languages and Programming. Proceedings, 1996. XII, 681 pages. 1996.

Vol. 1101: M. Wirsing, M. Nivat (Eds.), Algebraic Methodology and Software Technology. Proceedings, 1996. XII, 641 pages. 1996.

Vol. 1103: H. Ganzinger (Ed.), Rewriting Techniques and Applications. Proceedings, 1996. XI, 437 pages. 1996.